Christians and Jews under Islam

Christians and Jews under Islam

Youssef Courbage
and
Philippe Fargues

Translated by Judy Mabro

I.B.Tauris Publishers
LONDON • NEW YORK

Published in 1997 by
I.B.Tauris & Co Ltd
Victoria House
Bloomsbury Square
London WC1 4DZ

A full CIP record for this book is available from the British Library

ISBN 1 86064 013 3

Set in Monotype Garamond by Philip Armstrong, Sheffield

Printed and bound in Great Britain by WBC Ltd, Bridgend,
Mid Glamorgan

Contents

Tables and Figures

Figures

Preface

Since the overthrow of the Pahlavi dynasty in 1979 and the appearance of a supranational political Islam, an old and recurring confrontation seems to have returned to world politics and Christianity and Islam have come to be regarded once again as two irreconcilable blocs. Seen from the Christian North, Mediterranean Islam appears to maintain an undivided rule over the societies of the South. But is this apparent uniformity and continuity really rooted in history?

Faced with the current situation, the average European thinks of the expansion of Islam as a lightning conquest which was as much about political power as religious belief. But in fact, it took Islam nearly one thousand years to find acceptance among the peoples who now live under its sway and the intervening period was not one of continual violence and coercion. Nor was the process of Islamization ever fully completed. A number of non-Muslim communities still exist, defend their positions, and even prosper in the Arab East today.

The conquerors who came out of Arabia in the seventh century adopted a dual view of the world. In the territory which they occupied (*dar al-Islam*), the non-Muslim 'People of the Book'– Christians and Jews – were given protected status. The rest of the world, the non-Islamic territory, was regarded as a realm of potential war (*dar al-harb*) and Christians and Jews coming from there were looked upon as latent enemies of Islam. So territorial expansion and the propogation of Islam were two different things, of which the first was the more important. For a long time, the organization of war and of religious co-existence went hand in hand. Coptic peasants, Jacobite scribes and Jewish artisans were all obliged to pay a poll tax if they wanted to keep their own religion, and the money thus raised was vital to the expansion and consolidation of the empire. Nevertheless, the new religion gradually gained ground.

For the most part it did so peacefully and in three ways. The first was through conversion, a process which continued throughout the thousand years after the Islamic conquest and was driven by material or spiritual forces rather than coercion. The second was through marriage which, since Islamic law ruled that the children of a mixed marriage would be Muslim, was the supreme powerful contract through which Islam made progress. Finally, from the beginning of the twentieth century, Islam has gained ground almost exclusively through different rates of population growth among various religious communities. Massacres and expulsions have been excluded from this list because, although they did take place at various times and places, there were no large-scale occurences until the birth of modern Turkey.

The expansion and consolidation of Islam in the Arab East took nine centuries from the *hijra* (the flight of Muhammad from Mecca to Medina in AD 622) to the fall of the Mamluks in 1517 (Chapter 1). It began with armed Arab tribes repelling the two great seventh-century powers of the region – Byzantium and Persia. However, as their numbers were very small in comparison to the peoples they conquered and subsequently governed, the Arabs had to gain acceptance if they were to survive. The religious disputes which divided Christians in the Byzantine empire provided a fertile terrain for the new conquerors. The status that Islam from the outset created for Christians and Jews codified interconfessional relations. Its effects were, however, ambivalent. On the one hand it enabled religious communities to perpetuate themselves, while on the other hand it encouraged people to convert for opportunistic reasons, both material and social. However, the core which remained, proved to be very resilient.

Although events might have developed in the same way in the western part of the Islamic empire, in fact North Africa was completely dechristianized (Chapter 2). Far from the geographical heart of Islam, the Maghreb soon split into small homogeneous entities with the appearance of proto-nations. It was from North Africa that Islam first encroached upon European territory, in Spain, where, during the Reconquista, it experienced its first head-on collision with Latin Christianity. It was in the wake of the Re-conquista that the remnants of the Maghreb's Christian communities converted to Islam.

Latin and Arab Christianity came into direct contact with each other for the first time during the Crusades (Chapter 3). Although the ideological aim of the Crusaders had been to liberate their co-religionists from the yoke of Islam, Arab Christians had reservations about the Latin religious culture, and suffered harassment at the hands of the Latin Christians who were supposedly helping them. For this reason they weathered the shock of the invasion without a breakdown in relations with Islam, which by then had become the majority religion. However, the episode ended with the ordeal imposed by a fundamentalist Islam adopted by the Mamluks on Eastern Christendom, which reduced it in both size and influence.

When in the sixteenth century the Ottomans entered the Arab East after conquering the Balkans they came armed with a significant experience of confessional dialogue. From the moment they took Constantinople from the Byzantines they had recognized, against a background of Sunni orthodoxy, the collective existence of the religious minorities, establishing them each as individual 'nations' and granting them autonomy in matters relating to religion, law, culture and health. The Ottoman empire, which aimed to control society without taking over or changing it, thus allowed Arab Christendom to re-establish itself (Chapter 4).

In Turkey itself, the Ottomans reorganized a region – Anatolia where four centuries of anarchy had eroded Christianity (Chapter 5). Both Christianity and Judaism revived and flourished within the framework of this system. However, again in Anatolia, the secular nation-state which after the First World War emerged from the ruins of the empire sealed its destiny violently. The nation envisaged by the founders of the new Turkey aimed to bring together people who were as similar as possible and, as a result, age-old Armenian and Greek Christian communities disappeared in one tragic decade.

A third confrontation between Islam and the Latin church took place in the Maghreb during the colonial period (Chapter 6). Although it dominated Islam in its own territory, the French colonization was short-lived compared to the Frankish colonization of the Latin kingdoms. However, unlike the latter, it left a cultural and linguistic imprint which, thirty years later, continues to be significant.

A little later and further south, but on these same imperial ruins, the Jewish people also established a nation-state. Coming both from Christian Europe and Muslim countries, they were a reminder of the earlier intrusions of the Crusaders and colonialists. Confronted with the reality of Israel, Palestinian Muslims and Christians stood together and, among other forms of resistance, sought to redress their communal balance vis-à-vis the immigrant Jewish population through an exceptionally high birth rate (Chapter 7).

On each side of Israel today a diversity of confessions is concentrated along two axes. Along the Nile, and on the coastal areas of the Levant, Arab Christianity is now declining significantly (Chapter 8). During the nineteenth century, and at the beginning of the twentieth century, the comparatively early adoption among Christian communities of modern norms, and their generally advantageous economic circumstances, had lead to an increase of their nuimbers. Because in the second stage of the demographic transition it is associated with a small family size, the social progress which had formerly helped to advance it, now acts as a restraint. In addition, urbanization has had the effect of reducing the geographical space occupied by Christians, while enlarging their economic influence.

This history of the spread of Islam in the Middle East is not simply that of a succession of monotheisms, but also a series of incursions, both conspicuous and imperceptible. From the horsemen of Islam and the nomads of Arabia to the Crusaders, from the Mongols to the Turks, from the Euro-Latins to the Ashkenazis – all these episodes have had remarkably similar beginnings in the form of a newcomer, a minority group, which seizes power and arrives armed with a religion and a language. Subsequently, events proceed in different ways. In some cases the minority has become a demographic majority, or has taken over completely by a cultural rather than a demographic process. For example, is there any Tunisian today who does not feel Arab, or any Anatolian who does not feel Turkish? In other cases minorities have merged socially into the society they have subdued politically. In yet others, the minority has either departed or perished.

At the risk of losing their own culture to that of the conquered peoples, the Arabs and the Turks diffused them both, and this worked in favour of multiculturalism. The Europeans, whether the Crusaders or the *pied-noirs* in Algeria, either did not choose to do this or were not successful when they did. The result was the segregation of two cultures, a divided society and – in the end – the expulsion of the intruders. The third example of a refusal to mix – the Jewish colonization of Palestine – has been in existence for only half a century, too short a period to permit any prediction of the long-term future, but long enough to observe in what way it is different: while the Crusaders and the European settlers in Algeria remained in a minority in the land they ruled, the Jewish population is a large majority inside the recognized borders of Israel. If a dialogue is to be established here it will, therefore, depend more on international than communal relations.

Indigenous Christianity, formerly the majority religion in the Middle East, now very much the minority, has survived in some places and died out in others. Its decline, however, is not the outcome of an inevitable process, but rather of varying combinations of constant factors which have produced different outcomes. The fact that they existed in the region before the arrival of Islam enabled Eastern Christians to establish roots in Islamic societies which an alien imported Christianity could not do. Shared life-styles and social norms quickly made co-existence between Muslims and non-Muslims commonplace. The adoption of the language of the conqueror, whether Arabic or Turkish, was crucial to social intercourse. From the Nestorian translator to the Maronite encyclopaedist, many talents have borne witness to the reciprocal esteem between the language which was the vehicle of Islam, Arabic, and the religion which it encountered, Christianity. Loyalty to the state and refusal to offer allegiance to the invader both acted in their favour (although the Christian communities did not always display these characteristics).

The religious minorities have not, however, always been fully in control of their fate. Periods of fast decline occured after major episodes of European penetration, even where there was no open alliance between indigenous Christians and invaders. Each confrontation of this kind has been followed by a revival of Islamic fundamentalism. Almohad puritanism and the first victories of the Reconquista, Mamluk intransigence after the adventure of the Crusades, the pan-Islamism of Sultan Abdülhamid after the humiliation of the Ottoman Empire in North Africa and the Balkans, the current growth of Islamic neo-fundamentalism after the creation of Israel. These episodes of radicalization in state and society have all coincided, in one way or another, with a retreat of the Christian minorities. And yet, one long episode, the four centuries of the Ottoman empire, showed that decline could be followed by a revival.The division of the East into nation states has today brought a further dimunition of the Arab Christians; if history is repeated this may be nothing more than an eclipse.

The authors wish to thank the Institut National d'Etudes Demographiques and its documentation centre which enabled them to write this book.

CHAPTER ONE

The Installation of Islam in the Arab East

In the name of God, the Merciful and Compassionate! This is the
safeguard granted to the inhabitants of 'Alia [Jerusalem] by the servant
of God, 'Umar, commander of the faithful. They are given protection
of their persons, their churches, their crosses – whether these are in
good state or not – and their cult in general. No constraint will be
exercised against them in the matter of religion and no harm will be
done to any of them. The inhabitants of 'Alia will have to pay the *jizya*
in the same way as the inhabitants of other towns. It rests with them
to expel the Byzantines and robbers from their city. Those among the
latter who wish to remain there will be permitted on condition that
they pay the same *jizya* as the inhabitants of 'Alia. [Extract from the
Treaty of Capitulation of Jerusalem (633) recorded by Tabari, *Tarikh
al-rusul wa'l-muluk* (923).[1]]

At the time the Prophet Muhammad received his revelation Mecca
had, at the most, a few thousand inhabitants. Surrounded by desert
for hundreds of kilometres, the city lived by trade sending caravans
beyond the sky-line of sand dunes in search of far-off markets.
These same routes enabled the Prophet and his followers to travers
the Arabian peninsula, but with a different aim – to gather a
community of men. By the time of his death in 632 Muhammad
had brought most of Arabia under the hegemony of his new faith
and built the foundations of a religious state. Within less than three
decades his immediate successors, known to Muslims as the *Rashidun*
or rightly-guided caliphs, had created a world empire which extended
from the Indus to the Atlantic. Remarkably, this swift conquest was
accomplished by a small army of nomadic warriors. But the weakness
of their demographic base proved to be a source of strength for the
Arab–Muslim armies since, in order to impose the power of Islam
on much larger populations, they were obliged to rely on the support
of the local people and had necessarily to come to terms with ideas
and cultures that were different to their own.

Religion was firmly inscribed in the identity of the civilizations conquered by the Arabs. From the time of his first military break-throughs in the Arabian peninsula itself, Muhammad had to find a mode of religious coexistence with the Christians and Jews he encountered and the principles he established during his lifetime became the rules which were, to varying degrees, followed by the later Arab conquerors and Muslim heads of state. When he was forced out of Mecca in 622 the Prophet settled in Medina, an oasis with a large Jewish population. Here he initially attempted to establish perfect equality between his companions and the community which received them: 'To the Jews their religion, and to the Muslims theirs.' However, the Qur'anic revelation was rejected by the Jews who soon became openly hostile, forcing Muhammad to expel them. The Prophet's subsequent encounters with the 'People of the Book' were as a warrior. Before launching an attack he would offer them three choices – conversion, payment of a tribute, or to fight by the sword. If they did not choose conversion a treaty was concluded, either instead of a battle or after it, which established the conditions of surrender for the Christians and Jews – the only non-Muslims allowed to retain their religion at that time. The terms of these treaties were similar and imposed on the *dhimmi*, the people 'protected' by Islam, certain obligations.

Although over the generations the majority of the *dhimmi* were converted to Islam, Christianity remained important in the Arab East (the Mashreq). Here, its most significant concentration can be traced along two geographical axes, one from Luxor to Alexandria and the other from Acre to Aleppo. Often in rebellion against the decrees of a distant mother church, first in Rome and then in Byzantium, the Christians of this region paradoxically owe their survival to the dialogue they have maintained, over long centuries, with Islamic states, and to their ability to reconcile national loyalty and allegiance to their faith. Behind this capacity lie the long periods of history in which the Christian communities of the Arab world have been isolated from each other, and the numerous particularisms of the Eastern churches and their congregations which have developed as result.

Whether located on the banks of the Nile or the Orontes, Arab Christian communities are thus deeply marked by the history and culture of their region or city. This remains trues even though, from the time of the Pharaohs of the New Empire to Gamal Abd al-Naser, Egypt and Syria (including present-day Syria, Lebanon, Jordan,

Palestine and Israel) were often closely linked, with Egypt as the suzerain state and Syria the vassal. The relations between these two countries have produced important moments in history; indeed it was in one of their earliest phases of unity that monotheist thinking was established, first in the form of the ephemeral religion of the visionary Pharaoh Akhneton, and then as Judaism. Their periods of political unity could also last for long time. From the ninth to the sixteenth centuries, for example, under the independent dynasties which emerged from the heart of the vast and crumbling Abbasid empire – the Tulunids (864–904), Ikhshidids (935–69) Fatimids (909–1171), Ayyubids (1169–1260) and Mamluks (1250–1517) Egypt and Syria had parallel if not joint destinies. These seven centuries, and the ensuing five centuries of Ottoman rule, did not remove the particularities of the Arab churches, or of the two very different countries we know today. Yet it gave them a common characteristic, unique in the area between the Atlas mountains and the Himalayas: the coexistence of two religions which everywhere else are separated by national borders.

The Situation of Christian Communities on the Arrival of the Arabs

On the eve of the Arab conquests Byzantium and Sasanian Persia together occupied a large part of the Middle East – the former Egypt and the coastal regions of Syria, the latter Mesopotamia. These two empires had been engaged for almost a century in long wars against each other. Both coveted the interior of Syria and the city of Jerusalem had, at different times, passed from Byzantine to Persian control. The peoples of these regions were Christians with a small minority of Jews.[2] Most of the Christians were, from the point of view of the Byzantine state, heretics. In the fourth century the emperor Theodosius had adopted Christianity as the official religion of Byzantium and decreed that Constantinople, his capital, would be the second capital of the church. Theodosius had also imposed as the orthodox creed of the empire the doctrine, declared at the Council of Nicea in 325, of the consubstantiality of the Father and the Son – the belief that Christ had both a human and divine nature fully united in his person. Throughout the vast region that came under Byzantine sway the clergy had to submit to this official doctrine. Hence the ensuing theological debate naturally became a vehicle by which aspirations for political autonomy were expressed.

The most important schisms to arise after the Council of Nicea were the Nestorian and the Monophysite. Nestorianism originated at the beginning of the fifth century in the theology of Nestorius, a priest of Antioch. It maintained a sharper division between divine and human nature than the Nicean creed, believing that Christ was a man in whom the word of God dwelt. The Monophysites on the other hand, led by the bishops of Alexandria, believed that Christ had a single, uniquely divine nature. In Iraq the majority of people were probably Nestorians.[3] In Egypt and Syria a large proportion adopted monophysism, the Copts in the former and the Jacobites in the latter. The Greek church encompassed many of those who remained faithful to the original Nicean doctrine and were popularly known, from the Arabic, as the Melkites, or partisans of the 'king' of Byzantium. In this confusion of sects, the debate was also coloured by inevitable polytheistic memories.

On the fringes of the Byzantine and Sasanian empires, the religious and political situation was confused. The Ghassanids, who inhabited the present-day Syrian Jazira, were the vassals of Byzantium. They had become Christian and their leader was recognized as *phylarch* (commander) by Byzantium. The Lakhmids of Northern Arabia, also Christian, were respectively the vassals of Byzantium to the west and Persia to the east. To the south, in the desert, the empires no longer exercised any power. Here Christianity had only penetrated superficially. The sole emperor whom the Arabs had given to Rome, Philip II called 'the Arab' (244–9), who was a heathen in the eyes of his subjects, was said to have converted secretly. Later, in 356, Constantine had sent an ambassador, Theodophilus Indus, as far as Southern Arabia. Nestorian missions from Syria and Iraq had performed evangelizing work but, since they followed the trade routes, they touched only the fringes of the desert: to the north the approaches to the valleys of the Euphrates, the Orontes and the Jordan; to the east the shores of the Gulf and the Indian Ocean, where bishops were noted in Oman in 424 and in Bahrain in 575 and 676; to the south the mountains of Asir and Yemen. In the latter a king who converted to Judaism in 523 had more or less exterminated Christianity.[4] In the heart of the Arabian peninsula, Najd and Hijaz, there were few Christians and even fewer Christian communities. Only the small oasis of Najran, famous for a treaty[5] that Muhammad negotiated with its inhabitants, had been Christian since around the year 500.[6] Judaism, on the other hand, was of some importance in pre-Islamic Arabia, as can be seen clearly in the treaties concluded with the Muslim conqueror. Nevertheless, the large majority of the people of the peninsula almost certainly lived out of the reach of the two monotheisms.

When Islam came to the region that is today known as the Arab East, how many Christians and how many Jews did it actually encounter? There are a few testimonies, some of them tax accounts from the time of the first caliphs, which enable us to make a rough of estimate of the population in this troubled period preceding the advent of the Arabs.[7]

Conquerors are normally inheritors. When they subject a population, they generally appropriate rather than destroy the legacy of their past. The Arab–Muslim armies were no exception to this pattern. In Egypt they took over a land that had been centralized for around three thousand years and the moment that the country submitted to the army of the Muslim general Amr Ibn al-As he revived the administration. The first fiscal levies were recorded on papyrus and showed the total proceeds of the annual receipts of the *jizya*, the poll-tax levied on non-Muslims; 12 million dirhams immediately after the conquest. Several testimonies record individual totals, 24 Egyptian dirhams per person, on average. Assuming that one taxpayer represented on average a family of five, Egypt must have had a population of approximately 2.5 million, all non-Muslim.[8]

Given that, with its gift of the Nile, Egypt brings to mind a land of plenty that is highly populated, this may seem a derisory figure.[9] And indeed there have been much rosier estimates. In 66 BC the king of the Jews Herod Agrippa, impressed by Egypt's financial receipts, concluded that the country had a population of 'seven million, five hundred thousand souls' outside Alexandria, a figure that survived for centuries. Of Alexandria itself, a city that always inspired dreams of glory, Alfred Butler, the British historian of the Arab conquest, wrote: 'al-Amr prided himself on having crowned his conquest by seizing 4,000 palaces ... 400 theatres, 4,000 public baths, 40,000 rich Jewish taxpayers out of an estimated total population of 600,000 men, not including women and children.'[10] Yet the cultivated area and agricultural yields of the time could not have supported more than 5 to 6 million people and Egypt not only fed its own population but also exported a large agricultural surplus to Rome. A reasonable estimate of the population at the beginning of the Christian era would, therefore, be 4.5 million. A statement of agricultural production under Diocletian (284–305) shows a possible decline to 3.2 million inhabitants. The great plague of 542–600 must, therefore, have caused the loss of one-fifth of the country's total strength. Perhaps as a result of this, the Arab armies encountered very little resistance (except in Alexandria which the Byzantines held on to for several more years).

For Syria which, in comparison to Egypt , had always been restive in the face of authority, there is apparently no contemporary testimony providing information about the population. The only available document mentions the tax paid in the town of Homs, which was 85,000 dinars per annum. Since each man paid a tax of 1 dinar and adult men formed one-quarter of the population, the town and its surroundings may have comprised 340,000 individuals. Homs represented approximately one-twelfth of the country, so Syria may have had a population of around 4 million. Similar deductions enable us to estimate the population of Mesopotamia, the region corresponding to present-day Iraq and south-east Turkey, at 9.1 million at the advent of the caliphate.[11]

At the time of the Muslim revelation, therefore, the Arab East probably contained some 15 million Christians and less than 200,000 Jews (see Table 1.1).

Seven Centuries of Islamization

The Islamic conquest proceeded at great speed and twelve years after the death of the Prophet the Muslim–Arab armies had taken the whole of the contemporary Arab East: the Fertile Crescent in 640, Syria and Northern Mesopotamia in 641, Egypt in 642. Spiritual conquest did not, however, match this frantic progress. Although some historians have gone so far as to say that the majority of the population of the empire remained non-Muslim until the Crusades,[12] the reality is that Islam spread at different speeds and in different ways according to a complex of circumstances: some groups adopted it from the beginning, while others – either in whole or in part – maintained their old beliefs for several centuries.

Religious Uniformity in the Arabian Peninsula

The Tradition (*sunna*) of Islam relate that on his deathbed the Prophet had declared: 'Two religions must not co-exist in the Arabian peninsula.' It was, in fact, the second caliph Umar who in 640 expelled the Jews from the Hijaz and the Christians from Najran, denouncing the treaty which Muhammad had negotiated with them and according to which they had been assured the right to live on the land for ever.[13] If the Prophet had actually ordered the expulsion of the Christians and the Jews, why was it not implemented by Abu Bakr, his immediate successor, and why did Umar wait until the end of his caliphate to execute it?[14] Two centuries later, the great chroniclers of Islam believed that the whole of Central Arabia was emptied of Christians and Jews in the wake of Umar's action. But there are pieces of evidence to suggest that this was not quite the case. For example, it was a Christian of Medina, admittedly a slave, who assassinated Umar. During the reign of Mu'awiya, the founder of the Umayyad dynasty, a force of 200 Christians formed the police of Medina and in Mecca a 'cemetery for the infidels' existed for a long time.

Yet if non-Muslims did remain in the peninsula their numbers in the central region were small. It is almost certain that, three centuries after the revelation, only a tiny group of Christians remained at Najran. The Jews were confined to the periphery. A few dozen families are mentioned by medieval travellers in the Hadhramaut. In the twelfth century, Benjamin of Tudela reported that in the archipelago of Bahrain 500 Jews lived at Qays and 5,000 at al-Qatifa.[15] This is a clear exaggeration by a Jewish traveller; but it nevertheless indicates the strong impression that the community made on him. Aden, where the Jews were most prosperous in the twelfth century, still had 7,000 Jewish male taxpayers at the beginning of the Ottoman period,[16] perhaps 30,000 people altogether. Given the size of the Jewish community at the beginning of the twentieth century (2 to 3 per cent of the population) it is likely that they have always formed a notable proportion of the Yemeni population and that Yemen remained a significant home of Arab Judaism until the creation of the state of Israel.

Iraq from the Hijra to the Mongols

Iraq, which at time of the conquest was the most populous area in the region, has left us the least information. We must distinguish between Mesopotamia to the south and the mountains and foothills of the north, the areas which are today Shi'a and those which are Sunni and still retain a Christian minority. In the north under the first caliphs, the Nestorians remained strong enough to send missions to the Far East which are confirmed by funeral details found in Sian-Fu (China) and on the Malabar Coast (India). Furthermore, they had an important intellectual influence on the Muslim conquerors and through their translations transmitted Greek philosophy to the Arabs. In the south, by contrast, Islam spread rapidly. The extent of the conversions is demonstrated by the fall of receipts from the poll tax which under Caliph Umar I (634–44) amounted to between 100 and 120 million dirhams but under the Umayyad caliph Abd al-Malik (685–705) had declined to 40 million.[17] Two-thirds of the total population must therefore have converted to Islam during the first 50 years of the conquest. If we accept that towards the year 700 Iraq (understood in the widest geographical sense) had 9 million inhabitants, it may have consisted of 6 million Muslim converts and 3 million Christians.

Some historians believe that conversions were somewhat slower arguing that Egyptian, Persian and Aramaean converts did not outnumber Muslims of Arab origin until the beginning of the Abbasid caliphate (750–1258).[18] This is, however, doubtful. During this period there were apparently no more than 2 million Arabs (all, by this time, Muslims) in Egypt, Persia and Syria. To state that in this whole area of 20 million inhabitants the non-Arab Muslims were also no more than 2 million is to conclude that, one century after the conquest, barely 10 per cent of the conquered population had embraced the new religion. Ten per cent is a very small figure, especially if we accept another estimate which relates to the military. In 742–43, the 'Syrian' army (that is the total number of men, whether Syrian or not, commanded by the Umayyad caliph of Damascus), consisted of 530,500 men,[19] who with few exceptions were Muslim by law. Conscription during this period of political expansion was at a high level, affecting perhaps a quarter of men of arms-bearing age – who themselves represented 25 per cent of the total population. In order to supply troops on such a scale there must clearly have been between 8 and 10 million Muslims in the region. These estimates accord better with what we know of the reign of the Umayyad caliph Umar II (717–20).

Umar II was very pious and imposed policies which precipitated conversions throughout the caliphate recorded by many chroniclers. Coming to us from the first century of the hijra, a letter written by a Christian complains about the speed with which the peoples of the old Sasanian empire allowed themselves in this period to be seduced by Islam without even trying to resist it:

> Where is that great people of Merv, who though they beheld neither
> sword, nor fire, nor torture, captivated only by love for a moiety of their
> goods, have turned aside like fools from the true path and rushed headlong

into the pit of faithlesness, into everlasting destruction, and have utterly been brought to nought ... out of the many thousands who have the name of Christians, not one single victim was consecrated unto God by the shedding of his blood for the true faith.[20]

From the time the Umayyad Caliphate was established in 661, southern Iraq had a large commercial and cultural influence.[21] When in 750 the succeeding dynasty, the Abbasids, transferred the capital of the Islamic empire to Baghdad, this influence increased further and almost certainly explains the rapid propagation of the new religion in the surrounding area. Kufa, Basra and other Mesopotamian cities were originally simple garrison towns which controlled from afar a population with whom they had no contact. Under the Abbasids they became the centres of intense regional and international activity and attracted men from far and wide. People who had until then been kept aside by their new rulers came into contact with the Muslim religion and the Arabic language, adopted both and diffused them.

Was this period of economic prosperity and rapid Islamization accompanied by demographic growth? There is no clear answer to this question because, soon after the conquest, the burden of land taxation became heavier and brought about a rural exodus. The cultivated area thus decreased as the number of consumers in the cities grew. In the tenth century a long decline in the price of cereals commenced, a sure sign that the rate of population decrease had overtaken the rate at which people were abandoning the land. The fall in receipts from the land tax in southern Iraq reflected a general decline in activity: from 10.3 million gold dinars under Umar II, to 9.6 million at the end of the seventh century, 6.7 million at the advent of Harun al-Rashid (786), 4.5 million at the time of his death (809), and only 1.5 million in 918.[22] Baghdad would then have had a population that was ten times smaller in 956 than in the time of the caliph al-Muqtadir (908–32).

Iraq never got the chance to recover. A long series of troubles preceded the crumbling away of the Abbasid caliphate and the Mongol invasion (1258), which plunged the country into long-term chaos. After this it had, at most, 5 million inhabitants.[23] This long period of decline witnessed the withdrawal of Christianity from northern Mesopotamia, until then its main centre in Muslim lands.[24] The destinies of the Nestorian church and the Muslim caliphate were thus paradoxically interdependent, the decline of one being repeated by the other.

When the Mongols began their invasion of Muslim territories they were favourably inclined to Christianity. The Mongol Prince, Hülegü, the first Ilkhan of Iran and Iraq (1256–65), had taken a Christian wife and it was rumoured that he had converted in secret. Perhaps because of this the caliph chose a Nestorian, the Patriarch Mashisha II, to negotiate the surrender of Baghdad in 1285. During the pillaging of the city which nevertheless followed, thousands were slaughtered,[25] but the Christian quarters were saved. However, when in 1295 the Ilkhan Ghazan officially converted to Islam, the Nestorians' luck ran out. Christians in Mesopotamia faced in addition the semi-permanent hostility of the Kurdish population, which on more than one occasion almost ended in massacre.[26] These 'Protestants of the East'[27] continued to produce brilliant artistic or scientific figures but began to lose their demographic significance. Already by the fourteenth century the population of Iraq barely included more than the 2–3 per cent of Christians found by the Ottomans two centuries later.

The Co-existence of Religions in the Levant

The experience of Syria was very different. Christianity has until the present day remained important in Lebanon, Palestine and even Syria itself. In 661, only two decades after the capture of Syria, the Umayyads transferred the capital of the new Islamic empire from Medina to Damascus. The city remained the centre of the empire for just one century, enough time for the caliphs to draw up a more or less definitive map of the *dar al-Islam*, the land administered by Islam – that is, to mark out the borders (save a few alterations) of the people who would progressively become Muslim.

Paradoxically, despite its central position during this crucial period in the history of humanity, the Umayyad capital and, even more so, the Syrian hinterland, retained some of the features of a Christian land.[28] The taking of Damascus had been symbolic of the way in which events would unfold in the future. It is reported that the Muslims entered by two gates, one having resisted and the other capitulated. Lying between the two gates, the Basilica of St John was divided in two – one sanctuary for the Muslims and the other for the Christians. As a result, the Umayyad mosque was constructed on the remains of half of the cathedral, and the congregations of the two religions for a long time worshipped alongside each other. At Homs, the large church provided shelter for the services of the two religions for four centuries. It was not until the Crusades, and the atmosphere of suspicion they generated, that this practice, which testified to the great tolerance of the early Islamic rulers, ceased.[29]

A century after the conquest, the Muslim Arab population of Syria is said to have numbered only 200,000, to which must be added a few thousand *mawali* (converts to Islam) of Syrian origin.[30] This is certainly a symbolic figure, curiously identical to that advanced by the chroniclers and historians of other nomad conquests: 200,000 was also the number of Hilalians who invaded North Africa in the ninth century, and the Turkish Seljuks who over-ran Anatolia in the eleventh century. Nevertheless, the figure suggests how little the newly-established Islam had penetrated the body of Syrian Christianity: out of 4 million people, perhaps 250,000 (6 per cent of the population) were Muslim. The total strength of the population must not have changed significantly in the course of one century since it had been subjected to opposing influences – the emigration of Christians to Byzantium on the one hand and the arrival of tribes from Arabia on the other; a recurrence of the bubonic plague and inflows of wealth towards the centre of the Caliphate; the closure of opportunities in the Greek world and the opening of new ones in India and the Far East, within reach of the traders of Damascus now that Sasanian Persia had been opened and absorbed into the Muslim empire.

Under the influence of the caliph Umar II (717–20) the conquest, which was initially political, became spiritual. Violently snatched by the Abbasids, in 750 the central power was moved from Syria to Iraq, leaving the former in the hands of foreign garrisons, some of them tyrannical. Islam won over a part of the population by taking advantage of the political fragmentation that resulted from this situation, and as a result of the coercion exercised by the Abbasid caliph al-Mutawakkil (847–61).

The tribes were the first to convert. At the time of the conquest the Muslim army had to grant certain concessions in order to progress and many Christian tribes had been authorized to retain their religion in return for the military services they had given in Persia on the side of the soldiers of Islam. As time passed, however, the state made it more and more difficult for ethnic Arabs to escape Islam. In 779 the Abbasid caliph al-Mahdi forced one of the last Christian tribes, the Tanukhids from the region of Aleppo, to convert. 'Five thousand men renounced their faith,' reported the Jacobite historian of the Middle Ages, Bar Hebraeus.[31] Subsequently the towns, where the state had set up its administration and the population lived alongside the new religion, were Islamized. The towns of the interior adopted Islam sooner and more fervently than those on the Mediterranean coast, because 'the Arabs feared the sea',[32] and because Byzantium maintained multiple commercial and ecclesiastical relations in the ports facing Greece. The villages remained apart from the movement for longer, particularly in the mountains:

> ... always the home of the lost cause ... the Lebanon remained Christian in faith and Syriac in speech for centuries after the conquest. Only the physical conflict had ended with the conquest; the religious, the racial, the social and above all the linguistic conflicts were just beginning.[33]

Nevertheless, over Syria as a whole a Christian majority remained until the end of the third century of the hijra. The Jacobites even took advantage of the routes opened to them by the Sasanian defeat to send missions to the Far East – until then the preserve of the Nestorians. This evangelizing zeal was supported by population growth, shrewdly described by the ninth-century writer al-Jahiz: being more prolific than the polygamous Muslims, he noted, the monogamous Christians 'filled the land'.[34] Towards the year 900, the total population of Syria, which had certainly not changed much since the conquest,[35] would have been approximately 2 million Christians and as many Muslims.

The confessional geography of the contemporary Near East was established during the half millennium before the Crusades. At different times the mountain became either the refuge of a section of Christianity or its stronghold. The Maronites, Monothelites who had remained faithful to the resolutions of the Council of Chalcedon (451) and rejected both the dogma of the Monophysites and the liturgy of the Melkites, were confronted by the dominant currents of Eastern Christianity. In 694, the Byzantine army sacked their convents and allegedly massacred 500 of their monks.[36] The Maronites therefore started to leave the plain of Orontes to establish themselves on the northern foothills of Lebanon, in the Qadicha valley. They were soon joined by another group of Christians known as *marada* (rebels)[37] from the time when they were in opposition to Byzantium who, once established in Lebanon, adopted the Maronite rite, thus strengthening their community. The *marada* were driven to the mountain from the region of Mount Amanus, near Antioch after their capital, Jurjuma, had been razed by the cavalry of the caliph. This action violated an old pact concluded in 639 when the warriors of Islam had taken Antioch from the Byzantines and signed an agreement with the *marada* which made them their spies and allowed them to remain Christian without being subjected to the poll tax. Although they were 'infidels' they would have served in the Muslim army and had all the rights of soldiers, including a share in the spoils.[38]

Five hundred years later, the proximity of the Frankish kingdoms consolidated the Maronite presence in the north of Lebanon. But it was during fighting between Muslims under the Mamluks, towards the end of the Middle Ages, that the Maronites established a firm and lasting footing in the mountain, a 'Christian country' to which, centuries later they would retreat again during the Lebanese civil war between 1975 and 1990. The Mamluks, who in 1250 had succeeded the Ayyubids in Egypt and by 1291 had driven out the remaining Crusader states from the Levant, had decided to reduce dissidence in the Syrian province and to punish Frankish sympathies. In 1305, they expelled the Alawis (Shi'i heretics) from central Lebanon to the hinterland of Latakia and stopped the expansion of the Druzes (also heretics of Shi'i origin) and the Metawalis (Shi'i Twelvers)[39] in the Kesrouan. Paradoxically, while the Mamluks were intolerant in religious matters they opened territorial gaps which the Maronites were to fill. They thus, unwittingly, sowed the seeds of a Christian predominance in Lebanon.[40]

It was also under the Mamluks that Beirut, which was to become a large Christian metropolis in the nineteenth century, was opened to the West. Acre, Tyre and Tripoli had never recovered from the Crusades, and Beirut, helped also by its proximity of Cyprus, was the beneficiary. Once Europe lost its positions on the Syrian coast Cyprus became 'the meeting place of Western businessmen', a real entrepôt of international trade. Before it became a possession of Venice, the island spent several years under the suzerainty of the Mamluks (1426–72) who, anxious to develop commercial relations with Europe, profited from the interlude to develop a transit trade whose natural outlet would be Beirut. The Lusignan, a Cypriot aristocracy of French origin, then acquired the right to own various buildings in this city – commercial premises, houses, churches. Thus the way was prepared to establish (much later, under Süleiman the Magnificent and François I) privileged relations between the Eastern Christians and the West during the Renaissance.

Population trends in medieval Syria alternated between steep demographic decline and weak recovery. The Crusades were preceded by a long period of lethargy, which was reflected in the trend in food prices: only a continually falling population could have brought demand and prices down with it.[41] By the end of the eleventh and the beginning of the twelfth centuries, when it was invaded by the Franks, Syria was already drained of its energies and at the time of the first Crusade it had only 2.7 million inhabitants.[42] Two centuries of fighting Western Christianity were to exhaust it. As in Egypt, there was a marked improvement in the demographic situation under the first Mamluks. The effect of commercial activity, which was often very striking, should have triumphed over the impact of violent wars against the Mongols. However, in 1343 the population of Syria was only 1.2 million inhabitants.[43] In Sidon, Beirut and the Beqa'a, the Mamluk authority levied one soldier per 250 inhabitants. These provinces supplied 500 soldiers, which indicates that the population was 125,000. Together with Tripoli, Lebanon had a population of 150,000 and the whole of Syria was eight times more. Simplistic as it may be, this estimate corresponds with the results of the first census carried out by the Ottomans in 1580: 1.4 million inhabitants in the three *vilayat* (provinces) of Aleppo, Damascus and Tripoli.

The Black Death of 1348–9 killed 200,000 people, and possibly more[44] so Syria by then had no more than 1 million inhabitants, of which perhaps 100,000 were Christian. Indeed, their proportion at that time was probably close to the one shown in the Ottoman censuses, since the last large conversions had taken place under the first Mamluks. It was under this dynasty that Christianity in the Levant narrowly escaped extinction (see Table 1.2). The same was true of Judaism. At the end of the fifteenth century, the traveller Meshullam de Volterra reported that Damascus gave shelter to between 400 and 500 Jewish families,[45] say 2–2,500 people. In the whole country there would have been less than 10,000 Jews.

The Rapid Spread of Islam in Egypt

The destiny of Egypt has been remarkable. Swiftly conquered, it appeared that its Islamization would be fast and complete. But although it was less rebellious than the Maghreb and far closer to Arabia, it was in the end the only country in North Africa which never lost its Christian community.

When General Amr Ibn al-As landed in the Sinai, he found a country that was depopulated and weakened. The 4,000 horsemen

who accompanied him were certainly not sufficient for the invasion
he planned, but the 20,000 men he summoned as reinforcements
from Arabia met very little real resistance, except in Alexandria.
Defended by 50,000 men and still open to Byzantium on the sea,
the historian Aziz Atiya, founder of the Institute of Coptic Studies
in Cairo, writes that the city might have been held indefinitely were
it not for the duplicity of it governor, Cyrus.[46] Byzantium had made
the mistake of nominating Cyrus as both the patriarch and the
prefect of Alexandria. As representative of two reviled institutions
– the official (Melkite) religion and the tax authority – he must have
faced strong hostility from the Copts. He negotiated a surrender
whose terms dictated that hostages would be taken from the civilian
population.

The fiscal system of the new state was quickly established in the
first year of the conquest. The *jizya* (poll tax) gives us information
on the size of the non-Muslim population, and the *kharaj* (land tax
levied on all landlords whatever their religion), provides information
on the rural population. By adding the townsmen – then about 10
per cent of the inhabitants – we can estimate the total population.
These figures, however approximate, are very telling for they provide
us with markers that enable us to retrace a long and eventful history
(see Table 1.3). We can see that the *jizya* fell when the *kharaj* was
maintained, demonstrating the decline of Christianity despite demographic stability. In other words, Islam was propagated extremely
fast solely by means of conversions. More than half of the Copts
would have been converted in less than forty years – 26 per cent
between 644 and 661 and 33 per cent during the reign of Mu'awiya
between 661 and 680.

Aziz Atiya doubts that they could have abandoned their religion
so quickly. If, as all the chroniclers agree, the Copts welcomed the
conquerors who liberated them from the oppression of Byzantium,
they could not have intended to give up the faith that they had kept
in the face of persecution. The *jizya* may thus be an unreliable
indication of the number of taxpayers which was possibly affected
by factors other than population size, for example income.

The Arabs did not establish a tyrannical regime, and they
understood very well the significance of water in Egypt. The Treaty
of Capitulation they imposed at Babylon (Old Cairo) stipulated that
'the inhabitants of Misr [Egypt] were obliged to pay a *jizya* of 50
million as soon as the Nile flood ended … If at the time of the
flood the river did not reach its normal level, the tax would be

reduced proportionately.'[47] Thus, in certain years, the fall of the *jizya* could have been caused by a lowering of the level of the Nile. A deterioration of agriculture or a revaluation of the dinar could also explain in part the changing levels of tax receipts.[48] The governor of Egypt nevertheless watched the receipts of the state disappearing and worried about the rate of conversions: in order to maintain the level of public resources, the representative of the Muslim state himself encouraged the Copts to keep their religion.[49] However, other measures dissuaded them, for example the imposition in 705 of Arabic as the administrative language, which reduced Coptic to liturgical and domestic use.

The somewhat romantic interpretation of one of the first British historians of the Coptic church, E. L. Butcher, crumbles in the face of this tax evidence. He believed that deepening mysticism was the real cause of the decline of Christianity in Egypt, thus suggesting that Islamization had progressed very slowly. The large number of callings after the Islamic conquest to follow the monastic tradition of St Antony represented, he argued, a collective refusal of the future – in effect the 'suicide of a nation'.[50]

Towards the year 800, the population of Egypt was 77 per cent Muslim and only 22 per cent Christian – the remaining 1 per cent being Jews; this enables us to establish the revenue of the poll tax and the land tax for the same date. The statements of the *jizya* stop after that. From the ninth to the nineteenth century, it is possible to retrace the important stages of Egyptian demography, but not those of confessional distribution. Nevertheless it is clear that Christianity declined over the next eleven centuries from 22 to 8 per cent of the population in 1882.

The Arab conquest was not as favourable to population growth in Egypt as might be imagined. Of course, the increased opportunities to market its agricultural products in adjacent regions of the empire and in the cities which formed around the new administration benefited the population. But continuing crises of production prevented any permanent expansion. The peasantry were soon dominated by, and at the mercy of, an all-powerful military class. When the organizational capacity of this class disintegrated, which happened frequently once the prosperity that immediately followed the conquest had ended, the irrigation canals fell into disuse, agricultural production dropped and the people suffered. But the ups and downs affected everyone irrespective of their religion and it seems likely that the Christian population retained its relative demographic position until the advent of the Fatimid dynasty in 969. The Fatimids, who were Isma'ilis, were tolerant and maintained the tradition of community harmony both in relationship to the Sunnis, the majority of Egyptian Muslims, and the Christians. Indeed, they initiated what was to become common practice in Egypt – the incorporation of Copts into the higher administration of the state and the quasi-monopoly of the Egyptian Treasury by the Copts, which survived until the nineteenth century, dates from this period. This was a delicate position which exposed the Copts more than once to popular abuse: 'We can gain an idea of their number and their influence at all times by the constant complaints about the dishonesty of the Christian secretaries.'[51]

The Fatimid dynasty collapsed during one of the great catastrophes in the demographic history of Egypt, under the caliphs al-Hakim (996–1021) and al-Mustansir (1036–94). The unstable personality of the former plunged the country into chaos and brought religious hatred, while the severity of the famine to which al-Mustansir gave his name completed the break-up. In a single century Egypt lost one-third of its population, in perfect correlation with the fall in the volume of the Nile flood – from 1022 to 1121 the nilometer in Cairo continually showed a shortage of water. And during these troubled years Christianity suffered.

The first Crusades did not reach Egypt and its population recovered. Perhaps because of this its army was victorious when the Franks did venture into the country. However, when in 1169 Saladin was sent by the Zengid ruler of Syria, Nur al-Din, to take control of Egypt, he carried with him the climate of religious tension that the Crusaders had created in the Near East. At the beginning of his reign the Copts were made to suffer because they shared the religion of the Franks – although they never gave the slightest support to them. Under Saladin they were humiliated in their daily life, although not persecuted, and new 'mass'[52] conversions reduced their community. However, the atmosphere relaxed after Jerusalem was recaptured in 1187 and the Copts found favour with the hero of Muslim resistance to the Crusades, even supplying the architect who constructed the Muqattam citadel.

With the overthrow in 1250 of Saladin's house, the Ayyubid dynasty, Egypt embarked on a long period of rule by two successive Mamluk dynasties. Though different in many ways, under both these dynasties political life, the economy and the demographic situation progressed in perfect harmony. The Mamluks, literally 'the possessed', were originally slaves bought in the markets of Turkey to be reared as soldiers – a practice first used by the Abbasids. These slaves, who had initially formed a caste, became a growing power in the Ayyubid army and eventually overthrew the ruler naming one of their own officers as Sultan. The first Mamluk sultans were known as Bahrites (1250–1381). This was not a family name because, in its origins at least, the dynasty of these 'political eunuchs' was not reproduced by lineage. It was simply a place name, their barracks being situated on the bank of the river (*bahr*) Nile.[53] The Bahrite Mamluks brought back to Egypt the grandeur it had lost since antiquity. They successfully defended Syria against the Mongols, expelled the last Crusader states from the Syro–Palestinian littoral and extended their empire to the upper Euphrates and Cilicia.

The Mamluks also developed trade. Under the Ayyubids Egypt had begun to establish a position in the world economy that it maintained until the rounding of the Cape of Good Hope. Connecting the Mediterranean and the East Indies, two wealthy areas which were complementary but too distant to trade directly, the country was soon to become a commercial power. Alexandria, which had lost its glamour when it turned its back on the Greek world, began to revive from the trade with the Far East – a trend encouraged by the Mamluks who fostered good commercial relations with their former enemies, the Genoese, Venetians and Catalans. Population growth came with increasing wealth: by 1315 Egypt had once again more than 4 million inhabitants, although a plague in 1348 probably decimated one-third of the population.

Towards the end of the fourteenth century, the Mamluks changed their name by taking up residence in the citadel (*borj*) hence becoming the Borjites (1382–1517). Their ethnic origin changed to Circassian; but above all their politics changed. By intervening in economic activity and imposing an unbearable level of taxation, their state became a predator plunging Egypt into the period of palace intrigues and social devastation recorded a century later in the writings of al-Maqrizi.[54] In the great famine of 1403–4 perhaps half the population died. The plague and shortage of food sapped the strength of the Mamluk army which lost to Tamerlane at Damascus (1400), the Portuguese in the Red Sea (1500) and finally capitulated to the Turkish Ottomans (1517). The population of Cairo, which had doubled since the eleventh century, declined from 600,000 inhabitants in about 1340 to 430,000 at the beginning of the sixteenth century.[55] Leo the African,[56] who stayed in the city in 1526, provided a meticulous list of its neighbourhoods and the number of families in each – a total of 35,500, which corresponds to about 200,000 people. Clearly, the population growth had collapsed.

As for Christianity, the Mamluk era, which followed the defeat of the Crusades, was without doubt a period of rising Muslim religious feeling.[57] Being foreigners by origin, the Mamluks had only religion by which to legitimize their position with their Muslim subjects. In general, therefore, they were intolerant towards Christians. Neither the Bahrites nor the Borjites made any attempt to restrain the crowds when they pillaged churches.

Nevertheless, the condition of the Christians fluctuated in accordance with the general atmosphere. Baybars, the Mamluk general who drove the Mongols from Syria, became the triumphant head of state in Cairo and successfully buried his past. Under him the Copts, who had maintained a position of constant neutrality during the Frankish wars, rediscovered positions in the administration. As always, a kind of vicious circle was set in motion. When they gained office, the Copts accumulated wealth, which brought power and ostentation. The visibility of these wealthy 'infidels' jostled with the piety of the common people, who clamoured for their dismissal. The authorities willingly obliged. But each large dismissal of Copts paralysed the machinery of the state, and after a respectable interval the Mamluk authority would once again seek their services in order to restore efficiency.[58] The constant hostility of the ordinary people inevitably brought about new collective conversions, the last in the history of the country.

The Christians were not the only *dhimmi* of Egypt. There was also a Jewish community in the country, largely concentrated in Cairo. The rulers and the people generally treated them in the same way as the Christians. Relatively in favour until the reign of the Fatimid caliph al-Hakim, afterwards their situation oscillated according to events. Visiting Egypt in 1171, Benjamin of Tudela estimated that there were between 12 and 20 thousand of his co-religionists,[59] that is, about 1 per cent of the population. The Crusades subsequently damaged the Jewish community for, even though it was not involved, being non-Muslim it was naturally suspected of siding with the Franks. Communication with the enemies of Islam is a recurrent theme of the attacks against the *dhimmi*: '[The Jews] were not in sympathy with the Crusades, but [they] were also victims of the resentment which the Muslims had built up towards the *dhimmi*.'[60] In 1301 especially, they were the target of persecution. In 1481, the traveller Meshullam de Volterra estimated that they numbered only 5,000.[61] The rate of population growth of the Jewish community had therefore regressed considerably under the Mamluks. On the eve of the Ottoman conquest, the Jews represented no more than 0.2 per cent of the Egyptian population. However, many Jews were escaping from Spain under the Catholic kings, and a certain number found asylum in Egypt where they reinforced a rapidly weakening community.

Invaders or Liberators?

Although Islam was accepted in Arabia within a few decades, in Egypt and Syria it took almost a thousand for it to acquire the position that it holds there today. How could a handful of conquerors – however passionate their faith – have carried along with them a mass of people of such size and so remote? How could a point of equilibrium between the contrary pressures of Muslim expansion and Christian resistance have been found in Egypt and the Fertile Crescent?

From the time of the Prophet, Islam had established a fundamental distinction between the *dar al-Islam*, the land administered by the Muslim state, and the *dar al-harb*, the land of war or the land to be conquered. The war that extended the former at the expense of the latter was of very short duration and rapid victory was facilitated by the situation encountered by the first Muslim armies. The incessant wars between Byzantium and Persia on the eve of the Islamic conquest had exhausted both the military and the civilian populations. The armies of Constantinople and Ctesiphon could only offer weak resistance to the soldiers of the caliph, and the people, moving alternatively from one yoke to the other, but constantly held to ransom in order to finance military campaigns, were ready for a new master.

The background to these struggles for hegemony was the number of inextricable religious divisions in the region. In Iraq, the Nestorians lived uncomfortably with the Zoroastrianism of the Sasanian state, but also benefited from a certain protection in the face of the attacks from Byzantium. In Syria and Egypt revolt was brewing. Far from the centre of the empire, the people of these regions – even the Melkites who remained loyal to the official church – suffered heavy exploitation by Constantinople. Heretics who were nevertheless the majority they endured all kinds of persecution. Ruled over with a rod of iron by Byzantium, the theological protest of the

Monophysites thus took on the character of a proto-nationalism, Syrian among the Jacobites and Egyptian among the Copts. In this context, the arrival of the Arabs was accepted with hope, if not acclaimed with enthusiasm, a response that was still alive in Jacobite memory 500 years later when Michel the Syrian, a monk during the time of the third crusade, recalled 'the son of Ismaël who came from the south to deliver us'.[62]

Once Muslim power was established, the population moved immediately into the heart of the *dar al-Islam*. This did not, however, mean that they converted to Islam; on the contrary, because the law provided that non-Muslims would enjoy a special status it codified their existence. The conversion of the majority to Islam took several generations. It is known that coercion, although it was occasionally used, was rare in the history of Arab Islam. Rather, the institutions established by the conquerors and their successors, the social relations that were established over time between the different confessional groups and the shocks which over the years shook the Mediterranean world slowly produced their effect.

Some of the conquered people rapidly became Muslim and through conversion acquired full citizenship, perhaps without feeling any real rupture. For one thing the new religion stood in the tradition of Christianity and Judaism. It had been revealed in a language that was already familiar to the tribes of the steppes of Northern Arabia and the traders of the towns. According to Maxime Rodinson, Arab customs allowed and favoured adoption by clans of people of all types and origins who in this way became full-fledged Arabs. The wave of conversions slowly grew until it became irresistible.[63]

Another group kept their religion but accepted the change of power without any real resistance. Both the Copts and the Jacobites, for example, were neutral. Byzantium had deprived them of both their religious and their political freedom, while the Arabs proclaimed their intention of respecting the first – although at the price of alienating the second. All the treaties of capitulation stated without the slightest ambiguity that 'no constraint will be exercised in matters of religion'. And this promise was honoured, at least initially. Forced into a clandestine existence in the time of Byzantium, the Coptic Patriarch Benjamin reappeared in public under General Amr.

The Monophysite schisms, which had greatly assisted the Arab conquest, paradoxically slowed down Islamization. Accustomed to the domination of the king, their ecclesiastical institutions did not find it difficult to survive under Islam. The same factor thus explains both the success of the Muslim conquest and its limits. In Egypt on one hand and Syria on the other, Islam brought together the diverse Christian communities that it administered, and reinforced the alliances which could stand against it. It adopted an undifferentiated attitude to the Christians, whatever their sect. As a new religion, Islam considered the Christians to be uniformly unbelievers; as a new state, it treated them as *dhimmi*, all subject to the same rules. When, in 740, the Umayyad government forced the Melkites to break with the patriarch of Antioch, who was a refugee in Constantinople, and to elect an indigenous patriarch with no attachment to Byzantium, the Christian sects came into contact with each other once more.

A Progressively Muslim Society

> Fight against such of those who have been given the Scripture as believe not in Allah nor the Last Day, and forbid not that which Allah hath forbidden by His messenger, and follow not the religion of truth, until they pay the *jizya* readily, being brought low. (Qur'an, IX.29)

Many historians agree that the fiscal inequality introduced by the Qur'an between Muslims and non-Muslims was the main inducement to conversion, even if the amounts were relatively small at different times and places.[64] Christians and Jews could only avoid the payment of the poll tax, which remained in force until the reforms of 1839 in the Arab provinces of the Ottoman Empire and in 1855 in Egypt, by converting to Islam.

There were significant differences in the way taxation affected the non-Muslim population immediately after the conquest and when the Muslim state had been in existence for a long time. The treaties of capitulation introduced a fixed *jizya*. However, the administration which levied this tax also collected another, the *kharaj* – a land tax which everyone, Muslims as well as *dhimmi*, was obliged to pay. Since the Arabs did not bring their own administration with them to the territories they conquered, the tax collector was an indigenous person. The Arab rulers were only interested in the total amount of money collected and so they left the apportionment between the *jizya* and the *kharaj* to the judgement of the local collector. In the Egyptian countryside until the middle of the seventh century, the two taxes seem to have been confused and the converted were exempted from the *kharaj* as well as the *jizya*.[65] The main result of this was a stronger fiscal inequality in this country than elsewhere, which probably hastened conversions.[66] In Iraq, the rate of conversion to Islam was such that in order to retain the resources of the Treasury the governor had to impose the capitation tax even on those who had converted.[67]

The fiscal system had another, more pernicious, result. As conversions proceeded, the decline in the number of taxpayers liable to pay the *jizya* resulted in an increase in the amount due per capita. Taxation could become unbearable for those who were subjected to both the *jizya* and the *kharaj*, to the extent that they had to give up one or the other. In order to avoid the land tax, many convinced Christians left the countryside. It was probably in this early period that Christianity became significantly rooted in urban areas. The *jizya* had unexpectedly had the effect of producing social selection.

Poor Christians who could not afford to pay the tax became Muslim. In the original Muslim society, the non-Arab converts became *mawali*, subordinate to the Muslim Arab minority. For the majority of the *mawali* of low origin, the statute of subordination represented a social promotion.[68] Initially the less poor, but gradually the richer, Christians were the only ones with the material means to keep their religion if they wanted to. Thus the tax system of Islam may well have encouraged, by successive selection, the reproduction of a Christianity that was more and more bourgeois. Indeed, as Christianity retreated, a division of labour appeared that was confessionally based. In Syria more than in Egypt, the Christians were concentrated in certain professions abandoned by the Muslims, particularly in the liberal professions and banking.[69]

In the early stages after the conquest the converts were a minority who suffered certain social difficulties. For to convert to Islam cut the *mawla* from his origins, his family, his village or his neighbourhood. In time, however, social difficulties began to affect the non-converted. As the shackles of the Muslim administration extended and the proportion of Muslims increased, the status of the non-Muslim became more precarious. Everyday life became more closed to the minorities, official Islam became stricter and the ulema (religious scholars and doctors of law) more intolerant. It even became difficult for people to marry within their own religion since the number of marriageable people had declined so much. The law was absolutely inflexible on this point and therefore worked in favour of Muslim population growth: a *dhimmi* could only marry a Muslim woman after converting to Islam, while a Muslim could marry a *dhimmi* woman who had not converted and their children would be Muslim.

By a sort of snowball effect, social pressure therefore took over from the *jizya* as the cause of the later conversions. In its turn it produced another form of selection – no longer social, but religious. Those who remained Christian were less and less inclined to convert. Those who moved to Islam, whether rich or poor, found the change morally acceptable.[70] The statute of exception of the *dhimmi* had thus superimposed social on confessional differences, and reinforced the exclusion of the minorities. It had potentially radicalized society, and although through it the state legalized the difference between the confessions, social forces did not always accept it.

There were some violent episodes, some spectacular explosions of popular fanaticism, but the state was almost never a persecutor. The public authority sometimes decreed discriminatory measures whose origin went back to a famous convention of the caliph Umar II by which the *dhimmi* had agreed to various conditions: 'We will not attempt to look like Muslims by our dress We will not mount on saddles . . . We will not gird the sword . . . We will clip the front of our hair.' Umar had imposed these distinctive signs on the Christians to avoid them being confused with the Muslim soldiers when he had established a regular army from which non-Muslims were excluded by statute.[71] The building up of the state had been the reason for his measures, which quickly fell into oblivion. Their re-appearance in later years was nearly always during crises. In order to appease the clamour of the street, some caliphs did not hesitate to extol the piety of the people. Harun al-Rashid (786–809) for example, reinstated the convention of Umar by compelling the Christians to wear stipulated clothes. Charlemagne, it is said, took advantage of the occasion which presented itself to extend the influence of the Eastern empire. After an exchange of embassies with the Baghdad caliphate, he obtained permission to send regular aid to the Christians of Palestine and to finance various ecclesiastical institutions. 'It was reported that the leader of the infidels had transferred to Charlemagne the sovereignty of Jerusalem,' wrote Michelet.[72] The Holy City would thus have been covered with Latin foundations and grown into a veritable 'Carolingian protectorate – *lato sensu*'[73] with a charitable aim.

Other decrees excluded non-Muslims from public office. On this point the official doctrine of Islam is unambiguous: the Qur'an itself had established such exclusion by numerous injunctions not to take 'the infidels as associates'.[74] However, the facts are almost continually at odds with the precepts of the first caliphs, for the conquerors – being far-seeing politicians – understood the value of administrative continuity. 'The Arabs,' wrote the historian of the Middle Ages Ibn Khaldun, 'were rough, uneducated, and with few skills in the arts of writing and arithmetic; also they took Jews, Christians or freed foreigners to do their accounts.'[75] Levels of education would, of course, have converged fairly quickly, in theory enabling the public authorities to dispense with the services of non-Muslims. But more often they had recourse to them. The multitude of edicts which restate the Qur'anic prescription clearly demonstrate that this was not respected. Thus the Abbasid caliph al-Mutasim (833–842) had two Christian ministers, one in finance, while his successor al-Mutawakkil (847–861) dismissed all Christians from his administration.

History repeated itself eloquently. Exceptional circumstances, whether political troubles or economic crises, were required to justify purges – usually of short duration.[76] The only real persecution endured by the Copts (as well as many Muslims), under al-Hakim (996–1020), will remain in the Christian memory for a long time. 'For some time a great scarcity worried the people,' warned the old Druze man of the Lebanese mountain, before recounting to Nerval the legend of the caliph al-Hakim,[77] who allegedly became mad towards the year 1,000, proclaimed himself the divine incarnation expected one thousand years after Christ, secretly married (according to legend) his sister Sitt al-Mulk, and gave rise to a sect of adepts who assembled behind the preacher al-Darazi, from whom the Druzes took their name. Temperamental rather than methodical, al-Hakim banned religious processions one day, destroyed churches, deprived the *dhimmi* of the right to trade with Muslims, then authorized the Christians whom he had only the previous day forced to become apostates, to return to their religion. Another legend states that he was not stabbed to death by a Muslim, but in a place where he retreated after he converted to Christianity. Nerval used this as the epilogue to his narrative: 'The Copts claim that Jesus Christ appeared to al-Hakim, who begged forgiveness for his sins and did penitence for many years in the desert.'

The Mamluks showed themselves afterwards to be more severe than their predecessors towards Christianity. By the end of their reign, at the beginning of the sixteenth century, the scene had been set for its total disappearance. At that moment there was an unexpected reversal in the trend and the Ottoman empire, which was advancing towards Syria and Egypt, brought Christianity back to life.

Table 1.1: Population by Religion at the Beginning of the Arab Caliphate (in thousands)

Region	Total Population	Christians	Jews
Arabia	1,000	100	10
Syria	4,000	3,960	40
Mesopotamia	9,100	9,009	91
Egypt	2,700	2,673	27
Total	16,800	15,742	168

Sources: Total population, Josiah Cox Russell, 'Late Ancient and Medieval Population', *Transactions of the American Philosophical Society*, vol 48/111, 1958; Jews 1% of the total population, S. D. Goitein, 'Jewish Society and Institutions under Islam', *Journal of World History*, vol xi, 1968.

Table 1.2: Population by Religion in Syria, 633–1580 (in thousands)

Date	Total	Muslims	Christians	Jews
633	4,000	0	3,960	40
730	4,000	250	3,710	40
900	4,000	2,000	1,960	40
1199	2,700	n.d.	n.d.	n.d.
1343	1,200	1,068	120	12
1350	1,000	890	100	10
1580	1,419	1,291	115	13

Source: 1570–1580 Ottoman census of 1570–1590, Ömer Lütfi Barkan, 'Research on the Ottoman Fiscal Surveys' in M. A. Cook *Studies in the Economic History of the Middle East*, London, 1970; other sources are given in the text.

Table 1.3: Estimated Population of Egypt, from Antiquity to 1798
(in thousands)

Period	Total *jizya* (1,000 dirhams)	Christian and Jewish Population	Total *kharaj* (1,000 dirhams)	Total Population
1st century AD				4,500
4th century				3,000
600 AD				2,600
Arab conquest (641)	12,000	2,500		
Uthman (644–55)	13,000	2,500		
Mu'awiya (beginning)	9,000	1,875		
Mu'awiya (end)	5,000	1,040		
Hisham (743)			4,000	2,200*
Harun al-Rashid (787)	4,000	830		
Harun al-Rashid (813)	3,000	625	4,857	2,671*
al-Ma'mun (813–33)			4,257	2,365*
al-Mu'tazz Billah (869)			4,800	2,640*
Ibn Tulun (884)			4,300	2,365*
Mu'izz al-Din (975)			3,200	1,760*
al-Mustansir (1090)			3,061	1,683*
Saladin (1189)			4,277	2,351*
Muhammad (1315)				4,200
Barquq (1382)				3,150
Bonaparte (1798)				2,498

* Estimate from the total *kharaj* received.

Source: Josiah C. Russell, *The Population of Medieval Egypt in Medieval Demography*, AMS Press, New York, 1987

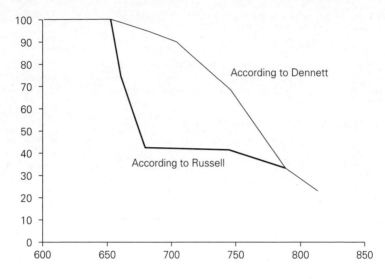

Figure 1.1: Percentage of non-Muslims in Egypt, 600–850

CHAPTER TWO

The Dechristianization of North Africa

The whole region, from the Maghreb al-Aqsa as far as Tripoli, or more precisely as far as Alexandria, and from the Roman Sea to the country of the black people, has been inhabited by the Berber race ... The Berbers, like all foreign nations, both east and west, were heathens. From time to time, however, they adopted the religion of their conquerors, for several great nations had held them in subjection. [Ibn Khaldun, *Histoire des Berbères et des dynasties musulmanes de l'Afrique septentrionale,* Paris, 1925.]

At the extreme West of the Muslim world, the furthest point from the epicentre of Islam and Arabism, Sunni orthodoxy today holds undisputed sway. Here the Christian past has been buried twice over, once by natural oblivion and once by deliberate silence.

The last real traces of an indigenous Christianity disappeared from the Maghreb eight centuries ago. Two generations have passed since the colonial occupation of the region by Europeans ended. Yet the memory of colonial violence is still so alive that, in the newly-independent states, official history hides, as though it were shameful, the thousand years during which Berbers were Christian, as well as the three thousand when Jews lived there. Such churches as still remain for the younger generation to see are relics of colonialism, the products of a foreign architecture which clearly has nothing in common with local culture. In Algiers, under the intrepid gaze of a statue of Charles Allemand Lavigerie (Archbishop from 1825 to 1892), neighbourhood teams play impromptu games of football in the square of Notre Dame d'Afrique. But 70 per cent of the city's population are too young to have seen the faithful of a religion other than their own enter the old synagogue converted into a mosque after independence. It is little more than thirty years since this vast Arab territory became wholly Muslim for the first time in history – thirty years which have come to seem like a peaceful eternity in the collective subconscious.

The Two Carthages

In 640, eight years after the death of the Prophet, the Arab armies approached North Africa from Egypt. They reached the Maghreb seven years later and by 711 they had conquered the whole region before moving on to occupy Spain, a process completed in 759. Most of the people they subjected in North Africa were Christian, although there were also small Jewish communities as well as tribes who had never adopted monotheism – or who had adopted and then abandoned it.

The Christian evangelization of the Roman province of Ifriqiya began in the second century on the coast, and from there it soon reached the interior. In about the year 200, Tertullian the Carthaginian, the first father of the Western Church, and the founder of Latin theology, is said to have claimed that Christians were already in a majority in the towns. But the 'towns' probably did not contain more than one-tenth of the population – certainly not the 60 per cent given by a French historian of the colonial period who wanted to show that France had restored an earlier Berber order that had been swept away by Islam.[1]

In the countryside, it is known that from a very early stage the Berbers had played the Church against the Roman Empire and developed a creed known as Donatism which taught fidelity to an original Christian purity it accused Rome of having betrayed.[2] Donatism became a kind of early nationalism rooted, like national liberation movements sixteen centuries later, in social protest. It also supported the Circoncellians, Berber peasants who were in revolt against large, Romanized landowners. The fact that Christianity had spread among the rural population does not mean, however, that the people were actually Christian: 'The quality of this faith' writes Abdallah Laraoui, 'can no more be judged by the faith of St Augustine than can the number of the faithful by the situation of Carthage.'[3]

Saint Augustine later returned the Berbers to the Roman faith. Born in Tagaste – known today as Suq al-Akhras in Algeria – Augustine died in 430 during the Vandal siege of his diocese, Hippone, near to present-day Annaba. Augustine's death at the hand of this Germanic tribe signalled a century-long period in which African Christianity was once more cut adrift from Rome. For the Vandals were Arianists, followers of a heretical doctrine preached by Arius (256–336), a priest of Alexandria who initiated an endless procession of Byzantine disputes by rejecting the doctrine of consubstantiality and thus challenging the idea of the divine nature of Christ. When Arius was excommunicated his heresy was transferred to the northern shores of the Mediterranean where it spread among the Germanic Vandal tribe who carried it back to North Africa via Andalusia. By 442 the Vandals had completely conquered the Maghreb and instituted a reign of persecution for the Berber Christians, pushing them back to the mountains. But Berber resistance strengthened their rejection of Arianism, and may well have served to reinforce their own faith. Eventually a Vandal king who favoured Catholicism, Hilderic, was enthroned at Carthage but promptly removed by his rival, Gelimer. At this point the Byzantine emperor Justinian, a committed Christian, responded to the situation by, in 533, sending his army under the command of Belisarius to reconquer Mediterranean Africa. Justinian was determined to extend Christianity to the tribes that had remained pagan and to regenerate the Latin orthodoxy of those who had been perverted by Arianism. His conversions, however, were made at the point of a sword and provoked constant Berber insurrections which it took the Byzantine army fifteen years to subdue.

Some 50 years later, at the beginning of the seventh century, Byzantine North Africa and Tripolitania together had 470 bishops. But this proliferation of high-level clergy did not necessarily reflect the size of the Christian congregation. One historian of the colonial period, Emile-Félix Gautier, who saw the pre-Islamic distinction between nomadic and sedentary groups, the Botr and the Baranes, as having existed since time immemorial argued that only the latter would have been truly Christianized: 'The Baranes were in prolonged contact with the two Carthages, the Punic and the Roman – that is to say with civilization. At the time of the Arab conquest they were Christian. Many of the Botr were Jews or Fetishists, known as "idolaters" by the Arab chroniclers.'[4] They would not embrace Islam with the same enthusiasm.

The Conversion of Tribes and Individuals

Describing the religious situation the Arabs encountered when they arrived in North Africa, Ibn Khaldun writes: 'Beside the ancient naturist and animist cults, beside the Carthaginian gods, orthodox and heretic Christianity, Talmudic and non-Talmudic Judaism all had their adepts.'[5] Ibn Khaldun, who lived 600 years after the Arab conquest, could not of course be precise about the confessional distribution of pre-Islamic North Africa. He suggested, however, that Christianity dominated widely. 'Also, we state that before the introduction of Islam, the Berbers of Ifriqiyya and the Maghreb lived under the domination of the Franks [Latins] and professed Christianity, the religion followed by the Franks and the Greeks [Byzantines].'[6]

Modern demographers have estimated the population of North Africa at the time of the Muslim conquest to have been 2 million, possibly a little more,[7] of whom the large majority, perhaps 1.5 million, were Christian. The Jews of the Maghreb were a small minority – around 20,000 or 1 per cent of the population.[8] This group undoubtedly included descendants of Jews from Palestine who had settled in the area when the Phoenicians ruled the southern coast of the Mediterranean from Tyre and Sidon, but it consisted largely of Judaized Berbers.[9]

Islam never eliminated Judaism – secular subjection to the Christian power had for long accustomed the Jewish community to minority status – but it destroyed Christianity. The question is whether it simply swept it away, or whether it disappeared by a slow process of erosion. The first history of the conquest was only begun six centuries after the event [10] and no contemporary account of the expansion of Islam has been recovered which gives an indication of the speed at which people adopted the religion. We can therefore only surmise the state of the religion and society in North Africa when the Arabs arrived armed with their new faith.

Roman Christianity survived the Vandal terror by relying on its own resources – not the mother church with which, owing to force of circumstance, it had not maintained relations for a century. The Byzantines had not been acclaimed as liberators and indeed their arrival had, as already noted, incurred lively opposition among the Berbers to whom Byzantium embodied the temporal, not the spiritual. Thus freed from ecclesiastical hierarchies, the African faith was able to follow its own path and to flourish as a mode of thought rather than as allegiance to a system of precepts. It was at the same time this weak institutional base that enabled Islam to advance Thus, notes the Arab historian Abdullah Laraoui: 'When, after being united in one state and around one credo, the Arabs left their desert peninsula, they behaved as heirs. Developed away from all contact with the Church, African Christianity slowly assumed the form of an abstract monotheism able to be satisfied with any dogma.'[11]

Islamization, in other words, would have cautiously extended the internal evolution of North African Christianity to the point at which the process would have passed almost unnoticed by the people themselves. This is an attractive thesis because it lays the foundation of North African Islam – which is today so well-rooted in personalities – on an original free choice. The reality, however, was perhaps rather more varied.[12]

The Maghreb in fact became Muslim by two distinct processes, which were probably of different length and depth – collective and individual conversion. The military conquest led to the political submission of whole Berber tribes with the surrender of their leaders. Conquests, however, always stir people to revolt, and the Arab conquest of the Maghreb was in this respect no exception. The new authority was confronted with repeated uprisings. Once proclaimed, Berber loyalty was interpreted by it as the unanimous and global adoption of the master and his faith. But it remained fragile. If the tribe rebelled, its political insubordination (*ridda*) was immediately denounced as apostasy (*irtidad*).[13] Significantly, the words *ridda* and *irtidad* come from the same root in Arabic and are closely related in meaning, reflecting the fact that Islam was born both as a religion and a state [14] and, even more important, that its Prophet was the founder of an empire.

It is nevertheless unclear whether the tribes took up arms in order to defend Christianity, or their freedom. Faltering between faith and war, frequent resurgences of pre-Islamic monotheisms (Judaism and Christianity) marked the first centuries of the hijra. 'In Ifriqiyya and the Maghreb,' writes Ibn Khaldun, 'the population consists of tribes, each of which is animated by a strong *asabiyya* [group feeling]. Ibn Abi Sarh inflicted a first defeat on them as well as the Franks [Romans], but this was unsuccessful for they continued to apostatize. They continually revolted when the Muslims dealt them heavy blows.'[15]

The epic of the Kahana gives a vivid impression of just how turbulent the history of these collective conversions must have been. In their progress to the west, the soldiers of the Arab general Hasan Ibn Nu'man faced not only the armies of Byzantium, but also stubborn resistance in the mountains. Grouped together under the military and political authority of the Kahana, a Jewish 'queen' and 'priestess'– a symbolic figure for such Algerian French-speaking intellectuals as the writer Kateb Yacine – the tribes of the Aurès kept the Arab army at a distance for four years (689–93). According to the legend, when she realized defeat was inevitable the queen herself chose resistance until death, but ordered her two sons to submit to the conqueror. Each son was charged with recruiting from their tribes 12,000 men who would be converted and placed under their command in order to lead the holy war alongside the Arabs. Ibn Khaldun attested that 'the offer of a general amnesty persuaded the vanquished people to embrace Islam and to provide a contingent of 12,000 warriors for Hasan. The sincerity of their conversion was proved by their later conduct.'[16]

We must be wary of reading into this story the common practice of Islamization of the Maghreb.[17] As with other legends, the significance of the Kahana lies less in the doubtful truth of the facts that it recounts than in the variety of interpretations to which it lends itself. The Judeo-Berber tradition, for example, retains only the resistance of the mother, who is the symbol of the patriotic loyalty of the Jewish community of the Maghreb. Gautier, on the other hand, referred only to the reversal of the sons when he wrote, with characteristic colonial arrogance, that:

> ... the Berbers, in the twentieth century as in the seventh, had no concept of the fatherland. The only thing about which the Berber felt passionately and was ready to give his life, was his clan, his family. Consequently everything is simple. In the imminent and inevitable disaster, the only thing that really matters, the clan, must be saved. The conqueror, whether Arab or French, would ask no more than to use the services of a family upon which it has exercised excessive influence.[18]

It is also possible to see an allegory of Islamization in the reconciliation of the two sides of the story – the honour of the queen and the conversion of her sons. Hoping to free themselves from distant masters, first Rome, then Byzantium, the tribes undoubtedly understood that Islam would preserve their autonomy and that a simple conversion would be sufficient for them to be accepted by the conquerors.

The principal religious opposition to the Arab conquerors was in fact neither Jewish nor Christian. On the contrary, it came from within Islam and asserted itself in the name of Islam against the practices of the centralized empire, in particular against the land tax. Various Berber tribes found themselves in sympathy with Kharijism,[19] which was spread by preachers from the other end of the Arab empire – Iraq, where a handful of rebels had refused to accept that the caliph Mu'awiya (the founder of the Umayyad dynasty) should be the successor to Ali, the fourth caliph and the son-in-law of the prophet. This dissident movement lead to the foundation in the Maghreb of small states that had a more or less ephemeral existence although some – like Sijilmassa and Tahert – enjoyed considerable prestige. Kharijism never united the region under one authority, but the rebellions it fuelled contributed to the restoration of a certain autonomy – economic and otherwise – in the Maghreb which had been successively stripped by Rome, the Vandals and Byzantium. It is partly because Islam offered this potential of independence that North Africa eventually adopted it definitively.[20]

Mass conversion to Islam was probably rare under the Umayyads, who ruled North Africa until 750. When it did happen it involved tribesmen, particularly nomads, who converted because they had a similar lifestyle to that of the first conquerors, themselves nomads in the Arabia they had left behind. But the view that mass conversions had occurred died hard. Thus when, twelve centuries after the Arab conquest, republican France set out to restore a 'Berber identity' it believed had been stifled by the Arabs, official history gave prominence to these collective conversions on the grounds that they demonstrated the fickleness of the Berbers

Islam for the most part gained ground by the much slower, less capricious process of individual conversions. Alongside the mountain and nomadic tribes – which were united by what Ibn Khaldun called a strong 'group cohesion' (*asabiyya*) and could only convert as a group – lived town and country people who joined the new religion in a different way. The *rum*, officials of the Byzantine administration, traders and artisans of the cities, and the *franj*, Latinized peasants, progressively joined Islam as individuals or as families. Enticement rather than force was the main impetus behind this process. There was certainly no awakening of a Punic memory that had been slumbering for more than a thousand years pushing 'the old civilized people of Ifriqiyya to follow the inclination of their deep instincts', and welcome a religion brought by the cousins of far-off ancestors from Phoenicia – a view found in Gautier's account that has been surprisingly persistent in contemporary historiography.[21] The material and moral advantages which the sedentary Berbers discovered – fiscal with exemption from the poll tax, and social with integration into a civil and political society that was increasingly Islamicized – were the real motive for their conversion.

In North Africa, as in the whole of the empire they were in the process of establishing, the Umayyads had to find a delicate balance between two conflicting demands of their occupation: to win the people over to Islam and to secure the revenues that they, as conquerors, acquired from the 'unbelief' of the conquered peoples – the *jizya*. We have already seen that in Egypt the problem of maintaining tax revenues paradoxically encouraged the Muslim state to slow down the rate of conversions. Since there is no similar testimony for the Maghreb we may perhaps conclude that here Islamization, in both the urban and rural areas, was relatively slow. Indeed it is only on the strength of texts written more than half a millennium after the conquest, and which almost certainly incorporate elements of legend (those of Ibn Khaldun and Ibn Abd al-Hakam) that we imagine there was a tidal wave of conversions. 'In the year 101 [719 AD, merely a generation after the military installation] the rest of the Berbers embraced Islam.'[22] Historians have for a long time been content to repeat this view. Gautier, for example, states that once Tariq Ibn Ziyad began the conquest of Spain, the Maghreb 'surrounded by two sparkling centres of Muslim civilization, Tunisia on one hand and Andalusia on the other, offered no more resistance to the religious and intellectual influence of Islam. The conversion was complete.'[23]

In reality a good part of the population probably remained Christian until the end of the Umayyad Empire in 750. The Arab conquerors enlarged their territory without enforcing religious uniformity, as Bernard Lewis argues: 'During the first centuries of the Muslim rule there were few or no attempts at forced conversion, the propagation of the faith being rather more by persuasion and incitement.'[24] The adoption of Islam, in other words, remained a matter of free choice, even if the economic motives for conversion were sometimes compelling. But alongside conversions, which probably took place at a moderate rate, demographic processes would have worked in favour of the Muslims from an early stage, through intermarriage. The Arab armies did not travel with their families and, while the Arab Muslims remained in a minority, limited matrimonial choice must have favoured intermarriage with the local population. The law in the Maghreb conformed in every way to that which prevailed in the East, forbidding the marriage of a Christian or Jewish man with a Muslim woman, but not that of a Muslim man with a *dhimmi* woman.[25] In the latter case the children of the couple would automatically be Muslims as well as the generations that followed them.

Nevertheless, Islam did not assert itself until a period beginning two centuries after the conquest, when the Abbasid caliph al-Mutawakkil (847-61) held sway over the East. The interminable wars of succession from the beginning of the ninth century and the increasing influence on the army of uncontrolled Turkish elements, had by this time created a climate of permanent terror in Baghdad and had caused the caliph to transfer his capital to Samarra. As a result, the authority of the caliphate broke down and the central power of the Arab Muslims was succeeded in the provinces by local dynasties whose autonomy was reinforced over time. To the west, the Idrisids of Fez (788–926) pacified vast areas, while to the East the Aghlabids spread out from Kairouan (801–909). Between the two, the kingdoms of the central Maghreb occupied smaller areas. Once they were established, these entities – because they were much smaller than the disintegrating empire – became inward looking and very soon homogenous. In these circumstances, the assimilation of minorities probably became a way for the regional powers to consolidate themselves. The reduction of differences in such states anticipated the spirit, if not the letter, of a process that was to become in the twentieth century a necessary stage in the construction of nation-states.

From Hilalians to Almohads

The arrival in the eleventh century of the Hilalian tribes, originally from Arabia, marked a turning point in the history of the Maghreb and triggered a process that was fatal to Christianity. The Banu Hilal were plunderers who had formerly been rife in the neighbourhood of Taif and were deported to Egypt in 930 to atone for their insubordination. They were allied with a heretical branch of the Isma'ilis, the Qarmatians, revolutionaries whose rebellion had shaken the Abbasid caliphate. The gentleness of the Nilotic people had not civilized their customs and a century later their reputation as bandits remained intact.

In order to rid himself of these unruly nomads, the Fatimid caliph of Cairo, al-Mustansir, who was facing the problem of starvation among his own people, dispatched them to punish his Zirid vassal al-Mu'izz, who had just seceded in Kairouan (1041). The story goes that 200,000 Hilalians were hurled into the Maghreb. 'All these events shattered the prosperity of Ifriqiyya, devastation abounded and a crowd of brigands on the roads stopped travellers and robbed them,' wrote Ibn Khaldun[26] who, two centuries later, recounted some of the tales he had heard of this period. Stories about the Banu Hilal still survive in North Africa today, kept alive by the last nomads of the Algerian high plateaux, themselves on the verge of becoming sedentarized.

Did the Banu Hilal bring insecurity to Ifriqiyya or did they find it there? Just as the Mongols later devastated the countryside in the East before sacking Baghdad, did they throw the Maghreb into a continuing chaos in which the obscurantism of the nomads eclipsed the sedentary civilization? Ibn Khaldun certainly made a clear distinction between the two nomadic Arab invasions. The first, in the seventh century, was a military invasion which brought garrisons and an administration to the towns. It was carried out by an army of single men who were eager to found mixed families and it was a physical and spiritual, not an ethnic conquest. The second, in the eleventh century, was an invasion of whole families – men, women and children – with their language. In short, it was a colonizing movement.

Accepting the Ibn Khaldun's distinction, but magnifying the demographic impact of the Hilalians, Gautier established a parallel distinction between this Arab nomadic colonization – 'the enemy of all government',[27] 'a predator which did not build its own nest but lived in someone else's'[28] – and the French republican one which organized the population and developed its resources. Caught in the spirit of anti-colonialism, the next generation of French historians adopted the opposite point of view and applied itself to minimizing the role of the nomads as devastators, to the point of almost reducing the Hilalian invasion to no more than a myth.

Whatever the case, it was the Banu Hilal who drove al-Mu'izz from his kingdom thus contributing, directly or indirectly, to a weakening of its borders. At the gates of the Christian world Sicily, which had been Muslim since 827, passed into the hands of the Normans without any reaction from Kairouan. Hired by the pope and the princes of Lombardy to push back Byzantium, the Normans gained a footing in Palermo, part of the Fatimid empire, in 1072 and occupied the whole of Sicily twenty years later. Around the same time, in Andalusia the first sounds of the Reconquista were heard. Toledo fell in 1085 – the first episode in the long intermittent struggle for Spain that ended with the fall of Granada four centuries later. Ten years after the fall of Toledo, Pope Urban II was advocating the crusade.

THE DECHRISTIANIZATION OF NORTH AFRICA

As was almost always the case in subsequent Arab and Turkish history, those Christians who remained on Muslim territory were to pay the price for sharing a religion with the enemies of Islam, even if they did not side with them. Whenever external threats arose, the situation of the Christian and Jewish minorities in North Africa deteriorated and they were subjected to all kinds of discrimination, not just fiscal. At different times, they had to accept prohibitions on clothing, on work, even on behaviour – for example they were obliged to ride side-saddle so that they could immediately be distinguished from Muslims, who alone were entitled to mount their horse in the way of a nobleman. From time to time there were persecutions and conversions took place on a massive scale. Nevertheless, the chronicles record no massacres or deportations comparable to those suffered by Christians in Anatolia ten centuries later, at the fall of the Ottoman Empire.

Nor did the Muslim Maghreb produce groups like the Moriscos and Maranos, the Spanish Muslims and Jews converted by force to Christianity under the Inquisition before their expulsion at the beginning of the seventeenth century. On the contrary, Islam was spread without such demographic trauma. Following the pattern of the conquest itself, conversions took place in the regions that were closest to the centre of Islam and then spread out towards the most distant of the occupied lands. Hence the last references to an indigenous Christianity go back to 1049 in Libya, 1091 in Tunisia, 1150 in Algeria and 1300 in Morocco.[29] A turning-point in the disappearance of these Christianities was the reign of the founder of the Almohad dynasty, Ibn Tumart, a fundamentalist who in 1121 established a small state in the south of Morocco and proclaimed himself the Mahdi, the Messiah. The Almohads conquered the whole of Morocco in 1130 then invaded Algeria in 1147 and Tunisia in 1160. They carried with them the puritanical teachings and intolerance of their founder and although their empire did not last for long it had a devastating impact on the Christian communities it encountered.

Among the regions to the West of the Nile, Islam spread most rapidly in Libya which the Muslim armies entered in 640. The country lost the core of its Christian population when a Berber tribe, the Louata, departed with its bishop to Morocco.[30] All traces of them had been removed by the time the Banu Hilal passed through in their march towards the west.

In Tunisia, Christianity seems to have survived until the eleventh century. Carthage, formerly a prestigious bishopric in which the last of a long line of Councils was held in 646, was conquered by the Arabs in 698. However, the See was maintained there for several more centuries even if the recollections of Europe and the Maghreb have together put this distant memory under seal. The Fatimid dynasty, which during the first half of the tenth century was centred on Kairouan, was probably as tolerant in its North African phase as it was in Egypt until the time of al-Hakim. Certainly in 990, the church in Carthage once again had a demographic and spiritual foundation sufficient for it to send a bishop to be consecrated in Rome. Letters dated 1053, 1073 and 1076 addressed by the pope to the bishops of Carthage, bear witness to Christian activity.[31] Another source which attests to it is Constantine the African, a Benedictine monk born in Tunisia in about 1015 who has given us numerous translations in Latin of Arabic medical texts. However in 1270, when Saint Louis died in front of the besieged Tunis,[32] Christianity had been almost extinguished for two centuries. The first blow came with the Norman conquest of Sicily (1072–91), after which the ruthless intolerance endured by the Muslims of the island led to the elimination of Berber Christianity in response.[33] By 1159 it only remained for the Almohad conqueror, Abd al-Mu'min, to raze the See of Carthage and force the remaining Christians into exile or apostasy.[34]

Algeria, the birthplace of Saint Augustine, had maintained a Catholic community throughout the time when the Kharijis, adherents of a pure Islam, were divided into small theocratic fiefs. Ibn Khaldun reported that in Tlemcen in 963, 'Various ancient monuments could be seen, of which some were found in the church ministered by the Christians.'[35] The country probably lost these Christians a little after the arrival of the Almohads in Algeria (1147). A long time after this, in 1512, Pope Julian II nominated a bishop to Constantine, but he soon abandoned his post for want of finding a sufficiently large congregation.[36] During the period of Ottoman rule other Christians lived in this region. These were Europeans captured in the Mediterranean by the corsairs of the Barbarossa brothers and held hostage in the hope of a large ransom. At the height of the trade there were thousands of Christian captives, perhaps as many as 30,000 in the prisons of Algiers and 10,000 in those of Tunis in 1650,[37] of which a certain number converted to Islam.

The martyrdom of Saint Marcellus at Tangier in 298 testifies to an early Christianization of this region. Ibn Khaldun states that as from 788 Idris I, father of the founding dynasty of Morocco, had eliminated Judaism, Christianity and Magism from the plains of Fez, Tadla and Chellah. A century later, under his descendant 'Umar b. Idris II, the church no longer existed as an organized institution, but Christianity survived among a part of the population, as well as, on occasion, priests.[38] Later the Almoravids, although they were the first dynasty to confront the Christian recovery in Muslim Europe did not attempt to extinguish Berber Christianity. In 1137, shortly before the final collapse of their dynasty, they had numerous Christian soldiers and slaves while Christians were still prominent among their merchants.[39] The Almohads would change all this.

Yet the Almohads recruited Christian mercenaries – with the authorization of the pope himself. The latter, it is true, still retained the hope of converting the Muslim people all the way up to the sultan, if the correspondence addressed to him is to be believed.[40] Even so, in 1237 the Franciscan and Dominican bishops left Morocco to reside in Spain and, from the beginning of the fourteenth century, no indigenous Christians were to be found outside Tangier and Ceuta. Henceforth, the only Christian presence in Morocco was that of the European captives and emissaries. Some of these founded families, and at the end of the fifteenth century in Rabat bells could be heard on Sundays from the church of Saint Francis – rung for the sultan's guard which consisted of the Christian descendants of the old mercenaries. By 1517 the Christian presence was sufficiently strong to found the convent of Saint Catherine at Safi. Returning under Moulay Isma'il (1672-1727), the Franciscans registered the deaths of captives in Morocco; between 1684 and 1693 they recorded 1,070, which suggests that the Christian population was of the order of 4,000 people. When relations with Europe were harmonious, the Christian community could even regain a significant size.

Berber Christianity therefore took more than five centuries to disappear from Muslim North Africa. The progressive division of the Maghreb into three states and the gigantic confrontation with European Christianity finally killed it off.

The Survival of Judaism

Unlike the Christians, the Jews did not disappear. A small minority under Byzantium (1 to 2 per cent), they remained the same under Islam. Except for some cases of mass conversion, for example that of the Jarawa of Aurès in 693, which was significant because it marked the defeat of the Kahana, the Judeo-Berber tribes kept their religion. Ibn Khaldun drew up a detailed, perhaps exhaustive, list: 'One part of the Berbers profess Judaism, the Djeraoua (a tribe which inhabits the Auras), the Nefousa of Ifriqiyya, the Fendelaoua, the Mediana, the Behloula, the Ghiatha and the Fezaz of Maghreb al-Acsa, etc.'[41]

Through nearly five centuries of Islamization, the history of Judaism in the Maghreb was relatively uneventful. In Morocco, times were easy under the Idrisids (789-974), but the situation changed at the beginning of the Almoravid reign. Sharing for one last time the lot of Christianity, the Jews later saw their situation temporarily deteriorating under Almohad puritanism. In 1232, no doubt for some futile motive that the chronicles have forgotten, there was a massacre of Jews at Marrakesh.[42] However, when the Merinids (1248–1465) came to power after the collapse of Islam in Cordoba (1236), a climate favourable to the Jews was established. The new sultans, who attempted to stop the Reconquista in Spain, and the Jews, who were persecuted by it, soon came together in their hatred of Christianity triumphant.

Pushed by the terror of the pogroms, Jews, including converts whose new adherence to Christianity aroused suspicion, began to flee Castille from the second half of the fourteenth century, and Andalusia after the fall of Grenada in 1492. For the most part they found refuge in Muslim territory – Istanbul, Palestine, North Africa. A little earlier the Spaniards had destroyed Tetuan (1401) and the Portuguese took Ceuta in 1415 before seizing Tangier in 1471. In a Mediterranean region which was breaking up, the Sephardic Jews established themselves for a long time next to Islam. The sultan of Fez, Abd al-Haq, even named a Jew, Aaron Ben Battas, as his prime minister; but his decision signalled the fall of his dynasty, the Merinids, when both the sovereign and his prime minister were assassinated.

Peace was maintained virtually without a break until the middle of the twentieth century. As if to demonstrate their integration into Muslim society the Jews had adopted the language of the Qur'an in a higher proportion than the Muslims themselves. In 1960, immediately before the emigration of their community to Israel, 88.5 per cent of Jewish Moroccans but only 64.1 per cent of the Muslims had Arabic as their mother tongue. Berbers who did not speak Arabic represented only 0.3 per cent of the Jews against 19 per cent of Muslims.[43] In Algeria, Tunisia and even in Libya, where the Berbers of the Jabal Nefussa were still Judaized at the time of the Arab conquest, the Jewish minorities had also held on until the second half of the twentieth century.

The Jewish community, which had been accustomed since the time of the Roman and Byzantine empires to the difficult condition of a minority, found within itself the moral resources and the ability to survive for a very long time under the Muslim power. This stable relationship, however, flourished in a favourable international context. By contrast to the Christians, no external power that threatened Islam appealed to the religion of the Jews. On the contrary, they had to face the intolerance of the Catholic kings side by side with the Muslims; the day when Grenada (the last bastion of Muslim resistance) fell, the Jews were expelled from Spain or forced to repudiate their faith in order to remain there – temporarily – and become Maranos. Their relative quietude in the Maghreb lasted until the time when Jewish nationalism confronted another, Arab Muslim, nationalism. The Crémieux Decree, which in 1870 gave the Jews of Algeria the citizenship of France, had already introduced a first wedge between their community and the Muslim population. Against their will perhaps, they were bound to the pieds-noirs until the exodus in the twentieth century precipitated by the birth of Israel. Condemnation of the new Zionist state was to become one of the rare – or rather the only – points of accord among Arab nationalists. A millennium later, the same dynamic which had caused the slow erosion of Christianity – identification with the enemy, whether real or imagined, by virtue of confessional identity – thrust Judaism into brutal exile.

CHAPTER THREE

The Crusades:
A Confrontation of Two Christianities

> For a long time Europe and Asia, the Christian and the Muslim religions, two sisters, two halves of humanity, had lost sight of each other. With the Crusades they found themselves face to face once more. Their first glance at each other was one of horror. [Jules Michelet, *Histoire de France*, 1876.]

> In modern times, the Israelis have looked to the Crusaders for the precursor of their national movement while, in the battle of their ancestors to regain the country, the Arabs look to them for encouragement in their anti-Zionist struggle. [Claude Cahen, *Orient et Occident au temps des Croisades*, 1983.]

At the turn of the millennium the division in the Mediterranean between a Christian north and Muslim south began to crystallize. The attempt to restore, under the banner of Islam, the unity which had existed around the sea under the Roman Empire was already showing signs of collapse. The Arabs were soon to cede land in Andalusia and Sicily, while the long struggle of the Turks against Byzantium continued. The invasion of the Holy Land by the Crusaders brought with it a new unifying project, this time from Europe. In the end, however, the Christian invasion of the south, like the Muslim invasion of the north, was a failure, perhaps because both conquerors shared the same shortcomings – they rejected the language and religion of the subjected peoples while they themselves were numerically weak. A third such venture, the French colonization of Algeria in the nineteenth century, also stumbled against similar obstacles.

A Scattering of Christian States

Conscious of the political dynamic that was emerging in the Mediterranean, Pope Urban II believed that the authority of the Church, even in Europe, would grow if Christian influence could be re-established in the East. In 1095 he therefore proclaimed the powerful ideal behind the invasion on which the Crusaders were soon to embark – to reinforce indigenous Christianity and weaken Islam:[1]

> It is an urgent task for you to provide your brothers of the East with the help so often promised and so crucially needed. The Turks and the Arabs have attacked them … and, entering further into the country of these Christians, have seven times vanquished them in battle, killed them and taken a large number of captives, as well as destroying the churches and devastating the kingdom.[2]

The Crusaders marched towards the East fired by these simplistic ideas and captured Jerusalem in 1099. They recognized that in order to keep the Holy City they would have to form a powerful Christian state in Palestine and that the viability of this state, its capacity to push back Islam, would rest on a strong Christian population. But the picture they carried, of a persecuted Christian population united in adversity and awaiting deliverance by Rome was false. Although Muslims by this time formed a small majority in Syria and Palestine,[3] they lived with the Christians in a climate of coexistence and much less tension than Europeans wanted to believe. Over centuries of conversion, social, administrative and intellectual life had been progressively influenced by the Arabic language and a Muslim ambience; there had been no rupture with the past and no manifest worsening of the situation of the non-converted.[4] The condition of the local Christians under Muslim rule had certainly not deteriorated to the extent that an armed intervention was necessary to rescue them. Indeed the Fatimids of Egypt, who at this time governed Jerusalem, maintained 'a greater level of tolerance than any society then practised'.[5]

During the military operations the Arab Christians wisely stood back.[6] Except for a few isolated cases there was no manifest collaboration with the Franks although instances of diplomatic dealings did arouse the suspicion of the Muslim ruling class. Before the assault on Jerusalem, for example, the Christians of the small village of Bethlehem sent a delegation to the Crusaders – an act that incited the Fatimid commander to decree, as a preventive measure, the confiscation of their assets and their expulsion to nearby villages. The Crusaders, who had an efficient spy service, also from time to time used the services of local Christians, but more often they recruited Muslims.

The Oriental Christians' lack of interest in the Latins reflected a split which was both material and spiritual. Commercial exchange between the two sides of the Mediterranean had ceased long before the Crusades as Levantine merchants progressively dropped their interests in the West for others in India and the Far East.[7] And on the spiritual front, virtually the only link between the two Christianities seemed to be the pilgrimage to the Holy Places. The Eastern Christians were by this time Arabs, both culturally and linguistically.[8] This is not to say that they were a homogeneous group – there was some rivalry between the various congregations with their different customs, beliefs and liturgies and Greek Orthodox services were celebrated in Greek, Jacobite services in Syriac. But whether schismatics like the Greek Orthodox, or heretics like the Jacobites and Armenians,[9] for the most part the Christians retained their distinctive characteristics throughout the period of the Crusades. Exceptionally, the Maronites of Lebanon, whose population at the time numbered about 40,000,[10] renounced their monothelete[11] creed in 1182 and joined with Rome. We do not know precisely how significant this event was from the point of view of the Crusaders. The chroniclers of the period had little to say about the Maronites, almost certainly because they were (by contrast to later centuries) a small minority of the Christian population which was dominated by the Greek Orthodox and the Jacobite churches and the Armenian, Nestorian and Copt communities. Whatever the case the Maronites' conversion came too late to be of any help (they were famed for their skill at archery) to the Crusaders, for Jerusalem was reconquered by the Muslims just five years later.

The First Crusade changed the composition of the local population. In Jerusalem and the coastal towns Muslims and Jews fought together against the Crusaders and were massacred.[12] None of the inhabitants of Beirut were to escape. In 1110 the Muslim population of Sidon (5,000 people) migrated to Egypt and Syria, although they had permission to stay on the spot by paying a tribute (a *jizya* in reverse). As for the Jews, who lived in the towns and in some parts of the countryside – in Galilee, Tiberias and Safad – the rare survivors were sold as slaves. In the rural areas there were no such massacres – the reputation of the Crusaders preceded them, and the Muslim peasants fled. By the end of the first Crusade, Western Christianity seemed to have achieved its primary objective – it found itself alone with the indigenous Christians in a region largely deserted by Islam.

Although the demographic weight of the Arab Christians increased temporarily in the Latin kingdoms, fortune did not smile on them. 'In Syria, the Crusaders also met Christians, but Christians from "heretical" churches, speaking the same language as the Muslims, and whom they did not intend to treat much better than they did the Muslims.'[13] Moreover, they often confused some of the Oriental Christians with Muslims and killed them on the grounds of their appearance. 'The Crusaders,' reported one witness, 'killed many Syrians who had beards and followed the law of Greece [the Greek Orthodox Church] ... because of their beards they were killed as if they were Saracens.'[14] For both economic and religious reasons the Crusaders had no intention of according Arab Christians a legal status equal to that of the Franks or superior to that of the indigenous Muslims and quickly established various forms of segregation institutionalized by distinct jurisdictions. The Christians of the towns had the status of free men – as did the handful of Muslims and Jews who had returned to the region – though all were liable to pay the poll tax, an obligation from which only the Franks were exempted. In the countryside, by contrast, the local peasants – whether Muslim or Christian – were equally ranked as villeins and subjected to enforced servitude, such as bondage to the land, forced labour or the payment of land tax. The Greek Orthodox clergy suffered the supreme humiliation of losing the Church of the Holy Sepulchre in Jerusalem to the Latin clergy. The Eastern churches were not, however, all in the same position since, like their Arab predecessors, the Crusaders were more distrustful of those with foreign support. The Monophysite Jacobite heresy was thus less troubled than the Orthodox schism which was backed by Byzantium.

The military operation of the Crusaders soon gave way to a long-lasting settlement. But this required an economic hinterland which the Franks could not provide by themselves. As the Latin states were consolidated along the Syro–Palestinian coast – to the south, the Kingdom of Jerusalem (1099–1187) and the county of Tripoli (1109–1289), to the north, the Principality of Antioch (1098–1268) and the county of Edessa (1098–1144), as well as, in their sphere of influence, the Kingdom of Armenia in Cilicia (1098–1375) – the Franks became more tolerant and began to deal more gently with the indigenous population, which had become economically indispensable to them. After the taking of Sidon in 1110, the killing and plundering which followed the First Crusade came to an end. Slowly the Muslims and Jews regained the Frank-dominated towns where, like the Christians, they had the right to autonomous jurisdiction. And in the countryside, the relatively small size of the Frankish population, together with the mistrust which coloured their relations with the Eastern Christians, who complained of 'the violence and wretched character of the Franks',[15] imposed a coexistence with the Muslim peasantry.

However, the violence of war gave way to social violence. The Muslim population was allowed to remain but was relegated to the lowest social and economic echelon. The land administration was overturned and ownership of the land passed from Muslims to the Franks. Seigneuries or simple Frank fiefdoms were constituted throughout the exodus, to Egypt or Syria, of the old landowners. The laws of the Kingdom of Jerusalem actually guaranteed to each knight the ownership of any land that he could conquer – an arrangement that prefigured the law relating to the property of those who were absent promulgated by Israel 800 years later in 1950. Towards the end of the Crusades, however, the situation of the Muslim population began to improve – quite considerably. The last generations of the Franks adapted better to the spirit of the place: 'We have been transformed from Europeans to inhabitants of the Orient. Yesterday's Italian or French has been transplanted and become a Galilean or Palestinian. The man from Reims or Chartres has become a Syrian or a citizen of Antioch. We have already forgotten our place of origin.'[16] Resigned to the overwhelming indifference of the West, these later Franks appear to have conceded ownership of the land more easily to the indigenous peasantry. This is what the Andalusian traveller Ibn Jubayr had to say:

We left Tibnin [Toron] by a road continually running along farms inhabited by Muslims who live in great comfort under the Franks – may Allah keep us from similar temptation! The conditions imposed on them are to give up half of the crop at the time of the harvest, and to pay a poll tax of one dinar and seven qirats, as well as a small tax on the fruit trees. The Muslims are masters of their dwellings and manage themselves as they wish. Such is the form of the farms and villages where they live in Frank territory. The hearts of many Muslims are filled with the temptation to establish themselves here when they see the condition of their brothers in the districts governed by the Muslims, for the state of these is quite the opposite of comfortable. The misfortune for the Muslims is that, in the country governed by their co-religionists, they must always complain about the injustices of their leaders, while they can only be satisfied with the behaviour of the Franks, in whose justice they can always trust.[17]

This text has often been quoted out of context by French historians in order to glorify colonial administration[18] implying that the alien administration of the French in North Africa, like that of the Franks in the Orient, could be praised, even by local people.

The Impossible Attempt to Settle the Holy Land

A more effective and a more durable way of colonizing the Holy Land than supporting indigenous Christianity was through European immigration. A demographic explosion in the year 1,000 had created in the West a pressure that encouraged territorial expansion and, in large measure, explains the response to Pope Urban's call to arms. Indeed when he encouraged a nobility without a future, in search of a new cause and wider horizons, to emigrate, he not only promised them 'eternal riches' but also spoke of 'the riches of the East' compared to the 'poverty of the Western world'.[19] But in the end the attempt to settle the Holy Land never overcame two obstacles which finally proved fatal – ultimately it did not attract enough Europeans and it was unable to establish roots.

In 1110, some years after they had arrived in the East, there were no more than 10,000 Franks – 300 knights, 1,200 foot soldiers and their families. Their numbers were notoriously insufficient against the Muslims of the conquered region and even more so against the multitudes of Syria (2.3 million inhabitants in the region which remained under Muslim control), Egypt (2.5 million) or Anatolia (4 million). But, fortunately for the invaders, in the early days of the Crusades these areas were split into enemy states. After three or four generations, on the eve of the fall of Jerusalem to Saladin in 1187, the Frank population had reached its maximum figure – around 120,000 – largely through migration

Until the Second Crusade (1148), the flow of European migrants was substantial enough to compensate for military losses and even to produce a surplus population. The main dynamic behind this movement was population growth,[20] especially among the European nobility – the source of the original Crusaders. The increasingly widespread practice of using wet-nurses reduced the period of *post partum* amenorrhoea among noble women, thus increasing their fertility and producing more aspiring knights.[21] The Crusades held out images of glittering wealth which growing competition between the younger sons of the nobility made more and more difficult to satisfy locally. Often coming from a modest background,[22] the

Crusaders were able to appropriate seigneuries and fiefdoms in the Holy Land which they could never dream of in the West and, because in the East they shared in political power, they could in addition acquire the privilege of levying taxes.

The military expeditions of the nobility brought in their train thousands of pilgrims from all over Europe who, alone or with their families, sought adventure overseas. Among them, the people from the northern part of the continent, who were the least informed about the East and least disposed to peaceful coexistence, made the greatest mark on the Crusades.[23] Exchanging their villein clothes for those of the bourgeoisie, these migrants soon constituted the mass of the expatriate population; altogether an estimated 100,000 people, mostly of this kind, joined the 20,000 of noble blood. In addition the society of the Franks included 500 Chevaliers of the monastic-military orders born out of the Crusade and created to keep order in Palestine – the Templars and the Hospitallers. Known originally as 'The Poor Chevaliers of Christ' the Templars – like the Hospitallers – acquired huge fiefdoms, such as the castle-fortress of Kerak, and soon stopped being poor.

Although it was strong in Europe, the natural growth of the Frank population showed signs of deficiency in the Levant. Increased mortality affected the nobility as well as other classes; all were victims of their inability to adapt to the climate. Estimates made from gravestones suggest that their life expectancy was 39 years – much lower than that of the Muslim population which reached 58 years.[24] Such a high death rate frequently interrupted the continuity of the administration of the seigneuries and fiefdoms, where minors still under tutelage were brought to replace their fathers who had died prematurely. It also affected population growth, since many died before they had children. Finally, the age and gender structure showed that males were more numerous than females among the Franks, but not among the local population. This increased the differences in the birth rate: fathers produced 1.75 sons among the Franks and 2.10 among the Muslims.[25]

Living in an environment which was hostile, or at best neutral, the Franks were obliged to concentrate their meagre forces in a few areas.[26] Three-quarters of the Frank population of the Kingdom of Jerusalem was concentrated in three towns: Jerusalem (20,000 inhabitants), Acre (40,000) and Tyre (30,000). The remaining quarter was distributed into about 30 small towns, villages and fortresses. In rural areas it was unusual to find Franks, although some villages –

today we would call them settlements – were established outside Arab villages. These Frank peasants enjoyed bourgeois status, unlike the Arabs, whether Muslim or Christian, who were considered to be ruffians.[27]

Since it was the only way to consolidate their presence in the Holy Land the Franks continually exhorted the people of Europe to join them; but their attempts to increase their population beyond a threshold of 120,000 were in vain. After the Second Crusade, the flow of migrants ceased. Moved by the lure of wealth rather than the spirit of the Crusade, the migrants of the thirteenth century preferred Constantinople, Cyprus or the Peloponnese, which were open to Frank colonization after the Fourth Crusade and the foundation of the Latin Empire of Constantinople in 1204. After the Crusaders' capture of Damietta in 1219, the grandees of the Kingdom of Jerusalem appealed to their ruler, King Amaury, as follows: 'Sire, let it be well known in France, in England, in Germany and throughout Christendom that you have this conquered land and that you need assistance in order to populate it.'[28] But such distressed appeals to Western Christendom to reinforce the ranks of the Crusaders proved ineffective

Even under duress, the Franks did not accept the help of Eastern Christians. So violent was their distrust that they rejected the offer of the King of Armenia to send 30,000 of his subjects to the Kingdom of Jerusalem, 'in order to guard the country, populate it with Christians, ensure its security and throw out the Saracens'[29] Differences of rite increased the hostility between the two opposing branches of Christianity. 'We expelled the Turks and the pagans, but we could not expel the heretics, Greeks and Armenians, Syrians and Jacobites,'[30] an anonymous Crusader stated learnedly. When issues of money were involved, the hostility reached its peak. By virtue of its dominant position, the Latin clergy tried to impose a tithe on the Armenians, who of course did not belong to the Roman Church. Meeting with the refusal of the Gregorian clergy,[31] the transplantation project, which would have revitalized the Kingdom of Jerusalem, was aborted.

In addition to rejecting Eastern Christians, the Franks denied themselves the help that might have come through the conversion of Muslims. The Crusaders occupied a realm that had been under Islamic rule for five centuries; but the religion itself had been instilled into society for a much shorter time. Many Muslims were descended from families who had converted only a few generations earlier.[32]

The Franks, however, behaved as though they knew nothing of this long, recent past of Christianity. The Latin clergy in practice hindered conversion by the humiliations they attached to it. The convert had either to remain in servitude or to enlist as an auxiliary in the Turcopoles, the light cavalry of the Franks[33] – an attitude that contrasted fundamentally with the pragmatism of Islam which had made conversion into an instrument of social advance.

The small number of migrants and their aloof attitude to the local population, whether Christian or Muslim, condemned the Franks to atrophy. They remained in the minority barely representing, in their own kingdom, one-third of a population of around 400,000.[34] Deprived of sorely needed new blood, whether in the form of settlers from the West or a healthy birth-rate in the East, they were placed in an untenable military position. In order to raise 2,000 cavalrymen and 20,000 foot-soldiers – the minimum required to resist enemy forces – they needed to mobilize the whole of the adult male population of the kingdom.[35] And yet their armed forces taxed the subject people beyond all reason whereas, in order to maintain the producers, they would have had to live on good terms with the neighbourhood, that is to assimilate and disappear as if they were a graft on the branch of local society. In the end, once Syria and Egypt had been united by Saladin, they had no choice but to engage in a war they could not hope to win.

The first real military rout of the Crusaders, at Hattin in 1187, put an end to the first Kingdom of Jerusalem and, almost a century after they had set out for the Holy Land marked the beginning of their decline. Another century elapsed before the defeat of Antioch (1268), Tripoli (1289) and finally the fatal wound inflicted at Acre (1291). The Frank population then completely disappeared (by escape, captivity or massacre) leaving only a few children of mixed marriages. Today their distant descendants can be met on the slopes of the Alawite country and Mount Lebanon where, it is said, the Patriarch Simon charitably received several families of the defeated Franks.[36]

The End of the Crusades and the Mongols

The Franks had set out to relieve Eastern Christianity, but far from realizing this aim,[37] their conquest ended in a considerable deterioration of the Christians' situation.

When the Muslims began to retake the Holy Land, they did not accuse the local Christians of collaboration. In fact successive Muslim reconquests were met with neutrality, sometimes collusion. Their subjection to the Franks had brought about a kind of complicity between the indigenous people of different confessions and Arab Christians looked upon the victories of Nur al-Din in the north and Saladin in the south as a first step towards their emancipation from the Frank religious yoke. The Christians of Jerusalem may well have come to an understanding with Saladin and assisted him in taking the city. For they and the Christians in nearby villages were allowed to stay in their homes and guard their possessions in return for payment of the poll tax, now transferred once again to the Muslim treasury. The Jews also benefited from the tolerance of Saladin. The sultan lifted the banishment the Crusaders, following an old Byzantine tradition, had imposed on them and encouraged them to resettle in the Holy Land.[38]

In the towns which had not yet fallen, this favourable treatment meant that the Franks regarded local Arab Christians with suspicion, as potential collaboraters.[39] Nevertheless, realizing after Saladin entered Jerusalem that they could not hope for victory with their forces alone, they attempted to turn the Christians in neighbouring Muslim countries against their rulers. These attempts were generally unsuccessful:[40] Outside the Crusader states, Christians and Jews under Muslim jurisdiction remained loyal to their rulers and their situation did not noticeably deteriorate.[41]

The beginnings of the Mongol invasion overlapped with the end of the Frank occupation and at this point relations between Muslims and Eastern Christians became strained, for the latter concluded some local agreements with the new invader. Today, because the Western world is dominant and Mongolia is a weak state that menaces no one, whenever Islam is threatened it is more ready to rail against the Crusaders than the Mongols. Muslims have forgotten that the Mongols flaunted a superficial Christianity before converting very rapidly to Islam, and that they were even more bloodthirsty than their Crusader predecessors. However brief and geographically limited, the collaboration of the Eastern Christians with the Mongols erased the advantages of their long period of reserve towards the Crusaders.[42]

The Franks had at first been tempted to join forces with these nomads from the steppes of Central Asia in order to trap their Muslim opponents in a pincer movement. In 1253, before the Mongols had reached the Anatolian border, Louis IX, who had attempted to capture Egypt in 1249, had sent the Franciscan

Guillaume de Rubrouck to the heart of Central Asia to explore their intentions.[43] The Mongol Hülegü, who conquered Baghdad in 1258, as well as his general, Kitbuka, were reputed to have affinities with Nestorian Christianity.[44] The Crusaders of the south, who had gathered around Acre, did not form an alliance with them and even facilitated the movement of Egyptian Mamluk troops toward Syria.[45] The Crusaders of the north, however, and the local Christians, mainly Armenians, made common cause with the khan and even provided him with soldiers. Did the Eastern Christians believe that these conquerors, who seemed to share their religion, could liberate them from both Muslim and Latin domination?

When they emerged victorious over the Mongols at Ayn Jallut in 1260, the Mamluks, who by this time had overthrown the Ayyubids, made the Christians pay for this collaboration.[46] Eschewing the tolerance shown by their Fatimid and Ayyubid predecessors who, despite the two Crusader invasions of Egypt, had not made life particularly hard for the Christians, they devastated the Armenian Kingdom of Cilicia and the Principality of Antioch without bothering to distinguish between Franks and indigenous Christians. It was during this period that the Maronites fled from the coast to their mountain sanctuary, from which they only started to re-emerge in the nineteenth century. The new masters of Egypt and Syria, as recently coverted military slaves, were armed with the neophyte's zeal and contributed greatly to the degradation of the conditions of life of its Arab Christian and Jewish subjects. Initially limited in scale, their extortions were soon directed at all Arab Christians, who for three centuries were exposed to a general hardening of Islam.

The widespread fanaticism stirred up by the traumas of the Crusader and Mongol invasions, influenced the thought of the theologian Ibn Taymiyya (1263–1328). Transposing his hatred of the Christian invaders onto their Arab co-religionists, he advocated restrictions on Christianity and even Judaism, attacked their holy books and violently opposed the construction and maintenance of churches and synagogues.[47] Some evocative titles stand out among his abundant philosophical writings: *The Book of Response to the Christians, The Problem of the Churches, The True Response to He who Altered the Religion of Christ, Shame to the People of the Gospel, To Keep away from the People from Hell.* This Islamic Luther must have inspired the Wahhabis of Arabia in the seventeenth century, and the Egyptian Islamists continue to claim him.[48]

In the popular literature, the famous tale of Baybars (1260–77), a picaresque novel and epic to the glory of the Mamluk leader who vanquished the Mongols and the Crusaders, puts forward an Islamist vision of the world. The adversaries whom he conquers, whether Christian or other, must convert immediately or be branded as criminals afflicted with all defects, who deserve neither respect nor pity.[49] 'He marched, followed by Baybars, until he arrived at the necropolis of the Christians, where the tombs were covered with enormous stones, like the curse that weighs upon the infidels.'[50] This is far from the delights of *The Thousand and One Nights* which reflected the serenity of the Abbasid period, still so evocative that in 1985 Islamist pressure in Egypt succeeded in banning the book.

Until the conquest of the Arab East by the Ottomans, proud rulers who had vanquished the Christian invaders, together with the ordinary people who venerated in their masters the slaves who had become kings, raised intolerance to new heights. In Damascus, the Christians paid for the welcome they had given to the Mongols with the destruction of the Church of Mary.[51] In Egypt, the Copts faced many tribulations. In 1301 and 1321, the people attacked churches and devastated convents, and in 1354 the authorities confiscated a large part of their possessions.[52]

Far from the theatre of the Crusades, at the borders of the Mamulk domain, sectarianism reached Iraq, now ruled by the Mongols. The initial sympathy of the khans towards the Christians, whom they exempted from the *jizya* and allowed to rebuild churches and open schools, let loose popular violence in 1267. The Jewish community, a member of which had even been nominated to head the Mongol government, was the object of similar street violence in 1291. When Ghazan Khan converted to Islam in 1295 the Christians and Jews found themselves brutally deprived of the protection of the prince who imposed clothing restrictions on non-Muslims and levied the *jizya* once more.[53]

In 1291, Acre was taken. With the Mongols pushed back from Syria and soon converted to Islam, the history of the Crusades reached its end. What remains of this knightly adventure? Some blue eyes among the Christian Maronites on the edges of the Qadisha and the Muslim Alawis in Mount Ansarieh; tons of Roman columns broken up and buried for ever in the walls of Sidon or Kerak; the patronym of a former president of the Republic of Lebanon, Suleiman Frangieh (1970–76); bread in the shape of a baguette, *frangi* bread, while elsewhere the unleavened form is preferred. The signs are too tenuous for the Arab East to preserve the traces of

Frank civilization. Levantine Christianity certainly suffered from it. As for Islam in power, it stopped being Arab for a long time.

CHAPTER FOUR

The Christian Recovery
in the Ottoman Arab East

Between the Ansari in the north and the Druze in the south, live a
small community of people known for a long time under the name of
Maouarné, or Maronites. The first [happy circumstance] is religion,
which places an insurmountable barrier between the Maronites and
the Muslims, and has prevented ambitious people from conniving with
foreigners in order to subjugate their nation. The second is the nature
of the country ... [The third is] the very weakness of this society
which from its origin has been surrounded by powerful enemies and
could only resist them by maintaining unity among its members ...
Thus, with customs taking the place of laws, the Maronites have been
protected until today from the oppression of despotism and the
disorder of anarchy. [Volney, *Voyage en Egypte et en Syrie*, 1787.]

At the end of the twentieth century, with the return of the question
of nationalities in the Balkans and of nations in the East, the
Ottoman Empire still casts its shadow over events. Neither its former
enemies nor its former subjects are indifferent to the memory of
the House of Osman. For Europeans, it embodies the decadence of
Islam. For Eastern Christians, however, it speaks of long lost days
of prosperity. Nor have the Jews forgotten the hospitality the Ottomans offered on two occasions when Christian Europe threatened
them – under the Catholic Kings of Spain and, 300 years later,
when anti-Semitism grew strong in republican France and Tsarist
Russia. Three quarters of a century after its collapse, the empire still
has its advocates among Christians and Jews in the Arab East who
regard the imperial alchemy, which dissociated the status of individuals from the status of the land, as the only hope for multi-
confessionalism.

Until the Ottomans conquered the Arab provinces in the sixteenth
century, the population of their Empire had a large Christian and
European majority. They could count on the support of the Greek

57

Orthodox patriarch in Istanbul and they had learned the art of coming to terms with their non-Muslim populations. Two Ottoman sultans, Selim I and then Süleiman the Magnificent rewrote the map of the East in barely twenty years. Syria was captured from the Mamluks in 1516, Egypt and its dependencies in Arabia in 1517. Algeria was added soon after, a gift from the corsair Barbarossa, and in 1534 Iraq was snatched from Persia. These victories made the sultan ruler of the largest Muslim state of the time – a state that, apart from slight differences of borders, covered the same territory as Justinian's Byzantium, but this time under Sunni rule.

Under the Mamluks Christianity had weakened in the Arab provinces of the new empire to the point that it was threatened with the kind of extinction we have already encountered in North Africa. Under the Ottomans, however, the trend of the previous millenium was reversed, enabling Christian communities to make an extraordinary recovery. When they took over the Fertile Crescent (present day Iraq, Israel, Gaza and the West Bank, Jordan, Lebanon and Syria) 7 per cent of the population was Christian; by the time the empire collapsed four centuries later, the religious minorities, although weakened in the eastern part of this region, were considerably strengthened in the west. In the Fertile Crescent, excluding Iraq, 20–30 per cent of the population was by this time Christian (see Tables 4.1 and 4.2, Figure 4.1). The Jews were 3.1 per cent of the total population, but concentrated mainly in Iraq where they represented 6.1 per cent. Egypt, always at odds with the rest of the Empire, did not experience a comparable revival; its Christian population was only 8 per cent of the total.

Politics and Censuses

From Istanbul the Ottomans ruled a huge territory and a great diversity of people. Periodic censuses of the population were an important means of exercising control over the provinces, enabling the Sublime Porte to keep a record of the number of taxpayers and the soldiers it could levy. But the maintenance of registers demanded an efficient administration which only a strong state could guarantee and the registers were correctly completed and recorded for only as long as Istanbul controlled the local powers.

In the Fertile Crescent a census campaign was conducted in the sixteenth century (1570–90) after the Ottomans had established their administration. This first systematic attempt to estimate the population of a Muslim territory took place one thousand years after the *hijra*.[1] It was preceded by smaller surveys, used by the sultans to assert their domination. Thus, in Damascus, according to a local chronicler, a comprehensive census was taken on Sunday 2 Ramadan 922 AH (1516) – the day after the army of Selim II entered the city.[2] In reality there must have been a greater time-lag between the suspension of fighting and the census, but this telescoping of the memory indicates the extent to which the Ottomans' power and organization created a sense of wonder among their subjects.

From the next century, a weakening of Ottoman power at the centre inhibited any such wide-scale operation. In any case, the spread of the *iltizam* system meant that the census was by this time less useful for tax purposes.[3] Under the *iltizam*, tax-farmers (*multazims*) purchased their office from the state for a fixed amount then reimbursed themselves, eventually making a profit, from the tax returns. The *multazims*' agents were generally locals and closely acquainted with the people of their districts. A system of this kind had no need of a census and no more were undertaken until 1831 under Sultan Mehmet II, the first reformer of the empire. This did not, however, include Syria, Palestine and Iraq. The modernizing and centralizing thrust of the Tanzimat reforms, which continued from 1840 until 1876, took place in the context of an empire that was shrinking in size as a result of foreign invasions and inde-pendence struggles in the provinces. The last grand Ottoman census, which was undertaken between 1881 and 1893 and covered the whole of the Mashreq, was the work of a crumbling Empire attempting to re-establish itself by making a count of its troops and taxpayers.[4] This extraordinarily rich body of documents[5] plots the distribution of the inhabitants[6] of each *caza* (canton)[7] by religion, specifying all the different Eastern rites practised by the Christians.

In Egypt the Mamluk administration left in place by the Ottomans after their conquest quickly assumed autonomy and defied the authority of the pasha nominated by the Porte to govern the country. Hesitant about allowing Istanbul the slightest pretext for authority, the Mamluks established a decentralized revenue system which rested on village committees charged with allocating the tax between inhabitants. This direct communal management had no need of a general census. When the sultan considered taking military measures against the Mamluks in 1785, he demanded a report on Egypt from Jazzar, the governor of Sidon.[8] But this document provides no statistical information on the population.

The first comprehensive demographic evaluation of Egypt was conducted by the French scholars who wrote the *Description de l'Egypte*. Inspired by scientific curiosity, these scholars concentrated on a thorough inventory of the inhabited sites of the province of Minya which they considered to be representative of the average and on the estimation of urban densities through several samples, upon which they based their estimates of the population. However, they had not the administrative infrastructure necessary to take a comprehensive census of individuals in order to produce a detailed account of the various religious communities. Their picture of denominational distribution was therefore less accurate than their estimate of the total population, itself understated. It was in fact Muhammad Ali, the founder of modern Egypt, who inaugurated the era of statistics in that country with a census taken in 1846 – a practice continued by his successors.

In the plain and the towns of the Levant, the Ottomans gathered statistics from an early date, but soon came up against the mountain where communities which did not profess the majority Islam – Christians and schismatic Muslims – had taken refuge. The most compact of these mountain regions, Mount Lebanon, was the subject of censuses in the sixteenth century,[9] but not in the nineteenth. By evading the census, the mountain people escaped not only its collective outcome – disclosure of the size, or in other words the strength, of the group – but also its consequence for individuals – the creation of a tax register. In this Christian fief, the poll tax imposed selectively by Islamic law was not collected as assiduously as in the plain, where Christians were in a minority. As Dominique Chevallier points out, for 'the minorities who had taken refuge in the mountain, to conceal their size was still a way of ensuring the autonomy of the social organization which allowed them to maintain, in order to perpetuate themselves, the type of structure where they conceived the existence and the identity of the individual in his group.'[10]

At the time when Istanbul took over the provincial statistics, a crisis was developing in Lebanon. At the end of a short period in which it had been governed by Egypt (1832–40), the country had become the target of European powers who were protective of the Eastern minorities. In order to arbitrate between rival communities, it was necessary to know their strength; demography became crucial. Estimates proliferated, based as much on conviction as on the registers held by the communities: everyone had something to prove.

Whereas the French sources provided coherent estimates - at least so far as trends were concerned – for the Maronites, the interested parties themselves inflated the figures. The Catholic authorities in Europe, moved by the events taking place on the other side of the Mediterranean, each tried to better the other. They were agreed on only one, but fundamental, point; that the population of Mount Lebanon at the time was about 80 per cent Christian (see Table 4.6).[11]

The Demographic Improvement

In 1580 the population of the Fertile Crescent was 92 per cent Muslim, 7 per cent Christian and 1 per cent Jewish. Nearly a millenium of Muslim administration had gradually done its work. Peaceful conversion, whether by enticement or simply for convenience, had been far more effective than the sudden, if rare, attacks of violence which had poisoned the atmosphere under the Mamluks. Confessional diversity was to be found mainly on the Mediterranean coast, which against all the odds maintained contact with Venice, Genoa and Christian Europe.

Whether Islamic schismatics or the People of the Book, the minorities of the East had established their quarters where the physical surroundings formed a citadel. Open to the coast, the *vilayat* of Tripoli[12] was 23 per cent Christian. Facing the desert, the other side of the mountain was more solidly Muslim: in the *vilayat* of Damascus, only 8 per cent of the population were Christians but the first Jewish community (2 per cent of the inhabitants) was there long before that in Baghdad. Other mountains, in the region of Mosul far from the shipping routes of Europe, had also supported a Christian presence. On the other hand, in the depths of the Syrian steppe Islam ruled almost undivided: Christians were less than 3 per cent in the *vilayat* of Aleppo, although their community experienced renewed growth under the direct administration of Istanbul.

After four centuries of Ottoman rule, the non-Muslim communities of the Fertile Crescent acquired considerable demographic importance. The Jewish population doubled and the Christian tripled: more than 20 per cent of the population were by that time Christian, and 2 per cent Jewish. While the Muslim population had increased by a factor of 1.2 Christian numbers had multiplied by 3.9 and Jewish by 2.9. In the early years of the empire the Jewish communities were swollen by the last exiles from Spain, who joined the small group of Jews which had always existed in Palestine. On the other hand, for the first time in the history of the *dar al-Islam* the Christian community grew from its own resources, that is the birth and death rate, and not through foreign migrants like the Crusaders of the past or the *pieds-noirs* of the future (see Table 4.3), so making the Ottoman centuries a long exception.

The geographical distribution of the Christian minorities emphasized the contrast with the past. As they flourished in areas that were economically prosperous and in contact with the outside world – the West more than the East – they slowly abandoned their remote strongholds for the Mediterranean coast to the west and the trading fringes of the nomadic *badia* region to the east. By 1881 Christians made up 40 per cent of the population of the regions facing the coastline (the *vilayat* of Beirut and the *mutasarrifiya* of Mount Lebanon), and 12 and 15 per cent of the *vilayats* of Aleppo and Damascus respectively. Situated nearer to Istanbul and therefore better protected by the imperial order, the Christians of Aleppo experienced the most surprising revival – 5.9 per thousand population growth per annum – while the Muslims increased only by only 0.2 per thousand. The Catholic families of Aleppo still relate today that in the sixteenth century Sultan Selim I, distressed to meet so few Christians in the city, had ordered that the community should be repopulated. This partly explains the astonishing diversity of origins that could still be found in 1914: 52 per cent of Christian Aleppans were Greek Catholic or Orthodox, 33 per cent Armenians and 14 per cent Syriac.[13] Such vigorous development compensated for the decline of the most far-off Christian communities, those which disappeared progressively from the *vilayat* of Baghdad.

Population growth was certainly not continuous throughout the four centuries of Ottoman rule. A strong push in the sixteenth century in the whole area of the Mediterranean and the Arab East was followed by a long period of stagnation. Epidemics and famine could, within a few weeks, cancel out decades of population growth. But towards the middle or end of the nineteenth century, it stabilized and then accelerated. During these three periods, the Christian communities did not maintain a constant advantage over their Muslim neighbours.

We possess only fragmentary information on trends in the earliest days of the empire. It is known that towards the middle of the sixteenth century, in about 30 mixed villages in the province of Damascus, population growth reached a peak with Christians multiplying at double the rate of Muslims: 20.3 per thousand per annum against 9.8 per thousand from 1533–59.[14] These were kindly times for the whole population, but the birth rate of the Christians must have been higher than that of the Muslims, or their death rate lower, as was the case in the nineteenth century. The towns, which were subject to heavy migration, all had different experiences: for example, the number of Christians increased in Damascus and Ramla, remained more or less constant in Beirut, Nablus and Gaza, and decreased in Jerusalem (see Table 4.9).

The normal death rate, that which applies outside plagues, did not begin to decline until it was affected by the economic and technical progress of the nineteenth century. Modernity reached the Arab East through its non-Muslim minorities. Both the Christian and Jewish communities therefore experienced a decline in their death rate, while their birth rate was maintained, half a century ahead of the Muslims. Furthermore, this demographic transition affected the comfortably-off classes before the ordinary people, the town-dwellers before the rural inhabitants. Since the Christian and Jewish communities were relatively prosperous and urbanized, economic and geographical factors, rather than religion itself, favoured them. But the very reasons that accounted for their early demographic recovery in the nineteenth century were to bring about their relative decline in the twentieth century when, in the next stage of the demographic transition, their birth rate began to fall.

The increased census taking in the last decades of Ottoman rule provides a detailed picture of the situation in Syria, Lebanon and Palestine. Between 1881 and 1914 in these three countries, the average annual increase of the Muslim population was 10 per thousand. Among the Christians it was 21 per thousand if we consider their natural increase and 14 per thousand if we look at the net balance[15] – relatively high rates of population growth. The gap between Muslims and Christians was reduced by emigration to the New World which involved large numbers of the excess population of the Lebanese mountain, mainly Christians: 3,000 departures were registered each year between 1860 and 1899, then 15,000 between 1900 and 1913.[16] The magnitude of this transfer by itself demonstrates the magnitude of the surplus of births over deaths.

Although the migration reduced Christian numbers, it also gave their population new life. In the early days at least, the Lebanese of the diaspora sent remittances to their home country which stimulated the economy of the mountain and enabled the birth rate to increase despite demographic pressure on an area with limited agricultural resources. Meanwhile, Palestine received more than 80,000 Jewish immigrants from Europe before the First World War – a reverse migration which meant that the Jewish population (23 per thousand average growth per annum) was increasing faster than the Christian, despite a lower rate of natural growth.[17] In Syria there were marked contrasts in the rate of population growth among religious minorities. The *vilayat* of Beirut attracted Christians from the *vilayat* of Damascus, where the Muslim population had become the most dynamic, and from Aleppo where the Christian population would soon reach its maximum level.

By contrast to the Fertile Crescent, the population of Egypt was stable. Under the Mamluks, the proportion of Christians had reached its lowest level; about 1 inhabitant out of 14 in the thirteenth century.[18] As for the birth and death rates, Copts and Muslims, whose standard of living and relationship to the land was much the same, were affected by more or less the same conditions.

According to Jomard, one of the authors of the prestigious *Description de l'Egypte*:

> The state of the population is one of the least favourable aspects of the Egyptian question. Rather than increasing or remaining stationary, it has been in decline. Without looking back to Antiquity, I start from the French expedition. According to the most likely calculations, Cairo contains 263,000 inhabitants, and the rest of the country 2,225,300. In all, less than 2.5 million,[19] which is a sad result of the Mamluks and the Ottoman invasion. Since the departure of the French, three or four violent plagues ... gave a slightly higher proportion (8 per cent).[20]

Jomard provided a table of the 'various nations which live in Egypt' besides the indigenous Muslims–Turks: 30–40,000; Mamluks and white slaves: 8,000; Copts: 160,000; Nubians and Negroes: 11–12,000; Armenians: 2,000; Syrians: 3–4,000; Greeks: 5,000; Jews: 3–4,000. In total, therefore, there were 170,000 Christians, about 6.7 per cent of the population as estimated by Jomard.[21] The first censuses of 1846 and 1882 gave a slightly higher proportion (8 per cent).

As in Turkey and the Levant, but to a lesser extent, modernization triggered a burst of population growth among the Christians. Early differentials appeared in the mortality rate by community in the Arab East. Until the nineteenth century, routine mortality had little to do with religion since medicine was still ineffective. Nevertheless,

in the face of crises - famine, epidemics and sometimes wars –
Christians and Jews found themselves, as urban communities, in a
relatively protected situation. The peasant population of the Arab
East farmed the margins of the desert where the vagaries of water
supply meant that they were exposed to recurrent crop failures. But
only really devastating famines affected the town-dwellers, especially
in those towns where foreign trade compensated for the fluctuations
in peasant production. In Syria and Palestine where the Christians
and Jews were more urban than the Muslims, they were better
provided for against the collapse of agricultural produce.

The towns, however, were devastated periodically by epidemics.
The small, narrow streets and unhealthy open drains encouraged the
transmission of infectious diseases whose spread was limited only
by people's behaviour. In the face of the plague, which was the
cause of the greatest destruction, indigenous Muslims and Christians
reacted differently. Muslims would maintain a collective front, and
the frequent contacts between their families exposed them all to
contagion. The Christians on the other hand isolated themselves.
Like the 'Franks', diplomats, traders or European artisans, they either
withdrew far from the infected town or, if the epidemic had not
allowed them enough time for flight, shut themselves up in their
house .

Pierre Plane, a French trader in Aleppo on the eve of the French
Revolution, describes the close confinement which spared the
Christians from the recurrent slaughter of epidemics: 'It is a question
of not leaving the house and not allowing anyone to enter ... These
are the only precautions that all the Franks and a number of
Christians and Jews have taken, and none of them were attacked by
the plague.'[22] Likewise, when Beirut was in the clutches of cholera
the Christians fled but the Muslims remained: 'Almost all the
Christians have fled to the mountain; also, in these days of renewed
outbreaks, the scourge is hitting the Muslims in particular,' it was
reported in a commercial letter from Beirut dated 1865.[23] These
were the diseases of the poor, diseases that simply drove away those
who had the material means to flee. Perhaps the greatest vulnerability
of the Muslims, therefore, was that they comprised the multitude of
the ordinary people of the towns.[24]

In Lebanon and possibly Iraq, the natural features of the region
also protected the Christians. The escarpments where they had
entrenched themselves provided protection not only from attacks
but also from the diseases of the plain and the towns – malaria and

cholera – which were killed off by the altitude. 'Thanks to the mountain refuge, health and sickness are also differentiated according to confession.'[25] Such inequality also existed on the African coast of the Mashreq. The plague of 1835 killed 35 per cent of Alexandrians, but with great discrimination: 55 per cent of Egyptian Muslims, 85 per cent of 'Berbers and Negroes' and only 11 per cent of Turks, 12 per cent of Copts, Armenians and Jews, 14 per cent of Greeks and 6 per cent of Europeans. Muslims suffered big losses but Christians were relatively spared.[26]

The fact that each group lived in its own separate district also played a role. In this multi-confessional society, religion remained an essential mark of collective identity. Having close economic relations, the minorities and the Muslims preserved their residential areas. In all the large cities of the Arab East, apart from Beirut, there was a Christian district and a Jewish district, a segregation that was generally accepted. In Cairo, a kind of spontaneous hierarchy existed, according to which Egyptian Muslims placed other Arab Muslims (North African and Syrian) closest to themselves. They were followed by the Turks, even though their language was not understood, and only then the Christian Arabs, whether Egyptian Copts or Syrian Catholics – that is to say both those who had for long centuries been part of Egyptian history and newly arrived immigrants.[27] These groups rarely met and as a result, epidemics which affected one would not reach the others.

War never became a cause of huge Muslim excess mortality in the Arab provinces of the Empire as it did in Anatolia. Until the campaigns of Muhammad Ali against the Porte, Arab contingents remained on the margin of large military operations. It was only when wars in the Caucasus and the Balkans broke out in 1876, to which men from all the provinces of the empire were summoned, that war became a cause of differentiation. Indeed, after the Tanzimat all Ottoman subjects were theoretically liable to mobilization. But Christians and Jews could gain exemption by paying the *badal* (exemption tax) and consequently the Muslims found themselves practically alone in combat. In addition, the Arab East experienced few civilian losses in the Ottoman period, for no significant conflicts broke out there, except those between the religious communities.

In the nineteenth century, first in Europe and from there through the spread of medical progress, a knowledge of how to cure illness was gradually acquired. Large natural catastrophes became less frequent and eventually disappeared. However, new inequalities emerged as knowledge, economic well-being and health began to reinforce each other. This was undoubtedly a decisive factor in the demographic advance at the end of the Ottoman period of the Christians and Jews who were better represented in the urban bourgeoisie and more educated than the Muslims. Infant mortality among the Armenians of Cairo[28] demonstrates the extent of progress among an urban minority: a rate of 140 per thousand between 1850 and 1900 and 115 per thousand in the period 1900–19, levels which the city as a whole did not reach until 1950 and 1960 respectively. The social distance which separated some of the Christian minorities from the masses of the city was also, at that time, a considerable demographic resource.

Evidence of differences in the birth rate is hard to come by. In a mixed canton of the Lebanese mountain in the mid-nineteenth century, the composition of the Christian population was 34.8 per cent men, 25.5 per cent women and 39.7 per cent children; that of the Druzes was 30.8 per cent men, 32.2 per cent women and 37 per cent children.[29] These figures show a low fertility rate among the Druzes – 1.15 children per woman against 1.55 among the Christians – which is confirmed by twentieth-century studies. The Druzes do not, of course, represent the majority of the Muslim population. We can nonetheless imagine that marital instability among Muslims affected fertility: polygamy, as the Abbasid writer al-Jahiz (776–868) brilliantly observed,[30] and divorce by repudiation, limited the Muslim birth-rate. At the beginning of the twentieth century, divorce broke up 30 per cent of marriages in Egypt and more than 40 per cent in Algeria.[31] The repudiated woman was put back on the marriage market, but only after the prescribed waiting period was observed and with less chance of finding a new husband. In this puritanical society, she frequently had to live out her divorce in sexual solitude. The opportunities offered by the formality of repudiation could thus persistently restrain the demographic vitality of the Muslim population.[32] In the Eastern churches divorce was either tightly bound up in legal procedures or quite simply forbidden, but either way the Christian family was spared.

Christian Reorganization in the Levant

In the Levant a new allocation of territorial space accompanied the growth of the Christian population. Four great demographic movements during the Ottoman period reshaped the spatial distribution of population into the pattern that we still know today. That most directly allied to demographic growth was the Maronite spread to the south, from the area defined by the Qadicha and Nahr al-Kalb rivers. The second movement was properly speaking a migration, which resulted from a religious split, namely the Catholic antischism in the Orthodox and Gregorian churches. The third and fourth were of political origin: the confessional violence which broke out in Damascus and Kurdistan.

In central Lebanon, the Maronites had formerly taken advantage of Sunni Mamluk repression to occupy Shi'i areas, a position which they reinforced under the Ottomans. Several armed incidents were accompanied by a limited exodus, notably in the Kesrouan (1677 and 1684), but the economy played the major part. The Shi'a were small peasants permanently in debt to traders from the coast; they paid these debts with their land and left to join the main body of their community on the other side of the mountain. They remained there until the second half of the twentieth century, when large numbers of them migrated to Beirut creating a band of poverty around the city.

The advantage which they had formerly drawn from the control of the territory by strict Mamluk Islam, the Maronites renewed but in a reverse situation. Whereas with the Mamluks they were deployed in favour of military action by the state, with the Ottomans it was the non-intervention of the public authority in the affairs of the mountain that offered them a series of opportunities. It was in the land of the Druzes to the south, the Shuf, that they would now be deployed. From the seventeenth century, propelled by vigorous population growth, the Maronite peasants settled on the lands of Druze feudal lords. Small farmers when they arrived, they benefited from a strangely progressive fiscal rule, the *mugharassa*, which allowed that after a certain time the agricultural labourer would be granted a part of the property. Rather than a 'real Maronite colonization of Lebanon',[33] this was a slow infiltration by successive generations on the land.

It passed unnoticed by the Druzes until they had become a clear minority in their fiefdoms. It was then that a decisive event took place in the history of the country, the battle Ayn Dara in 1711 in which two Druze armies confronted each other. From time immemorial the Druzes had been grouped under two rival authorities: the Qaysites, originally from the north, and the Yemenites, originally from the south. More mythical than real, this division cut through all the tribes that had originated in the Arabian Peninsula. The combat at Ayn Dara was fratricidal and still lives on in the collective memory; it set against each other the two branches of the Druzes rallied by two rival families, the Chehabs and the Alameddins. The Chehab's victory opened a new page of Maronite history. The defeated warriors of the Alameddins, together with those who had supported them, were exiled beyond Mount Hermon in the Hawran, clearing their villages for new Maronite farmers.

As a result of the conflicts which had divided the Druzes, the demography of the Maronites was the greatest winner and their political position was enhanced. Although the Chehab family were Druze emirs they were Sunnis who, from 1756 began to convert to Maronitism.[34] From 1770, for the first time since the coming of Islam and uniquely in the Arab East, Lebanon was therefore governed by a Christian, Emir Yusif Shihab (Chehab). And it has continued to be so ever since.[35] Officially Sunni like his successors, the emir had modestly kept his new religion to himself.

The favours that the emirs granted to the Christians turned Lebanon into a haven for various communities in flight. In the wake of the Maronite expansion, there was a wave of migration from the interior of Syria. This largely involved families belonging to the Greek Catholic community, a paradoxical neologism used to describe the Uniates who abandoned Orthodoxy, rallied to Rome and then established a separate church in 1701. The hostility of the Orthodox Christians towards these renegades degenerated into threats, persecution and riots in which the churches of one Christian sect were burned down by Christians of another rite. As a result of these incidents, a section of the urban bourgeoisie emigrated to Egypt and Lebanon. The Greek Orthodox followed them to join the small nucleus which had always existed in the plain of Tripoli. At almost the same time, an early Armenian community – the neo-Catholics chased from Cilicia by similar events – was established in Lebanon (1737–48).

The arrival in Lebanon of other Christians from Syria in 1810 was triggered by completely different developments. The Wahhabis,[36] a fundamentalist sect from Arabia brought up on the writings of Ibn Taymiyya, having sacked the Shi'i Holy Places in Iraq were threatening Damascus. In the Syrian capital and in all the cities where it had spread, the Wahhabi terror brought back old, long forgotten, discriminatory measures. Once again subjected to all manner of persecution,[37] Christians left Syria en masse for Beirut and Mount Lebanon encouraged by Emir Bashir II who was himself secretly converted to Christianity.

The confessional map of what was to become Greater Lebanon was thus almost in place from the first third of the nineteenth century. A British colonel who had access to the tax registers in 1835 described the situation then: Islam dominated in the plain and Christianity in the mountain. The coastal towns all had a Sunni majority and a large Greek Orthodox minority, but Beirut henceforth counted as many Christians as Muslims. To the east of the Anti-Lebanon, Syria was Sunni by a large majority. The eighteenth century had undoubtedly emphasized homogeneity, for the impoverishment of the Ottoman authority had allowed nomadism to develop. This pushed back ever more to the west the limits of the steppe and the cultivated areas and, with them, religious diversity.

In 1832, Shortly after the Wahhabi episode, Syria was brought under the authority of the Egyptian dynasty of Muhammad Ali. As soon as he entered Damascus, Muhammad Ali's son Ibrahim Pasha, who was a modernist, abolished some of the discriminatory practices that were a hangover from another age and established greater equality between the religions, notably in the duty to do military service. Muslims, and for the first time, Christians were all summoned to serve the flag. The measure collided head on with the tribal patronage of a society where mobilization existed only to defend a fiefdom.

Encouraged by the Porte and by Great Britain, the Druzes first rose up against Ibrahim Pasha, whom they accused of favouring the Christians. They were convinced that the Shi'a would come to their help in a region where they had lost their preeminent position since the eighteenth century. On the eve of battle, they discovered that their ranks were thinning out: the political situation suddenly clarified the demographic position. From Latakia to Tripoli and from Sidon to the Hawran, the Egyptian governor had faced revolt from communities who were opposed to each other on every point except the unanimous rejection of conscription.

The general disarmament, which was decided on too late in 1840, could not stop the insurrection. The crisis gave the European powers more influence in the religious game, in which their consuls became indispensable actors: those of France and Austria on the side of the Catholics, those of Russia and England on the side of the Orthodox and the Druzes respectively.

In order to avoid fresh shocks, Istanbul drafted an preliminary plan to separate the potential combatants. The Porte nominated two *qaimaqam*, one Maronite and the other Druze, who had authority over the members of their own community without being limited territorially. Such a concept, which dissociated the status of the people from that of the territory, conflicted with European notions of the nation state. On European recommendation Lebanon was therefore divided into two administrative units, each *qaimaqam* governing the whole population of the district, whatever their religion. 'This was to officially organize civil war in the country.'[38] For the first but not the last time, the Beirut–Damascus road became a 'green line',[39] intended to divide the country into two homogeneous regions – Maronite in the north and Druzes in the south.

This division was based on a rather summary political geography. Many Druze villages dotted the Christian Metn (a district to the north-east of Beirut), while the Maronites were the majority not only in their own *qaimaqamiyya*, but also in that of the Druzes. The largest Christian town at the time, Deir al-Qamar, was located in the only district with a Druze majority – the Shuf. This is where the Maronites suffered their greatest losses in the course of the civil war which broke out in 1860: 2,000 civilians were killed on 20 June alone. After four weeks of fighting the illusion of religious uniformity on which the partition of the country was established had become a reality: there were practically no Christians left in the Druze *qaimaqamiyya*, but 15,000 deaths and 100,000 refugees.[40]

On the ground, the conflicts of 1860 worked indisputably to the advantage of the Druzes. However, the support the Christians found outside the country transformed their defeat into an instrument of expansion. The massacres had aroused the anger of Europe. France sent troops to Beirut and the European chanceries put pressure on the Ottoman government to grant, under their guarantee, the autonomy of 'Lesser Lebanon'.[41] Eight *mutasarrif* (governors) succeeded each other from 1861 to 1915, all Catholics selected from the cream of the Ottoman administration. The first and the last were Armenian and in between there were three Aleppines, one Albanian, one Italian and one Pole nominated to this high office. Under this regime, the country experienced its longest period of peace and Christianity its most vigorous growth.

Far away to the east, in the hinterland of Mosul, another secular *modus vivendi* had tottered with the arrival of European missionaries. Nothing except their religion distinguished the Nestorians from the Kurds. Living together on the same mountain, one group Christian, the other Muslim, they all endured the same rigours of a hard life.

But the Presbyterian church, first British then American, lifted the Nestorians out of the oblivion into which they had fallen. The missions which soon followed from 1820 brought them close to the Western powers, but aroused the suspicion of the Kurds. A first massacre of Christian villagers took place in 1843. The army of the governor of Mosul, despatched under pressure from the British consul, could only stand and watch. Twenty thousand Nestorians and some Chaldeans perished,[42] a prelude to the near disappearance of their community in the East in 1933.[43] Was this massacre attributable to a Kurdish pre-nationalism?[44] More probably it was caused by the anarchy which had slowly established itself on the remote mountain slopes before they were taken in hand by the central government in Istanbul in 1869.

While they did not experience the same radical fate, the Jacobites nevertheless suffered from the climate of religious violence which spread in Kurdistan towards the middle of the nineteenth century. They too blended socially into their environment,[45] but the fact that they shared the religion of the Nestorians meant that they were exposed. The Jacobites underwent a slow demographic decline: from 300,000 at the end of the seventeenth century, their population declined to 120,000 by the end of the nineteenth century.[46] In 1920, their patriarch left Iraq to establish himself at Homs in Syria, the country which today houses the greater part of their community (86,000 people in 1992 out of a congregation that totals 167,000).[47]

A Successful Outcome for the Minorities

The conversions that had historically been the principle dynamic behind the spread of Islam hardly occurred under the Ottomans, for their main cause disappeared. The poll tax, the *jizya*, remained theoretically in force until the Tanzimat officially abolished it – but it was no longer a burden: the main tax was one that which hit capital and production without any differentiation by religion.

In the Lebanese mountain where Ottoman administration was indirect, the emir was the *multazim* (tax farmer) and he subcontracted his function to local notables. The hierarchies that existed in the heart of society enabled intermediaries – Maronites or Druzes depending on the dominant religion in the region – to levy taxes. In the Christian areas, the tax collector was therefore Christian. Consequently, the differential financial system which had worked so much in favour of conversion in the past progressively lost its significance. For all intents and purposes, the tax became the *miri* (of the prince)[48] or of the Treasury as we would call it today – in other words it had been secularized. The same term came to designate a great variety of taxes: on land, production, birth and death certificates and so on. The tax collector therefore conducted only one fiscal transaction. From that time to keep one's own religion was no longer seen as a distinct and calculable cost.

The situation was entirely different in Egypt where the tax collector in direct contact with the Muslim or Christian taxpayer was almost always a Copt. The law fixed the administrative framework for the deduction, as well as the proportions destined respectively to the Ottoman pasha – the representative of the sultan – the army and the local government, that is to say to the Mamluks. But it did not decree the precise rules of imposition. Only the total amount of the village tax was decided; the division between the inhabitants was arbitrated by a tripartite committee composed of the Coptic collector (*sarraf*), the mayor of the village (*sheikh al-balad*) and the lawyer defending the interests of the villagers (*shahed*).

This distribution of roles placed the *sarrafs* in an ambiguous position where unpopularity contended with notoriety. They were often accused of cupidity while their impartiality in village quarrels was valued, especially since the *sheikh al-balad* was frequently an involved party. One French traveller estimated – with obvious exaggeration – the number of individuals who made their living in Egypt from collecting taxes at 30,000, and went so far as to hold them responsible for depopulation: it was, he observed, likely to be the *sarraf* rather than the Mamluk who discouraged the peasant from producing.[49] Not only was the base of the financial administration generally Copt, but also its top echelons. For four years Muhammad Ali had Girgis al-Gawhari as his treasurer, a leading figure in the Coptic bourgeoisie who attracted the sympathy of the people with his gentleness in fiscal matters, but whom the governor had to get rid of for the same reason.[50]

Apart from the tax system, the whole institutional apparatus of the Ottoman Empire was transformed. The religious minorities never formed nations in the sense that the nation is understood today, endowed with a territory,[51] but they benefited from the institution of the *millet*, by which the Ottoman power delegated its authority on all questions relating to the status of the individual.to the spiritual head of each of the communities that it recognized. From marriage to inheritance as well as education, all the affairs of the family came under the jurisdiction of the *millet*. The status of the *dhimmi*, which previously linked the minorities individually to the Muslim authority, was transformed into a collective pact between the sultan and the communities. From being merely a large number of individuals, the Christians and Jews became recognized groups in society.

Unlike the *millet*, which strengthened the communities from the inside, the capitulations enticed them to the outside. In 1535, in order to reward him for having brought the Empire into the European theatre, Süleiman the Magnificent granted trading privileges to François I. In order to guarantee French traders respect of their persons and interests, the consuls of France first saw their jurisdiction widened in commercial, civil and penal matters. Only 18 years after conquering Syria, the Ottomans had agreed to give up some of their sovereignty on the question of the minorities. In 1740, the Capitulations no longer came under the largesse of the sultan but became a pure and simple obligation, when at the request of the King of France and not on his own initiative, the sultan had to renew the treaty. France soon made use of the Capitulations to establish itself as a protector, not only of its nationals in the Levant but also of those professing the same religion as them – Maronites and Catholics of the Eastern rite. Doubly 'protected', by the sultan and the King of France, they became the appointed intermediaries of Islam and Christianity, especially in economic matters. Meanwhile other European powers had obtained similar concessions, in particular Great Britain, Austria and Russia, each establishing itself as the protector of a religious minority: in this way the Capitulations became a key institution for the promotion of a trading bourgeoisie among the minorities of the East.

The Capitulations progressively created a mistrust of the Christian communities. This appeared sporadically, nearly always on the occasion of a far-off confrontation between Islam and Christianity. Thus, in 1799, the aggression against the Christians of Damascus was committed as a 'reprisal' against the entry of Bonaparte into Egypt. 'With Saint-Jean-d'Acre taken, the French army would have flown to Damascus and Aleppo,' recalled Bonaparte. 'It would have been on the Euphrates in a flash; the Christians of Syria, the Druze, the Christians of Armenia would have joined it; these populations were going to be shaken ... I would have reached Constantinople and India, I would have changed the face of the world!'[52] The Greek revolt in 1821, the French landing in Algiers, the British attacks against the Moghul empire in India and various other events which humiliated Islam worldwide, also affected interconfessional relations in Syria.[53]

When the Ottomans conquered Syria and Egypt, it was not known that the Near East would soon be on the margins of the great trade routes. The discovery of America had just opened up fabulous resources, and the route around the Cape of Good Hope removed the necessity of paying a tribute to camel-drivers for transit. The Levant lost its position as a crossroads of trade but it became provincialized rather than isolated. The Ottomans were the masters of an immense empire. When it came under their authority the Arab East found itself in a single stroke involved in a vast trade network – internal trade perhaps, but on a large scale. From Tunis to Salonika and from Aleppo to Belgrade, the most varied and complementary merchandise circulated along the imperial routes.

The modest size of transactions with the Christian West disguised the multitude of internal transactions, and this distorts our perception of the expansion of Ottoman trade. On the eve of Bonaparte's expedition, non-Ottoman Europe was the smallest of Egypt's partners (14 per cent of its trade), far behind the East (36 per cent) and the Ottoman Mediterranean (50 per cent).[54] Of the French ships chartered at Alexandria by the Ottomans, only 2.5 per cent were destined for Europe; from Asia Minor to North Africa, all the others sailed within Ottoman waters.[55] Several Arab towns occupied, or more precisely were able to conquer, a central position. Connecting the ships and the caravans, Alexandria and Beirut on the coast, Aleppo, Mosul, Damascus and Cairo on the desert, all experienced economic and, consequently, population growth out of all proportion to the meagre resources that they could have drawn from their rural environment.[56] The number of caravanserai in Cairo increased from 57 in the time of the Mamluk sultans to 360 at the end of the seventeenth century.[57]

To the north, the failure of the the siege of Vienna in 1683 heralded the difficulties and soon the disintegration of the empire in Europe. The mass of its trading was therefore moved to the Orient – Alexandria and Aleppo became the new pivots. The Red Sea, 'holy sea of the Muslims, forbidden to Christians,'[58] was no longer the royal spice route but had found a substitute product - the coffee of Arabia, which was exported from Mocha in Arab sailing boats which set off for Suez. There the Syrian, Armenian, Greek or Jewish agents took delivery of it and the French traders only came at the end of the journey.

Wealthier than Egypt, Ottoman Asia was also more impenetrable.

Its interior did not attract European traders, who were only present on the coast and the area immediately behind. Their connections ended at Damascus and Aleppo, where the immense caravan network of Islam began. Thus, the local merchants were a necessary part of the relay system of trading. While the Muslims were responsible for the main body of internal trade, the Christians and some Jews specialized in transactions with the 'Franks'. A Christian bourgeoisie that looked to Europe developed, not against the Empire but for it. Although very modest compared to the two worlds that it brought together – the Empire and Europe – this was a large intermediary role for the Christian communities of the East, who were pre-disposed to trade with these new partners in the west because of their religious links.

On the edge of the steppes where the camel-drivers dismounted, the Christian and Jewish populations were increasing in some of the large towns. To consider only Damascus, in 1569 there were 6,300 Christians and 3,300 Jews among 52,400 inhabitants[59] (see Table 4.8). Two centuries later the Christians had tripled (22,000) while the population of the city had not even doubled in size and the number of Jews had remained almost stable (4,000).[60] Of course the communities did not consist entirely of traders. In Jerusalem in the sixteenth century Christians, Jews and Muslims worked alongside each other in all the usual trades of the city – blacksmiths, masons, butchers and spinners.[61]

Well before Beirut, but more modestly, the Christians of Aleppo had also been flourishing. The consulates which were established by the Venetians, the French, the English and the Dutch between 1548 and 1613 opened this city of the interior to Europe. The direct authority of Istanbul guaranteed religious co-existence. The natural partners of their 'Frank' coreligionists, the Ottoman Christians (Melkites and Syrian Catholics, but also Maronites and Armenians) engaged in prosperous activities. Evidence of this can still be seen today in the ostentation of the houses in the districts of Jdaideh and Aziziyeh. As a reciprocal obligation, the Aleppines founded a colony in Livorno.

In Egypt the Copts never constituted such a successful bourgeoisie as the Christians in Syria. On the whole they remained rural and provincial. In Cairo they did not control international trade but generally occupied unobtrusive positions, such as clerks to the administration or the Muslim aristocracy, neighbourhood traders or small artisans. The statements of inheritance demonstrate their modest wealth compared to that of the Muslims: the possessions that a Coptic artisan left to his heirs were exactly one-third of those of a Muslim of the same profession.[62]

The real dominant class among the Christians of Egypt was of Syrian origin. Escaping from their strained relations with the Orthodox Christians, numerous Melkite families left Damascus and, in particular, Aleppo. Like those who, also from Aleppo, would take the road to Beirut two centuries later, it was a financial and intellectual elite who deserted Syria. In one generation they successfully constructed for themselves a major economic and social role in Cairo. They quickly displaced the Jews as customs farmers and played a considerable part in the import-export trade. The Syrian Catholics of Egypt had enough influence to negotiate, with the support of Muhammad Ali who wanted to distance himself from Istanbul, their liberation from the Orthodox *millet* (1816).

Beirut was a small village when the Ottomans arrived: 4,200 inhabitants, of which 10 per cent were Christian.[63] Two hundred and fifty years later, Volney found only 6,000 inhabitants there, for 'two inconvenient factors condemned Beirut never to be more than a mediocre place; on one hand it is dominated by a line of hills ... on the other hand it lacks water in the interior.'[64] But the voluntarism of Ibrahim Pasha, the son of Muhammad Ali, succeeded in changing this. With the Egyptian occupation the town witnessed an economic and demographic growth that was unique in the Arab world.[65] At the same time Beirut became the most Christian of the regional capitals (see Table 4.10). Towards the middle of the nineteenth century, or perhaps a little earlier,[66] the Christian population achieved parity with the Muslims for the first time, then became a two-thirds majority which was maintained until the French mandate. The town became a centre of economic prosperity and cultural brilliance an, despite occasional reports of brawls between *abadayas*, the hot-heads of the various religions, it was peaceful.[67]

The Maronites found a haven in Beirut, where they could hide temporarily from the traumas in the mountain. But the Christian bourgeoisie was at first Orthodox. From the nineteenth century, it acquired all the features of a modern capitalist class, accumulating capital and creating commercial banks. Vigorous financial activity in the four corners of the empire through family branches guaranteed it both real estate and an international network. Beirut attracted Ottoman Orthodoxy from afar, as can be seen from the variety of origin of the family names.

The Orthodox community owed this exceptional energy to the fact of belonging to the first Christian church in the empire,[68] the only one which arose from a patriarchate established in its heart, in Istanbul, which never looked to Rome for protection. The Greek Catholics, the Maronites and the communities of the Latin rite were probably closer to the Western chancelleries, in fact too close; the advantages which these communities received from the protection of Capitulations rather than the Ottoman *millet* certainly facilitated their commercial contacts, but they were prejudicial to public confidence. As for the Sunni bourgeoisie of Beirut, being part of the huge Sunni majority of the Arab and Turkish East, it was towards Egypt and the interior region of the empire that it extended its commercial network. The cream of Beirut society was inter-related, not yet through marriage but through business.

The trading cities were not alone in offering Christian demography the advantages of a link with Europe. This was also true also of the Lebanese mountain, where the population was emerging from subsistence economy.[69] The cultivation of mulberry trees and the breeding of silk-worms destined – after the Egyptian administration lifted the prohibition on export in 1833 – for European markets provided the community with the resources to free it from the hazards of food production. Thus the Maronites extended the limits of traditional demography. Silk was a trading as well as an agricultural activity, and from 1850 it became a small industry. French and some Lebanese companies despatched the cocoon or the thread from Beirut to Marseilles and then on to the factories in Lyons, so laying the basis for a new integration of the Maronite community. Its town and country branches were united in an economic network and incorporated into an international relationship.

Population growth was so great that the mountain became too small. When the breeding of silkworms collapsed in crisis, the most simple mountain dwellers were forced to emigrate overseas where they soon established the beginnings of a new prosperity. These early emigrants, some of whom took an active part in the construction of capitalism in Latin America, are similar to the families from one valley in the French alps who emigrated to Mexico at the end of the nineteenth century.[70]

The modernization of the Arab East was as much cultural as economic. Many Muslim and Christian Ottoman subjects were challenged by the overtaking of the empire by Europe, which was so evident in the nineteenth century. Since knowledge had to be repossessed, cultural relations with Europe naturally developed beside commerce. It was in particular the Christians who established them. In this connection, the opening of the Maronite college in Rome in 1584 under Pope Gregory III had been a founding act. Much later, Muhammad Ali sent contingents of Egyptian students to study in France.[71] But it was through the founding of the first religious educational establishments (in 1834 in Lebanon, 1854 in Egypt) by American missionaries, soon followed by French, Italian and British, that Western influence reached the people and helped to bring about a change in customs, in particular practices that would reduce the mortality rate. The Catholic missions played a large role in the spread of education, not only for the Maronites and Greek Catholics but also the Orthodox and Muslims. However, inequalities in education quickly became apparent between regions and, within regions, between religions.[72] Everywhere the Christians moved considerably ahead of the Muslims (see Table 4.7). The behaviour of the Jews was more constant: they received less schooling than the average in the *vilayat* where instruction was widespread (Beirut, Baghdad, Mosul), but were at the head in the most backward *vilayat* (Aleppo and Basra).

There is another side to the picture for the confrontation between rich and poor took on a religious aspect. The Tanzimat had unexpected effects. The Christian bourgeoisie which had been formed through several generations of contact with Europe consolidated its wealth, often at the expense of a class of small entrepreneurs who were frequently Muslim: 'The European industry imported by the Christians practically eliminated indigenous manufacture.'[73] The envy caused by the economic situation of the Christian elite had previously been tempered by a certain sympathy for its subjected status. When political equality was suddenly proclaimed, economic inequality became a provocation and jealousy was no longer balanced by compassion. The *ulama* stood up against the change in the Islamic character of the state represented by these secular reforms and ordinary people opposed the freedom of worship flaunted by the Christians – the church bells that began to ring again, the employment of Muslim slaves in the houses of Christians – in short, the pride that replaced their previous humble status. The clamour in the streets increased. During the war in the mountain, Beirut witnessed the first exodus of Christians to the Kesrouan and in Damascus there were massacres in which 5,500 Christians were killed. There would probably have been many more if the Algerian Emir Abd al-

Qadir, who had retired to Damascus after his exile from Algeria, had not offered to mediate to bring an end to the killing. He thus demonstrated that it was possible to declare holy war against France in the Maghreb and later to protect Christians in the Arab East.

The economic and demographic recovery of the Eastern Christians took place in a singular international context which ended with the First World War. The colonial and expansionist West had established its hegemony while proclaiming its Christianity. Economic and missionary victory went hand in hand. The Enlightenment, however, brought about the ideas that would triumph at the beginning of the twentieth century. Secularism and, much later, democracy became the new religions and both gave demography a right over politics.[74] By means of complex mechanisms they would slow down Christian progress.

Table 4.1: Population of the Arab Provinces of the Ottoman Empire, 1570–90 and 1881–2

Province	Population in 1580			Population in 1881–1882**		
	Muslims	Christians	Jews	Muslims	Christians	Jews
Aleppo	643,285	16,930	1,165	690,184	99,269	9,913
Tripoli, Beirut*	195,070	58,840	1,535	537,388	367,701	3,541
Damascus	452,155	39,335	10,440	338,931	61,576	6,368
Baghdad	319,990	20,175	3,015	298,704	3,326	25,364
Mosul	98,305	0	0	329,186	14,464	8,572
Basra				158,496	758	880
Total	1,708,805	135,280	16,155	2,352,889	547,094	54,638

*   Including Mount Lebanon, removed from the *vilaya* of Beirut in 1881–2.
** 1987 for Basra

Sources: 1580: Ö. L. Barkan, 'Research on the Ottoman Fiscal Surveys' in M. A. Cook *Studies in the Economic History of the Middle East*, London, 1970; 1881–1882 K. Karpat, *Ottoman Population*, excluding Mount Lebanon: see note to Table 4.2

Table 4.2: Population of Syria, Lebanon and Palestine in 1580, 1882 and 1914

Religion	Total Number			Percentage of Population			Growth Rate (per thousand per annum)	
	1580	1882	1914	1580	1882	1914	1580–1882	1882–1914
Muslims	1,290,510	1,536,441	2,150,569	91.0	74.2	71.6	0.6	10.3
Christians	115,105	507,939	794,131	8.1	24.5	26.4	4.9	13.8
Jews	13,140	27,382	58,644	0.9	1.3	2.0	2.4	23.4

Sources: Ottoman censuses for the *vilayat* of Beirut, Damascus and Aleppo; 1570–1590: O. L. Barkan, 'Ottoman Fiscal Surveys'; 1881–1883: K. Karpat, *Ottoman Population, 1830–1914: Demographic and Social Characteristics*, Madison, 1985; Mount Lebanon: 1882 Interpolation Armée française/Cuinet (Y. Courbage and P. Fargues, *Situation démographique au Liban*), 1914: Table 5.4

Table 4.3: Rate of Population Growth by Religion and Province between 1570–90 and 1881–2

Province	Muslims	Christians	Jews
Aleppo	0.2	5.9	7.1
Tripoli/Beirut*	3.4	6.1	2.8
Damascus	-1.0	1.5	-1.6
Baghdad	-0.2	- 6.0	7.1
Basra**	1.5		
Total	1.1	4.6	4.0

* Including Mount Lebanon in 1881–1882. ** 1580–1897 for Basra.

Table 4.4: Population of Egypt by Religion, 1914

Mohafazat	Muslims	Christians	Jews	Total
Cairo	600,777	121,587	26,529	748,893
Alexandria	307,898	90,571	21,808	420,277
Port Said	50,005	16,923	535	67,462
Suez	22,131	4,764	132	27,028
Damietta	22,947	484	7	23,438
Dakahlia	939,680	23,516	841	964,037
Sharquia	911,905	20,085	291	932,280
Kalyubia	488,477	11,360	281	500,118
Gharbia	1,573,460	31,436	1,479	1,606,375
Menufia	1,009,436	32,364	45	1,041,845
Behera	838,902	13,568	216	852,686
Isma'ilia	10,494	3,904	70	14,468
Giza	489,582	14,951	349	504,882
Beni Suef	404,281	24,353	82	428,716
Fayum	464,071	23,310	71	487,453
Minia	603,592	128,974	143	732,709
Asyut	747,577	210,128	99	957,804
Sohag	704,659	137,347	112	842,118
Qena	753,795	66,030	90	819,916
Aswan	240,315	6,733	113	247,161
Desert	29,742	392	2	30,136
Total	11,213,725	982,780	53,296	12,249,801

Sources: Interpolation between 1907 and 1917 censuses.

Table 4.6: Estimated Population of Mount Lebanon by Religion, 1816–95

Date	Author	Total Population	Christians					Druzes	Muslims		
			Maronites	Catholics	Orthodox	Protestants	Sub Total		Sunnis	Shi'is	Sub Total
1816	Corancez							70,000			
1833	Douin	215,000	130,000		10,000		140,000	65,000	2,500	3,000	70,500
1840	Laurent	218,622					173,586	30,170	8,775	14,866***	45,036
1847	Bourrée	193,935					153,030	26,445		5,395	40,615
1847	Guys	300,919					237,726	40,524		22,569**	63,193
1847	Chidiak*	107,593					77,682	12,911		17,000***	29,911
1860	Karam	441,500	350,000				350,000	40,000			40,000
1860	Anon.*	105,055					84,569	12,607		7,897***	20,486
1860	French army	269,980	172,500	20,400	27,100		220,000	28,560	7,795	13,220	49,575
1863	Maronites	262,000	206,000		24,000**		230,000	24,000		7,000***	31,000
1895	Cuinet	399,530	229,680	34,670	54,208	738	319,296	49,812	13,576	16,846	80,234

* Males only; ** Non-Maronite Christians; *** Sunnis and Shi'is

Sources: 1816 to 1863, Dominique Chevallier, *La Société du Mont Liban à l'époque de la révolution industrielle en Europe*, Paris, 1971; 1895, Vital Cuinet, *Syrie, Liban et Palestine: Geographie Administrative, Statistique et Raisonnée*, Paris, 1896 (p. 149).

Table 4.5: Fertile Crescent: Population by Religion and Province, 1914

Country	Wilaya	Caza/Sanjak	Muslims	Christians	Jews	Total
Jordan			123,179	13,016	0	136,195
	Damascus	Kerak (s)	66,023	8,205	0	74,228
		Ajlun (c)	57,156	4,811	0	61,967
West Bank–Gaza			354,838	36,504	19,183	410,525
	Beirut	Nablus (S)	151,552	2,982	29	154,563
	Jerusalem	Jerusalem (c)	70,270	32,461	18,190	120,921
		Hebron (c)	55,720	3	721	56,444
		Gaza (c)	77,296	1,058	243	78,597
Israel			160,643	32,952	12,488	206,083
	Beirut	Acre (s)	97,885	25,609	10,383	133,877
	Jerusalem	Jaffa (c)	62,758	7,343	2,105	72,206
Lebanon			364,413	502,101	4,647	871,161
	Beirut	Beirut (s)	145,484	63,819	4,568	213,871
		Tripoli (c)	50,004	17,293	72	67,369
		Akkar (c)	19,920	21,968	0	41,888
	Damascus	Hasbaya (c)	9,405	5,843	6	15,254
		Rachaya (c)	5,490	4139	0	9,629
		Ba'albek (c)	18,667	6,429	1	25,097
		Beca'a (c)	19,113	10,226	0	29,339
	Mount-Lebanon (Ohannes Samneh)		96,330	372,384	0	468,714

Table 4.5: Fertile Crescent: Population by Religion and Province, 1914 (continued)

Country	Wilaya	Caza/Sanjak	Muslims	Christians	Jews	Total
Syria	Beirut	Latakia (s)	1,173,473	134,546	20,181	1,328,200
		Safita (c)	134,738	11,393	0	146,131
		Qala'a Husn (c)	32,254	5,162	0	37,416
			16,477	13,281	0	29,758
	Aleppo	Aleppo (s)	286,183	34,795	10,046	331,024
	Deir Ezzor	Deir Ezzor (s)	65,770	522	2	66,294
	Damascus	Damascus (c)	197,507	14,988	10,129	222,624
		Zabadani (c)	14,329	1,690	0	16,019
		Wadi Sham (c)	13,528	2,770	0	16,298
		Kuneitra (c)	33,534	1,378	4	34,916
		Duma (c)	35,350	3,008	0	38,358
		Nebek (c)	40,139	6,205	0	46,344
		Hama (s)	176,509	29,763	0	206,272
		Hawran (Ajlun)	112,517	9,577	0	122,094
	Urfa	Raqqa (c)	14,638	14	0	14,652
Iraq		Baghdad*	1,030,222	33,608	69,240	1,133,070
		Basra*	414,045	5,612	54,322	473,980
		Mosul*	188,478	997	1311	190,786
			427,698	26,999	13,607	468,304
Total Fertile Crescent			3,206,768	752,727	125,739	4,085,234

* No census in 1914: Projections of 1881–1882 (Baghdad) and 1897 (Basra, Mosul)

Source: 1914 Ottoman censuses

Table 4.7: Schooling by Religion and Province at end-Nineteenth Century

Region	Total Population	Pupils	Rate of Schooling (per cent)
Vilayet of Beirut			
Muslims	336,468	30,933	40.0
Christians	166,443	21,496	64.6
Jews	25,136	1,908	38.0
Mutasarrifiya of Mount Lebanon			
Muslims	80,234	3,580	22.3
Christians	319,297	30,172	47.2
Vilayet of Aleppo			
Muslims	465,346	11,599	12.5
Christians	117,809	3,770	16.0
Jews	19,265	1,180	30.6
Vilayet of Mosul			
Muslims	264,280	4,190	7.9
Christians	30,000	2,355	39.3
Jews	6,000	40	3.3
Vilayet of Baghdad			
Muslims	789,500	9,700	6.1
Christians	7,000	650	46.4
Jews	53,500	1,467	13.7
Vilayet of Basra			
Muslims	939,650	4,940	2.6
Christians	5,850	115	9.8
Jews	4,500	140	15.6

* Rate of primary education: Pupils 20% of total population.

Source: Total population and pupils, Vital Cuinet, *Syrie, Liban et Palestine.*

Table 4.8: Population of Damascus by Religion, 1543, 1548, 1569

Year	1543	1548	1569
Total numbers			
Muslims	43,706	49,243	42,822
Christians	3,307	4,320	6,290
Jews	3,084	3,096	3,332
Total	50,097	56,659	52,444
Percentage share			
Muslims	87.2	86.9	81.7
Christians	6.6	7.6	12.0
Jews	6.2	5.5	6.4
Total	100.0	100.0	100.0

Source: M. A. Bakhit 'The Christian Population of the Province of Damascus in the 16th Century' in Benjamin Braude and Bernard Lewis, *Christians and Jews in the Ottoman Empire*, vol II, New York, 1982 (p. 146)

Table 4.9: Population of Jerusalem under the Ottomans by Religion, 1525–1914 (per cent)

Date	Muslims	Christians	Jews
1525	66.0	12.7	21.3
1538	76.0	9.4	14.6
1553	75.5	12.2	12.2
1562	78.3	12.1	9.5
1596	97.2	2.8	0.0
1882	67.1	24.2	8.8
1914	58.1	26.8	15.0

Sources: Ottoman censuses, 1525–1596, A. Cohen and B. Lewis, 1882–1914: Kemal Karpat, *Ottoman Population, 1830–1914: Demographic and Social Characteristics*, Madison, 1985.

Table 4.10: Percentage of Christians in Beirut, Sixteenth, Nineteenth and Twentieth Centuries

Date	Per Cent	Date	Per Cent
1523	9.7	1838	45.0
1530	11.0	1846	47.0
1543	3.3	1860	58.0
1568	14.8	1881	57.0
1596	13.1	1882	58.0
		1889	64.0
		1889	66.0
		1895	63.0
		1908	48.0
		1912	54.0
		1917	60.0
		1920	66.0
		1922	45.0

Sources: 16th century: M. A. Bakhit, ' The Population of the Province of Damascus'; 19–20th century, L. Tarazi Fawaz, *Merchants and Migrants in Nineteenth-Century Beirut*, Cambridge, Mass., 1983.

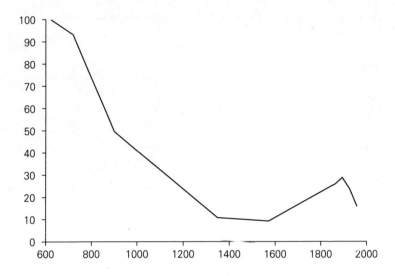

Figure 4.1: Percentage of Christians in Syria, Lebanon and Palestine, from the Hijra to date

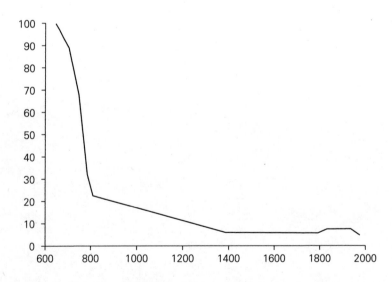

Figure 4.2: Percentage of Christians in Egypt, from the Hijra to date

CHAPTER FIVE

From Multinational Empire to Secular Republic: The Lost Christianity of Turkey

The Osmanli state is the greatest and most characteristic Near Eastern Empire there has ever been. In its present decline, it has become nothing but a blight to all the countries and people who remain under its sway, but originally it displayed an ability for strong government which satisfied the supreme need of the distracted Near Eastern world. This was the secret of its amazing power of assimilation, and this quality in turn increased its power of organisation, for it enabled the Osmanlis to monopolise all the vestiges of political genius that survived in the Near East.
[Arnold Toynbee in *The Treatment of Armenians in the Ottoman Empire*, London, 1916]

From the battle of Mantzikert in 1071, where the Seljuk Turks defeated the Byzantines, until the First World War when the Ottoman Empire collapsed, a multinational and multi-confessional state was progressively created on the eastern shores of the Mediterranean. In the fourteenth century the Turkish empire, lead by the Ottomans, left its Anatolian cradle[1] to conquer first the Christian Balkans and then its Arab and Muslim flanks. Throughout the period of conquest the Ottomans subdued Christian populations in growing numbers although they did not force them to convert but instead involved them in power. When, between 1914 and 1924, a secular state emerged from the debris of the Ottoman Empire a millenium of multi-confessional history was swept away in only ten years. In today's religiously uniform Turkey, hardly three-quarters of a century after the birth of the modern state, it is hard to remember that such a large Christian presence existed so recently. Turkish Christianity has, in effect, become a subject that survives only in the work of scholars. In particular, few remember that the region's minorities were neither confined to the marches of the empire nor to the cosmopolitan districts of the Mediterranean coast, but were firmly established in the Turkish 'heartland', in Anatolia itself (see Figure 5.1).

Christians Become a Minority

For almost four centuries Byzantium had resisted the intermittent pressures of the caliph's army and in the eleventh century the vast majority of the 7 to 8 million inhabitants of Anatolia were still Christian.[2] By the time Constantinople fell to the Ottomans in 1453 there were no more than 400,000 Christians in the region – Anatolian Christianity had literally disintegrated.

This transformation was not in itself surprising – the Middle East and North Africa had experienced changes just as spectacular. It was, however, unusual in Ottoman history. Although the empire occupied the Balkans almost continually for 500 years, they remained Christian except in three enclaves: Albania, Bosnia and Dobroudja. But whereas Rumelia was taken in one decisive attack and would have benefited from the immediate imposition of what was, by then, an efficient Ottoman state apparatus which protected its Christian identity,[3] Anatolia was won by a long process of erosion. The anarchy into which the region sank before the fifteenth-century Ottoman unification, the ebb and flow of dynasties and a series of disorderly migrations all created obstacles for the establishment of the institutions through which Ottoman Islam would later preserve Christianity.

The first wave of the Turkish invasion ocurred during the second half of the eleventh century and took the form of nomad raids, migration and settlement, mainly in the east and centre of Anatolia. These incursions eventually reduced Byzantium to a few fortified towns – Constantinople, Nicea and Trebizond – and resulted in the establishment in 1098 of the Seljuk sultanate of Rum centred on Konya.[4] The Seljuks might well have adopted Byzantine ways and become absorbed into the culture in which they settled; instead they chose to erase Hellenistic influence and slowly converted the peoples they subdued to Islam.

Nevertheless, under the Seljuks the erosion of Christianity in Anatolia was not, on the whole, a brutal process. In *Le Livre des merveilles* (The Book of Marvels),[5] Marco Polo recounted how, 200 years after the battle of Mantzikert, the Turks were still a minority in a country which remained Greek and Armenian. And, perhaps indicating an abiding admiration for the people they had defeated, almost three centuries after the invasion the Seljuks continued to call their country 'Rome' even though, since the Crusades, Christendom had insisted on calling it Turkey.

Once the Seljuks had asserted their authority over Anatolia and the Byzantine threat had retreated, inter-denominational relations were not marked with the animosity and exclusion that was later to develop. The capture of women in the course of the Turkish raids, and the procreation which inevitably followed, created blood ties, a relationship between Muslims and Christians which completely disappeared when the communities segmented. Ordinary people were not the only ones involved in this process; half the aristocratic Muslim families who governed the Seljuk sultanate in the fourteenth century were of Greek origin.[6] Furthermore, although the Seljuks hesitated to recruit Christians into their administration, their rule does not seem to have resulted in a deterioration in the conditions of life for their Christian subjects. But the break in communications with Constantinople, a city that had been the spiritual beacon for most of the Orthodox population of Anatolia, resulted in a number of them adopting the Turkish language and Muslim religion.

This period of relative stability and harmony was eventually disrupted by invasions of Anatolia by Crusaders, Mamluks and Mongols all against a background of Byzantine resistance organized from the remaining fortresses. The most devastating of these incursions, in the middle of the thirteenth century, was that of the Mongols, who were now Islamized and were lead by Tamerlane.[7] The Mongols reduced the Seljuks to vassals and destroyed their state structure. In these centuries of disintegration, borders were eliminated in Anatolia and the plateaux was opened up to further migrations of Islamized Turks who enlarged the area in which they practised nomadism and created a number of small frontier warrior states, one of which was eventually to become the kernel of the Ottoman Empire.

This multiplicity of warring groups shattered Anatolia. Already split between ethnic groups and various heresies, its Christian population did not stand up well to local alliances with various invaders and the repression which inevitably followed when the latter found themselves losing. It is estimated that on the eve of these great jolts, in 1200, 43 per cent of the inhabitants of Anatolia were still Christian.[8] In their wake the Turkish language progressively replaced Greek, Armenian and Persian and Islam was established as the dominant religion.

Migration of Turks or Conversion of Christians?

One of the historical puzzles that surrounds the Islamization of Anatolia is whether the Turks pushed aside the indigenous people, or simply their language and religion. This debate was reopened by Mustafa Kemal Atatürk while he was in the process of building the Turkish Republic in the 1920s and continues today: are the real roots of the population of twentieth-century Turkey Turkish or Hellenic? Did Islamization take place as result of population change or conversion?

The nation-state of the twentieth century based its legitimacy on the Turkoman nomads who poured into Asia Minor, by implication labelling as disloyal those people who were not both Turkish and Muslim – the Armenians, the Greeks and the Kurds. In the early years of the century nationalists – both Turkists and the Turanists[9] – had created the fiction of a homogeneous nation. How could they regard themselves as descendants of the *ikdich* – the Islamized Greeks – which in popular and administrative usage indicated a hybrid person, as little deserving of respect as a mule? The Ottomanists on the other hand continued to believe in a multi-ethnic empire – a sentiment so widespread that even the Young Turks expressed it when they came to power in 1908. Thus, one deputy of the National Assembly was anxious to maintain the teaching of classical Greek literature which, he argued, was not the patrimony of the Greeks alone, while another declared his pride that the assembly included the translator of the *Iliad* into Arabic, the Lebanese Suleiman Boustani.[10]

The creed of the post-war Kemalist state,[11] however, clearly asserted that the Turkish people came from,

> ... movements of migration on a large scale and modifications in the racial composition of the population, for the Turks are never content to administer as colonies the greater part of the conquered lands while maintaining within them armies of occupation and missionaries. On the contrary they settle there, work the land and leave numerous descendants, so making it their native land.[12]

Although the supporting evidence is scanty, this theme appears in an article by the historian Ömer Lütfi Barkan:

> We hope to have proved the existence of a large population in Anatolia by the need felt by the Turks to extend to the West, to settle in western Anatolia and in the eastern part of the Balkan peninsula, regions which

they transformed into a genuine homeland ... We do not believe that the Muslims who had formerly conquered and occupied Spain and the Mediterranean islands comprised only some Berber tribes chased from Africa and Arab nomads.[13]

The Byzantine population had no region to migrate to, so the question is whether it was massacred or merged with the conquerors. Official Kemalist history is unable to accept either of these hypotheses, and therefore remains silent on the subject. Other historians maintain that the new religious affinity was achieved by conversions alone.

> Calling the Osmanlis Turks, and regarding them as invaders upon the soil of Europe, is a historical error which has persisted so long that the Osmanlis themselves have fallen into it! They have always distinguished themselves from the Turks.[14]

Demography can provide a filter through which we can evaluate this dispute and measure the extent of immigration and conversion. An early witness, al-Umari, an Arab who travelled in Anatolia at the beginning of the fourteenth century, estimated the number of Turkomans at between 152,000 and 555,500. Claude Cahen, a specialist in pre-Ottoman history, puts the Turkoman population at 200–300,000 and speaks of tens of thousands of Tartars and several thousand Persians. This was the total number of Muslims who invaded the country in two waves between the eleventh and thirteenth centuries.

The small size of the total number is never discussed: 'It is generally difficult to imagine that the movements of people during this period could have involved more than some tens of thousands of individuals, at the most two or three hundred thousand, even if the texts give an impression of enormous size.'[15] We should remember that all migration is limited by the capacity of the reservoir which feeds it. In the steppe the nomads had left the economy was meagre. It could not possibly have maintained a large population and therefore could not have sent large numbers out.[16] It is certain that in the following century the migration stopped, for the bubonic plague in Central Asia permanently reduced the Turkoman ranks.[17] So the ethnic Turkish element could not in any way have made up the 70 per cent that has been suggested by the Turkish historian Osman Turan.[18]

Nomadic advances elsewhere gave a similar illusion of size for the same reason: the societies they encountered were in a state of anomie. The Arabs in the Near East and North Africa, the Berbers

in Spain, the Hilalians in the Maghreb and the Mongols over half
the known world – in all these cases the numbers of the invaders
were small but their organization was superior. When the Ottoman
leader Orkhan (1326–62) crossed the Dardanelles to invade Europe,
he raised his troops in Anatolia – as many as half a million men it
is claimed. The nomads from Central Asia, cut off from their
hinterland, would have been unable to supply him. Consequently he
recruited his soldiers from among the conquered peoples, notably
the Greeks.[19] Islamization was well and truly progressing.

There can be no doubt that when the first Turks arrived in
Anatolia, there was a very large Christian population: 7 million people
under Byzantium in the eleventh century. Much later, in 1520, after
an era of anarchy and depopulation, the Ottoman census showed
that Anatolia had a population of almost 5 million, but by then only
400,000 were Christian. The large numbers of Christians in Byzantine
Asia Minor was not, however, matched by unity among them.[20]
Byzantine society was fragmented into different rites, languages and
social orders, from the elite latifundia to the serf peasantry. In fact,
there was no genuine military front. While Byzantium certainly
attempted to avoid the attacks of the Turks, the combatants of the
two camps made pacts. Under the Christian *akritai* and Muslim *ghazi*
an 'original frontier culture' flourished;[21] there was no barrier to
prevent the entry of a new religion and so proselytism had a free
rein. If only one in seven Christians in each generation had
abandoned their religion, whether voluntarily by conversion or
involuntarily by birth in a mixed marriage, this would have sufficed
for the 7 million Christians in 1071 to become the 400,000 of 1520
– and by the same token, for the 200,000 Muslim immigrants to
have become, without any subsequent additions from Central Asia,
4.6 million (see Figure 5.2).

Christians converted individually, in families, or whole villages at
a time. Conviction, opportunism and, in the case of captives taken
into slavery, compulsion, all brought about the change. Contemporary
accounts are very contradictory and partisan, but they all comment
on the great mixture of the population. Marco Polo, who travelled
to the east among other things for the sake of the papacy, believed
that Christians were still the masters and the Turks were at the
bottom of the social ladder:

> In the province of Turcomania [centre of Anatolia] there are three types
> of people; the Turkomans who revere Mahomet and keep to his law; they
> live like animals in every way; they are ignorant people with a barbaric

language different from all others ... The others are Armenians, imperfect Christians, and the Greeks, who dwell mingled into the towns and villages and live from commerce and as artisans. The latter have many possessions. [The Armenians] are great eaters and drinkers. They have plenty of red and white wine and indulge in heavy drinking.[22]

Some years later, the Moroccan Ibn Battuta, 'the traveller of Islam', observing the city of Ladhik (today's Denizil), had a completely different view of the subjected and enslaved Christians:

Most of the artisans there are Greek women, for in [the city] there are many Greeks who are subject to the Muslims and who pay dues to the sultan, including the *jizya* and other taxes. The distinctive mark of the Greeks there is their wearing of tall pointed hats ... The people of this city make no effort to stamp out immorality – indeed the same applies to the whole population of these regions. They buy beautiful Greek slaves and put them out to prostitution and each girl has to pay a regular due to her master.[23]

Whether as free individuals or slaves, Christian women married Turks. Being Muslim according to the law, their descendants helped to swell the ranks of Islam. The impact of massacres and displacements of the Christian population from Anatolia was never as significant as that of mixed marriages. The displacements particularly involved Greek aristocrats, and generally spared the Armenians and Christian Arabs who were less disposed to serve Byzantium. Like the Arabs conquerors of the Mashreq, in order to maintain the poll tax revenues the Turks did not enforce Islamization.[24] However, the progressive weakening of Seljuk authority on one hand, and the disintegrating authority of the Byzantine church on the other, encouraged conversions in the conquered territories. The heirs of Greece and Rome, the conquered people effectively lost for ever the illusion of being at the centre of the universe. Their co-religionists on the other side of the border were now subjects of a Byzantine empire whose former grandeur had shrunk to the city of Con-stantinople and the pockets of Nicea and Trebizond. Disheartened, many of them converted, 'for men follow the religion of their king' as Ibn Battuta pointed out when he visited Anatolia in the fourteenth century, some decades before Ibn Khaldun generalized this statement to the whole of humanity.[25]

The conquered Christians also found themselves abandoned by a clergy which deserted its impoverished flock and migrated to Constantinople with no intention of returning. The churches in the

Turkish territory had become too poor to enable the Orthodox clergy to maintain itself.[26] Occasionally invited by the Seljuks to rejoin their parish after a peace had been concluded with Byzantium, the clergy usually declined the offer. Consequently church lands were deemed to be vacant and were integrated into the *waqf*, the inalienable estates in Islam, and credited to the charitable works or social and cultural institutions by which Islam entered into contact with the people. In this way the patrimony of the Orthodox church passed into the service of proselytizing Islam:[27] the new religion was as successful at occupying the sites abandoned by the former religion as it was at attracting the people.

The Islam offered to the defeated 'infidels' was eminently tolerant, even of heresies. Official Sunnism was dominant only in the towns where it permeated the administration. Elsewhere, Christians lived alongside a popular religion that was benevolent, influenced by Shamanism, Buddhism, Manichaeism, and even by Nestorian Christianity.[28] Muslims and Christians shared places of worship, recognized the same saints, celebrated the same feasts, and even shared the ritual of baptism. The mysticism and syncretism of the Mevlevi order of Jalal al-Din Rumi and the Bektashi order of Haji Bektash[29] did more to spread Islam than the *jizya* of the prince.[30] Finally, Islam progressed not only through genuine conversions, but also crypto-Christianity – which existed until the First World War.[31] By its extent and complexity, the process of conversions extended to all the regions and all classes of society. A good part of the Turks of Turkey are, in short, of Byzantine ancestry.

The conversions of the eleventh to the fifteenth centuries deserve particular attention because of a curious similarity with other experiences. Resembling in some ways the tenth and eleventh-century conversions in North Africa, they could have been encouraged by a disintegration of the central power. Almost continually the subject of dispute between the Byzantines, the Seljuk Turks, the Turkoman nomads, the Danishmand Turks, Mongols, Armenians from Greater and Lesser Armenia, Franks from Antioch and Edesse, and Latins from Constantinople, as well as a dozen rival Turkish tribes, Anatolia witnessed a blossoming of syncretic beliefs indifferent to orthodoxy, which would be transformed across the generations into Muslim faith. Christianity was, in short, weakened by the tolerance of this Islam while, paradoxically, the Sunni orthodoxy of the Ottomans, which created order from all this anarchy, not only maintained but also strengthened it.

The Rise of Christianity in The Ottoman Millet

When they deserted the capital of the old Roman empire of the East, the Byzantines left Constantinople a village in distress, with about 70,000 inhabitants.[32] Immediately after the Ottoman conquest a further 50,000 Greeks were taken into captivity and dispersed across the empire. However, Istanbul, as the city was now named, was soon repopulated and after only a century of Muslim rule it became the foremost metropolis in the world with 700,000 inhabitants (see Table 5.1).[33] By a paradox of history it was also one of the three great Christian cities, for more than one-third of its population was Orthodox. Until the First World War about 40 per cent of the population were non-Muslim, both Christians and Jews.

Once Byzantium had been destroyed,[34] the Ottomans sought the participation of their old enemies in government. Officially Muslim, the empire became, de facto, a sort of Greco–Turkish diarchy which lasted until the uprising and independence of Greece (1821–30).[35] After the taking of Constantinople, the diarchy was consecrated by the enthronement of the Greek Orthodox patriarch at the head of the first of the Christian *millet*[36] of the empire. Ever since, this high personage of the state has wielded spiritual and temporal authority over the Orthodox Christians of the empire, from the Adriatic Sea to the Persian Gulf. 'In contrast to the situation prevailing during the Byzantine period, the patriarch was no longer the humble servant of the emperor, but a recognized and respected member of the sultan's bureaucracy enjoying full jurisdiction over his followers.'[37] The promotion of the patriarch and the affirmation of the pre-eminence of the Greek over the other Christianities was a strategic calculation. The sultan rewarded him as the head of the anti-Roman party at a time when the empire was above all European and the papacy and its military arm, Venice, were seeking to drive Islam from the Balkans.

But the Ottomans were also driven by a spiritual impetus: to enlarge the *dar al-Islam* at the expense of the *dar al-harb*, that is to say to fight against Christianity outside the Empire.

> From its foundation to its fall, the Ottoman Empire was a state dedicated to the advancement or the defence of the power and faith of Islam. For six centuries, the Ottomans were almost constantly at war with the Christian West ... This centuries-long struggle, with its origins in the very roots of Turkish Islam, could not fail to affect the whole structure of Turkish society and institutions.[38]

The whole apparatus of empire, its military and civil organization, its tax system and its land structure, was driven by the need to occupy, through conquest and colonization, the lands of the Christian enemy. The keystone of the edifice was to increase the Muslim population of the world to the detriment of the Christian. In practise, however, in all its Asian possessions including the Arab lands, Ottoman policy unwittingly worked in the opposite direction.

By the nineteenth century, in Istanbul and in Anatolia, the Christian and Jewish population had grown once again thanks to the stability and security offered by the *millet* system. That is to say, four centuries under the rule of Islam had enabled Christianity to regenerate itself from the inside. From the 8 per cent recorded in the censuses of 1520 and 1570, by 1881 the Christian population of Anatolia had reached 16 per cent (see Tables 5.2 and 5.6).[39] This startling reversal was produced by a spectacular fall in conversions and by population renewal. The institution of the three main *millet*, Greek Orthodox (1454), Armenian (1461) and Jewish, put an end to arbitrary authority and disorder. The Christian and Jewish religious authorities had, within their *millet*, exclusive control of worship, schools and the judicial system. They administered estates that had become as inalienable as those in Islam. Conversions which had been instigated by fear or social pressure no longer had any meaning; those which came from economic motives had already taken place before the capture of Constantinople.[40]

Ouside the *millet* system the Ottoman sultans were content to respect Qur'anic precepts towards non-Muslims.[41] In fact they did this more faithfully and with greater rectitude than any Abbasid caliph.[42] In their favourable interpretation,[43] these precepts guaranteed that, where the People of the Book were concerned, all compulsion in religion and forced conversions were forbidden. The notable exception to this pattern was the institution of the *devshirme*, an authoritarian formula for recruiting Christians to the service of the empire which forced them into apostasy.

Weak population growth in the Ottoman Empire compared to the mass of Christianity outside compelled the sultan to be lenient towards Christians within. But was this 'moral rectitude'[44] or military wisdom? With more than 38 million Christians at the end of the sixteenth century, the western Mediterranean was stronger and had more influence than the lands of Ottoman Islam whose population was only 22 million of which, furthermore, the majority were Christian. 'Too many men on one side and not enough horses; on the other side too many horses and not enough men! The tolerance of Islam perhaps arose from this disequilibrium: it would have been happy to accept any men, whoever they were, as long as they were easily available.'[45]

On the other side of the Mediterranean, religious zeal combined with the ulterior motives of mercantile activity had inspired the authorities and the impoverished class when they first drove the Muslims and Jews from Spain (1492–95). Soon a demographic disequilibrium, the reverse of that of the Ottomans, strengthened the extreme intolerance of the Reconquista: between 1530 and 1594 the Spanish population doubled.[46] The Catholic kings reverted to their old behaviour in 1609–11 when they expelled the Moorish and Marrane descendants (who had converted to Christianity) of those Muslims and Jews who had been able to escape on the first boats. The Ottoman Empire, which was then underpopulated, enthusiastically received a large number of these exiles.

Being particularly concerned about their feeble population growth, the Ottomans did not sufficiently appreciate the disequilibrium within their borders. They had two instruments destined to invigorate their population – the *surgun* and the *devshirme* – which had delayed effects on the confessional balance of the empire. The *surgun* – an administrative decision to transfer whole communities – was intended to regenerate devastated regions, of which Istanbul was one, and restore them to their former glory. 'The sultan ordained that families should be sent to him there, rich or poor and from every province … This policy was not confined to Turks and Muslims. Greeks and other Christians were authorized – sometimes encouraged – to settle in the city.'[47] For those who were displaced, the *surgun* brought little happiness, but the Ottoman state placed its highest interests over those of the family. It had a global conception of regional development, according to which it moved individuals around like pawns.[48] In the end the *surgun* had unexpected side-effects favourable to both Judaism and Ottoman Christianity, simply because it brought the Jews of Salonika, the Greeks of the Peloponnese and the Armenians of Angora closer to the seat of power.

The institution of *devshirme* – a tribute levy of young male Christians who were converted to Islam and enlisted by force, the less fortunate into the Janissaries and the more fortunate into the administration – was undoubtedly a cruel practice. However, the targeted people, Albanian, Bosnian or Greeks, were quick to find in it a way of improving their social condition. Poor villagers, it is said, would even, before the call-up, ask the recruiting officer to take their son rather than that of a neighbour.[49] At least half a dozen Ottoman grand viziers and a series of high officials of Albanian or Bosnian origin suffered the trials of the *devshirme*.

In its upper echelons the Ottoman state wanted to maintain the monopoly of Islam; but it was constrained by weak population growth. In this context, the Christians converted by *devshirme* were a means of enabling the Muslim elite to renew itself. By the same token, the abolition of the *devshirme* in 1638 seriously threatened the Islamic character of the elite since it deprived the civil administration and the army, whose ranks were devastated during the war, of the new blood of young converts. This was clear 30 years later when the Sublime Porte appointed a Christian Dragoman for the first time in 1669. Far from being reduced to the simple task of translator (*turjman*), this position soon became equivalent to a minister of foreign affairs. The holder of the post was generally a Greek aristocrat close to the Greek Orthodox patriarch, and played an important role in foreign and domestic politics. Since he was not obliged to renounce his religion, the gates of the top administration were opened to the Christians of the Greek Orthodox *millet*.

Although it was diffused at first, the growing influence of this incorporated elite – whether recently converted or still Christian – was soon openly exercised. The Janissary converts to Islam rallied to the Bektachi, the adepts of the most syncretic of the Muslim orders who provided them with chaplains. While fighting the Christian enemy in the *dar al-harb*, they used their influence and profited from their friendships to protect Christianity in the *dar al-Islam*. Later, diverse solidarity networks spread the rewards of this re-Christianization from the top to the bottom of the social structure. Christian population growth resumed, receiving a strong stimulus from the autonomy of the *millet* and the benevolence – or connivance – of officials who were more and more frequently Christian.

The conquests of the empire in Arab lands[50] in 1516 and 1517 could have increased the relative size of the Muslim population as well as the Islamic character of politics. Until then the heart of the empire had been situated in Europe – in Istanbul and Rumelia; now it moved to the furthest poles, from Belgrade to Cairo and to Tlemcen. On the edges of the empire, Anatolia at this point entered a period of stable demographic growth.

THE LOST CHRISTIANITY OF TURKEY   103

With the peace of Süleiman (1520–66), the Mongol devastation was forgotten. The Anatolian population, according to the Ottoman census, grew from 5 to 6.8 million inhabitants between the periods 1520–35 and 1570–80. The Ottomans did not, of course, have at their disposal the sophisticated methods of modern statistics and while the censuses of the sixteenth century are extremely valuable, they must be used with caution. It is possible that the second census (1570–80) was more complete than the first (1520–35), in which case the population growth was overestimated. But at the same time there is no reason why Turkey should have been the exception in the Mediterranean world which was, during this period, experiencing an unprecedented demographic expansion. In Anatolia, as we have seen, the Christians formed 8 per cent of the population and their rate of growth was marginally greater than that of the Muslims (9.8 per thousand against 9.3 per thousand per annum). The situation in Rumelia, however, was quite different. For there the effect of the immigration of Anatolian Turks and the Turkish colonization of Dobroudja – the north-eastern region of Bulgaria – was that Muslim population growth, at 11.8 per thousand, was much higher than that of the Christians (5.1 per thousand) and the Jews (6.3 per thousand).

The censuses conducted in the nineteenth century show that the Christian advantage in Asia Minor endured throughout the Ottoman period. Because no intermediate census was undertaken, there is unfortunately no record of the population growth for 250 years, but partial operations do provide some information on this long interlude.[51] The different religions remained unequal before the law, particularly in tax affairs, with the *dhimmi* paying for their right to 'infidelity' in hard cash. The accounts of the *jizya* and of land transactions, which all mention religion,[52] demonstrate the dynamism of the Christian population (see Table 5.3). Far from emigrating en masse, they remained in the countryside and the towns. The cities of the Aegean Sea, in particular Izmir, whose population was nearly one-quarter non-Muslim, welcomed Greeks from the Peloponnese, Armenians from eastern Anatolia or Iran and Sephardic Jews from Spain whose ancestors had settled in Salonika. The coast of the Black Sea was less fortunate, for it was subjected to the backlash of political instability and the wars with Persia. Christians were thus obliged to emigrate from Trebizond and from 15,000 in the census of 1609, only 2,500 remained in the town at the beginning of the seventeenth century.

From The Tanzimat to the Young Turks: Religious Plurality

Proximate to the West, which was in the middle of a technological revolution, the Ottoman Empire was by the nineteenth century entering the last phase of its long history. Recognized as viceroy of Egypt by the Sublime Porte, Muhammad Ali, an ex-officer of the Ottoman army, had been close to making a vassal of the sultan.[53] Through Muhammad Ali's policy of modernization Egypt was launched into the industrial era at a time when Istanbul was undergoing a difficult evolution. The Christian and Jewish communities were the first to feel the attraction of modernity. The tensions that arose from this two-speed development were reinforced by the emergence of Balkan and Caucasian nationalisms. Fifty years after the French Revolution, the idea of equality had followed the path that the idea of democracy would follow at the end of the twentieth century: in order to participate in the concert of nations, it was necessary to reform. The Ottomans abolished the statutes of religious discrimination by a series of fiscal and civic reforms, the Tanzimat of 1839 and 1856, anticipating – by a paradox similar to that which restored Christianity under the authority of Islam – the secularism that in the twentieth century would definitively oust Christianity from Turkey. The Tanzimat reforms were crowned by Ottomanism, the first un-Islamic (if not anti-Islamic) secular doctrine which inspired the fairly short-lived Constitution of 1876. This was intended to establish a limited monarchy, whose subjects would all be considered as 'Ottomans, whatever their religion or their belief'.[54]

Equality might have brought a convergence of behaviour, perhaps even of population dynamics. However, the effect of the Tanzimat was totally different. The minorities benefited out of all proportion to their size in the population from an almost hundred-fold expansion of the bureaucracy. The secularization of the judicial system remained a dead letter and that of education brought about a lightning growth of Christian schools which were tolerated, even encouraged, by the men of the Tanzimat. On the other hand, the obligation of military service continued to weigh on the Muslims alone, for the minorities had eagerly accepted the exchange of the old *jizya* against the *badal askari* (redemption of military service), the payments for which were identical. Finally, the new provincial administration fell under the supervision of local councils in which non-Muslims were equal in number to the Muslims, that is to say over-represented.[55] This measure was not neutral vis-à-vis demography, for these councils took decisions on local management and resources – from health to culture – changing everything that would speed up the demographic transition. Without linking the minorities more firmly to the Empire, the Tanzimat helped to reinforce their demographic vitality. The censuses conducted in the nineteenth century prove this.

The census of 1831, which was intended principally to count the male population (Muslims of arms-bearing age and non-Muslims subject to the poll tax), showed that Anatolia was, by this time, 12 per cent Christian compared with 8 per cent in the sixteenth century. This picture of the distribution of population by religion can be accepted as reasonably accurate since both Muslims and Christians, for different reasons, had an interest in avoiding the count, while the censuses taken at the end of the century also confirmed the rise of the minorities. Stimulated by the modernization of the state apparatus and by the solicitous attitude of the European powers towards the religious minorities, censuses and estimates of the population abounded during the second half of the nineteenth century, from the Balkans to Tripolitania.[56] The censuses of 1881–82 and 1906–7 as well as the enumeration of 1914 provide a valuable tool with which to reconstruct the position of the Christian population in the eastern Mediterranean, both Turkish[57] and Arab,[58] on the eve of the catastrophe which was looming in Turkey.

Around 1881 the non-Muslim population, especially Greeks and Armenians, reached the peak of their growth. By that date they made up 21 per cent of the population in the territory of present-day Turkey (see Tables 5.4 a, b, c). The whole of the population of the Anatolian provinces increased between 1831 and 1881–93 (at a rate of 15.7 per thousand per annum),[59] but, as always in Ottoman history, the Christians grew more quickly (19.8 per thousand) than the Muslims (15 per thousand).

However, the shocks caused by the rise of nationalism soon imperilled Anatolia's two Christian minorities. The massacres of the Armenians in 1894–6 at first cut back their growth, but the total strength of their population nevertheless increased by 4.8 per thousand per annum between 1881 and 1906 (see Table 5.5). The Balkans war in 1912 then reduced the rate of population growth among the Greeks (4.4 per thousand between 1906 and 1914). For both groups, this slowing down of demographic growth was above all the result of emigration (300,000 departures),[60] which in turn was a response to insecurity. The Greeks and Armenians emigrated to

Greece, Egypt, Syria, Western Europe and Russia, or further afield to the Americas. The only one of the minorities to increase in size during this period, the Jews, experienced three decades of demographic growth comparable to that of the Muslims.

Istanbul nevertheless maintained its cosmopolitan tradition. As in the reign of Süleiman the Magnificent, the non-Muslims there represented more than 40 per cent of the inhabitants (see Table 5.6).[61] From the end of the nineteenth century, however, a new phenomenon developed – the immigration, especially to Istanbul, of Muslims fleeing from the neighbouring Christian world.[62] They poured out of Romania, Montenegro, Serbia, Bosnia, Bulgaria and Thessaly in the Balkans. Tens of thousands of Greek Muslims from Crete and 500,000 Circassians from the Caucasus also migrated. In total, more than 2 million fled. These migrations in the opposite direction[63] coincided with a radical political change.

Let us consider the relationships that might have existed between politics and demography in the empire at the end of the century. The politician is always more aware of abrupt changes than long-term tendencies. In circles of power, great attention was paid to any arrivals of Muslims. Exiles from regions that had been defeated militarily, they could not pass unseen since they were arriving in the capital. Yet at the same time, the politicians were not at all alarmed by the higher natural growth of the Christian communities, which was not immediately noticeable. Just before the great changes to come it reached 12 per thousand, while that of the Muslims was in the region of 9 per thousand. The Christian population thus doubled in 50 years, the Muslim in 65 years. This growth coincided with the time when, under Sultan Abdülhamid (1876–1909), the Ottoman state began a policy of 're-Islamization'. But as these figures show, Abdülhamid's radicalism cannot be explained by the growing Muslim numerical supremacy as a result of immigration from the Balkans. Indeed, the reversal of the official ideology had come earlier, when the Christian population growth was still the most dynamic. The policy of re-Islamization was, therefore, initially adopted for political rather than demographic reasons.

Differential population growth arose from the stratification instituted by the system of the *millet*. In Ottoman society with its pronounced hierarchical system, at the top of which stood the military, the Muslim majority and the Christian and Jewish minorities pursued different professions. Agriculture and the army fell in the main to Muslims; industry, commerce and services to the minorities.

As from the seventeenth century, the administration employed members of all religions. This division of society was mildly questioned from the second half of the nineteenth century; although the Muslims had accepted it as a privilege it was in reality prejudicial to them. It is not taxes, but wars that kill people; this noble activity forced Muslim men into a long period of military service, 20 years or more, but reduced to 12 in 1829 when the Janissary corps was dissolved in a blood bath. Their obligation to serve in the army took young men far from their homes and, since 12 per cent of the male population could be mobilized, reduced the marriage and birth rate among Muslims.[64] Furthermore, the frequent armed conflicts in Turkish history increased the Muslim death rate, already high in times of peace as a result of epidemics which produced more fatalities among them than among Christians or Jews, for the same reasons as in the Arab world.[65]

Although it was discriminatory in principle, in reality the *jizya* was less burdensome than war. Many were exempted from the tax, for example ministers of religion and those who worked in the administration and public utilities (security, maintenance of roads and bridges, breeding of falcons and the like). In practice only about one-third actually paid the *jizya*.[66] Free from military service, the Christian and Jewish minorities had far greater opportunities to be socially mobile, helped by the quasi-monopoly they maintained over the most dynamic sectors of the society and economy:

> Their commercial genius gave them a virtual monopoly over commerce and a considerable share of the wealth of the country ... The talents of the Armenian were truly indispensable to his masters and the general tolerance which the Turk accorded him showed that this fact was recognized. In reality, the Christian, intellectual, Armenian subject, and the Muslim master who was the farmer lived alongside each other in a fairly precarious relationship, but one which was not without mutual advantages.[67]

In this way the minorities were able to form themselves into an influential middle class while the protection of the European powers strengthened their role in other respects.[68]

Can we find in the population statistics any indication of a higher standard of living among the minorities? This was certainly the case in Istanbul. In 1876–9, the mortality rate of Muslims (21 per thousand) was much higher than that of the minorities (12 per thousand), especially for women. As in the Arab provinces, the illiteracy of the large majority of Muslims contrasted with the decisive progress achieved by the Christians and Jews in the nineteenth century, particularly as a result of the institutions created by the Christian missionaries and the Alliance Israélite Universelle (see Table 5.7). Health could not fail to be affected. But mortality was not the only factor. The weak growth of the Muslim population was also a result of lower fertility. This may well surprise us today when there is a widespread association between Islam and population explosion.

The early appearance of Malthusian choices among Muslim families in Istanbul at the end of the nineteenth century has recently been established.[69] At the time some observers had already remarked on it, and attributed the effects to conscription and, above all, to the fact that 'Turkish women of the lower classes try very mischievous means to avoid having many children.'[70] One hundred years later, an estimate that would have been impossible at the time proves them right: fertility in the Ottoman provinces varied in inverse relation to the proportion of Muslims.[71]

However, exceptional demographic growth could not guarantee the Christians' position. Their political survival was difficult to conceive outside the institutional mould of the *millet* system. From the moment the nation-state was born, Ottoman Christianity disintegrated. Before they disappeared in 1914, the minorities numbered 3 million. Although they were spread throughout Turkey, they were nevertheless close to constituting two compact groups. One of these were the Greeks – in Istanbul, in European Turkey and on the coasts of the Aegean and Black Seas, as well as some communities in the interior of Anatolia as far as the heart of the Armenian lands. The second were the Armenians, whose communities stretched from the Caucasus to the Mediterranean. There were also numerous towns and villages where Christians were mixed with Muslims, both Turkish and Kurdish. While the Greeks did not know Turkish,[72] half the Armenians had adopted it,[73] although this did not necessarily mean a complete integration of their communities.

At the turn of the twentieth century several nationalisms confronted each other. Some had no concrete territorial basis. Ottomanism dreamed of uniting around the sultan all Ottoman Muslims, Christians and Jews whether Turkish or non-Turkish; pan-Islamism wanted to assemble all the world's Muslims around the sultan/caliph; pan-Turkism broadened the definition of the nation to include all the Turks of Central Asia and the nebulous ideology of pan-Turanism claimed the unity of all people speaking a language of Turkish origin, from Mongolia to Hungary. Three nationalisms, however, had a specific territorial vision: Greek, which sought to establish a Greater Greece on the two coasts of the Aegean sea; Armenian, which wanted a state formed of Greater and Lesser Armenia, and Turkish. Both Greek and Armenian nationalism were victims of a demographic illusion common among the Christian minorities of the East: the Greeks overestimated their growth rate and the Armenians their number. Caught between the two the Turks were nevertheless in a majority everywhere. Abandoning the banner of Islam they rallied around a secular Turkish nationalism which was for the first time territorial. Anatolia, which had never been disputed, suddenly found itself coveted three times over.[74]

The End of the Christian Presence

When eastern Armenia (Erivan and Karabakh) passed to the protection of Orthodox Russia in 1830 it experienced national, religious and cultural renewal as well as economic expansion. Eastern Armenia and independent Greece were the two active poles of nationalism. The Armenians and the Ottoman Greeks were thus torn between loyalty to the empire and the new aspirations for independence which became more intense around the First World War when the Ottomanist doctrine disappeared. More than 3 million Ottoman Christians died or were exiled as a result of the clash of nationalisms and the birth of modern Turkey.

Our only reliable estimate of the size of the Armenian population of Turkey after the First World War is 77,000 in 1927, a figure provided by the first census of the Republic of Turkey. What was the size of the population of which these were survivors? The last census conducted by the Ottomans in 1914 gives a figure of 1.2 million, while the Armenian patriarch in 1882 claimed 2.4 million.[75] Known not long before as *millet-i sadika* (the loyal nation) – 'of all the nations subject to the Porte, that which has the most common interests with the Turks and is most directly interested in maintaining them'[76] – the Armenian community was in 1915–16 brutally deported from Turkey to the Arab periphery. The extent of the massacres it suffered during the exodus continues to this day to sustain an argument between Armenians and Turks. If any Armenians remained in Anatolia after the deportation and slaughter, the erroneous policies of the Russians, Americans and French at the end of the war soon hastened their disappearance.[77]

In order to understand the extent of the massacre, it would be necessary to know the number of Armenians in Turkey before the hostilities and the number exiled from Turkey afterwards. The estimates which are used to support the Armenian and the Turkish arguments contradict each other. The Armenians express doubts about the Ottoman figures and claim that their obligation to pay the *badal* encouraged Christians to hide themselves from the agents of the state. Using the patriarch's figures, their estimates usually vary between 1.8 and 2.1 million Armenians on the eve of the war.[78] Arnold Toynbee, who was not an Armenian, suggested a population of 1.6 to 2 million.[79] The Turks on the other hand still endorse the 1914 figure and insist on 1.3 million.[80] It is difficult to reconcile these figures if we accept the statements of the American Committee for Relief to the Armenians and Syrians which pointed out in 1915: 'The estimates of the Turkish government are generally considered to be too low and those of the Armenian patriarch as being sometimes too high, with a tendency in the first case to minimize and in the second to exaggerate the number and importance of the Armenian population.'[81]

An American scholar who reconsidered the issue in the 1980s has carefully examined the Ottoman data with the aid of modern demographic methods.[82] He estimated the Armenian population at 1.6 million and concluded that there had been no deliberate falsification, but rather a normal under-estimate arising from the enumeration techniques of the time. If we deduct from this the 77,000 Armenians counted in the 1927 census, we find that the population was reduced by about 1.5 million people as a result of the massacre itself as well as emigration (whether enforced or voluntary) and conversion.

The respective importance of the massacres and the deportations is the subject of lively controversy. Immediately after the events the British historian Arnold Toynbee and the German pastor Lepsius estimated the refugees in Syria, Russia and Persia, who had been counted on arrival by the charitable organizations, as well as those who remained in Turkey either because they had the luck to live in a large city, Istanbul or Smyrna, where 'it was difficult to suppress them in front of so many witnesses,'[83] or because they escaped death by converting to Islam.[84] Toynbee calculated a total of 660,000 people massacred and Lepsius 1 million.[85]

The Turkish argument, recently put forward, acknowledges that deportation took place but describes it as 'relocation'. It also admits the size of the operation – 703,000 people of both sexes and of all ages according to the official Ottoman source[86] – that is almost 70 per cent of Armenians.[87] However, it regards the deportation as a fact of war, inevitable given the Armenian collusion with the Russian enemy. This argument also accepts that more than 300,000 Armenians died,[88] but disputes that they did so at the hands of Turks. Far from being a massacre orchestrated from on high, the deaths were a side-effect of the war, a consequence of epidemics or debilitation during the exodus, or a result of battles between armies and rival militias. The regular Turkish army, according to this argument, was not responsible so much as bands of uncontrolled Kurds or highway bandits.

Western scholars today give equal weight to the sufferings of the Turks and the Armenians: 'To mention the sufferings of one group and avoid those of another gives a false picture of what was a human, not simply an ethnic disaster.'[89] One scholar has reworked the calculations to arrive at a total of 584,000 Armenian victims (see Table 5.8).[90] However, his estimate should be revised slightly upwards, for in his reconstruction of the Armenian population living in Turkey on the eve of the war he has omitted those who resided in Istanbul and European Turkey.[91] If they are included – as they must be – the result is a probable figure of 688,000 victims, which is close to that put forward by Toynbee at the time of the crisis.

The remnants of the Armenian population continued to shrink after the deportations and massacres. Those who left had no right to return. In 1965, the last census to mention religion numbered the Armenians at 64,000 of whom only 32,000 spoke Armenian. They have disappeared from the countryside in the historic Greater and Lesser Armenia and their community now lives in the former Ottoman capital, Istanbul.

As for the prosperous Greek community of Turkey, after the war it paid the price for the inordinate ambition of the Greek government. Not only did it underestimate an enemy which had just suffered defeat, but despite all the evidence it believed that demographic growth favoured the Greeks. Prime Minister Eleftherios Venizelos believed it to be well known that 'Owing to the breeding qualities of the Greeks, the [Greek] population of Smyrna before the end of the century would exceed the total population of the whole of the Turkish Empire.'[92]

Strengthened by these certitudes and under the protection of the allied troops, the Greeks attempted to rebuild Greater Greece after occupying western Anatolia. The Greco–Turkish war of 1920–22 routed the occupiers and was ended by the Treaty of Lausanne of 1923, which in one of its clauses envisaged a huge population exchange: the Turks of Greece for the Greeks of Turkey.

Looking back to the time of Greek independence in 1830, the Greeks of Istanbul and Asia Minor had already lost some of their positions and their *millet* was overshadowed by that of the Armenians. Nevertheless they remained for a century, despite the entreaties of Greece which often incited them to sedition. In spite of aggressive nationalism, the Greeks preferred the comfort of the Bosphorous or Anatolia to the liberty so recently acquired on the unwelcoming shores of Morea or Epire. They were even reinforced by immigrants arriving from secessionist Greece, for the Ottoman rulers wanted to maintain their multinational edifice.

A century later Mustafa Kemal showed less magnanimity. In the wake of the First World War the Greeks of Turkey suffered from the ineptitude of the Greek government. In addition, after the elimination of the Armenians, Atatürk wanted to finalize the process of ethnic homogenization begun under the Young Turks. In this country until recently governed by the *millet*, where religion created identity, religious uniformity had to be achieved before secularism could be proclaimed by a modernist leader.[93] The agreement Atatürk concluded with Greece after his victory in 1922 envisaged a population exchange. The 464,000 Turks or Muslims in Greece, with the exception of those in western Thrace, would be redirected to Turkey[94] in exchange for all the Greeks of Turkey – 1,344 million people, not including Istanbul – who would be sent to Greece. As a result, by 1927 there were no more than 10,000 Greeks in Anatolia.

In most cases it was the language they spoke that indicated which people would be deported. But, in a republic which promised a secular future, religion also served to identify the Greeks of inner Anatolia.

> If we take the denominations 'Greek' and 'Turk' in their western meaning, and not in that which prevailed in the Near East, the famous population exchange between Greece and Turkey comes to represent not a repatriation of Greeks to Greece and Turks to Turkey, but rather a deportation of Christian Turks and Muslim Greeks.[95]

Many of those deported did not even know the Greek language, they were well and truly Turks of the Christian religion.

For a long time Istanbul retained the memory of Constantinople, the capital of Orthodoxy. Its Greek population was more favoured and in principle escaped from the exchanges. In 1914, it was about 200,000 people.[96] But, driven back to the metropolis and deprived of its Anatolian hinterland, how long could it survive? Over time, despite the protection offered by the Lausanne Treaty, its size was constantly diminished: 130,000 in 1927 and only 86,000 in 1965.[97] Eventually, under cover of multiple periods of tension between Greece and Turkey – notably the Cyprus crises – the expulsion of Greeks of Hellenic nationality[98] hastened the decline of the community. By the end of the 1960s, only a few hundred old people and women married to Greeks of Turkish nationality remained. These expulsions also precipitated an exodus of Greeks of Turkish nationality. Their number is unknown, but it was undoubtedly significant. With the virtual disappearance of the religious minorities Turkish censuses are no longer of any use in tracing the religion of the population, which has become a redundant variable. [99] But the fall in the number of pupils in Greek schools – from 5,000 in 1965 to 800 in 1983 – confirms (if it were needed) the quasi-disappearance of the Greek community which today has no more than around 8,000 members.

Until the 1920s, the Greek community and the Armenian survivors of Istanbul were not extinct demographically speaking. Nevertheless, it seemed highly unlikely that the new Turkish state would keep to the agreement regarding the Greeks of Istanbul and look after these last Armenians. Indeed, in this city which remained the economic heart of the country despite the transfer of the capital to Ankara, the Christians still dominated the economy: 50 per cent of investments were Greek and 20 per cent Armenian; together they held nine-tenths of the employment in foreign concessions.[100] The weak Turkish participation had already coloured the nationalism of the Young Turks with economic demands.

Mustafa Kemal and his successors, pushing the minorities to leave, created a Turkish bourgeoisie. Like cadres of the FLN on the liberation of Algeria and the Arab Socialist Union in Naser's Egypt several decades later, this new class was able to avoid a long stage of capital accumulation by acquiring cheaply the property left by those who were exiled.[101] Vexatious measures reached a peak with the tax on capital in 1942, the *varlik vergisi*, which was regulated according to religion and nationality. Taxpayers were divided into Muslims, non-Muslims and *dönme*, those Jews who converted to Islam in the sixteenth century after the arrival of a strange messiah,

Sabbataï Zevi. Non-Muslims were taxed up to ten times more than the Muslims, the *dönme* double.[102] Accompanied by racist press campaigns which attacked the 'Jorgis and the Kyriakos' (Greeks), the 'Artins' (Armenians) and the 'Solomons' (Jews), these measures persuaded people to leave the country, including the Jews who until then had been spared by the regime. Today no more 20,000 Jews remain in Turkey

Far from reassuring the remaining members of minority communities, who for several centuries had been accustomed to administrative and religious autonomy, secularism put them in an increasingly precarious situation. The abolition of the caliphate by the republic was naturally followed by the expulsion of the Greek Orthodox patriarch from Istanbul. Although temporary, the measure toppled one of the last symbols of Orthodoxy. It was soon followed by the appointment of Turkish teachers and associated head-teachers in the Greek schools – when they were not simply closed – or by the suppression of Greek literary society. Secularism was always selective. Despite the adoption of a new secular civil code for all Turks, and despite the abolition of the state religion, the authorities continued to enter religion on identity cards and to exercise diverse pressures to dissuade non-Muslims from aspiring to a position in the civil or military administration.[103] A legacy of the Tanzimat, their participation in the state apparatus, especially the Ottoman office of statistics – which had in turn a Jewish, an Armenian and an American director – diminished considerably. Even in the private sector foreign enterprises were required to employ a minimum quota of Muslims.

Of all the catastrophes that have occurred during the history of Christianity in the world of Islam since the hijra, the ten years between 1914 and 1924 which marked the disappearance of the Armenian and Greek communities from Turkey were the most notable. The human cost – 3 million people, massacred or displaced – and the total unexpectedness of events came as the final break in Muslim history. There are two paradoxes here. First, the disappearance of the Christians conflicted with the transformations that were taking shape. Indeed, it had taken place under two modernist regimes, the Young Turk[104] and the Kemalist, which had replaced a regime that had legitimized Islam and were both infused with secularism. There was nothing in their demographic trends to suggest that the Christians would vanish in this way. The second is that triumphant Islam had prided itself on a communal life with the Christians and Jews; Islam in decline, that which understood at the end of the nineteenth century that the global battle was lost, drove back the religious minorities. From the sixteenth to the nineteenth century, before it became the sick man of the chancelleries of Europe, the Empire had without doubt created a unique structure, capable of ensuring civil peace. Christian and Jewish communities benefited demographically. Thanks to the *millet* system, which reserved military service for the Muslims but exempted the minorities in exchange for the poll tax, their natural rate of growth was high. Even more important, thanks to strong social mobility these minorities increasingly took on the appearance of a 'people as class'.[105] Their natural rate of growth was so vigorous that it even enabled them to counterbalance the increase in the Muslim population, which had been swollen by migration from the border regions that the empire lost.

In the end the Christians became victims of the pauperization of the Turkish people and of their ambivalent feelings of admiration and revulsion towards the Western model, of which the Christian community was the most visible representative. After the massacres and the population exchanges, in 1927 the non-Muslim population of Turkey was still as large as 340,000. If they had not emigrated, they would today number 1.2 million Turkish Christians and Jews.[106] In fact, there are no more than 145,000, say 0.2 per cent of the population (see Table 5.9). Beyond retaliatory measures taken by governments, it is worth considering the fate of minorities that become too small. After passing a critical threshold, are they driven of necessity to extinction? The marriage market shrinks as well as social advancement; while children continue to be born, they are destined to become emigrants.

Table 5.1: Population of Istanbul by Religion, Fifteenth, Sixteenth and
Seventeenth Centuries

	1478 Population	%	1520–1535 Population	%	1550 Population	%	1691 Population	%
Muslims	47,960	60.0	231,850	58.0	300,000	57.7	390,000	58.2
Christians	23,714	29.6	125,542	31.4	200,000	38.5	280,000	41.8
Jews	8,326	10.4	42,608	10.6	20,000	3.8		
Total	80,000	100.0	400,000	100.0	520,000	100.0	670,000	100.0

Source: Calculated from Robert Mantran, *La Vie quotidienne à Istanbul au siecle de Solomon le Magnifique*, Paris, 1990.

Table 5.2: Population (in thousands) and Annual Growth Rates of Anatolia by Religion and Province, 1520–35, 1570–80

Province	Numbers			Total	Percentages		
	Muslims	Christians	Jews		Muslims	Christians	Jews
1520–1535							
Anatolia	2,328.5	42.5	1.5	2,372.5	98.1	1.8	0.0
Karaman*	717.5	15.5		733.0	97.9	2.1	0.0
Zulkadrive**	334.5	13.0		347.5	96.3	3.7	0.0
Rum-i Kadim ***	497.5	33.0		530.5	93.8	6.2	0.0
Rum-i Hadis****	126.0	254.0		380.0	33.2	66.8	0.0
Total	4,004.0	358.0	1.5	4,363.5	91.8	8.2	0.0
1570–1580							
Anatolia	3,258.7	101.5	2.5	3,362.7	96.9	3.0	0.1
Karaman*	1273.0	67.0	0.0	1340.0	95.0	5.0	0.0
Zulkadrive**	544.5	21.0	0.0	565.5	96.3	3.7	0.0
Rum-i Kadim***	857.0	91.0	0.0	948.0	90.4	9.6	0.0
Rum-i Hadis****	296.0	290.5	0.0	586.5	50.5	49.5	0.0
Total	6,229.2	571.0	2.5	6,802.7	91.6	8.4	0.0

* Karaman: Konya, Aksehir, Kayseri. **Zulkadrive: Kirsehir, Maras. *** Rum-i Kadim: Amsya, Tokat, Canik. **** Rum-i Hadis: Trebizond, Kemah, Malatya

Table 5.2: (continued)

Province	Annual Growth Rate between 1520–1535 and 1570–1580 (per thousand)			
	Muslims	Christians	Jews	Total
Anatolia	7.1	18.3	10.8	7.3
Karaman*	12.1	30.8		12.7
Zulkadrive**-	10.3	10.1		10.3
Rum-i Kadim***	11.4	21.4		12.2
Rum-i Hadis****	18.0	2.8		9.1
Total	9.3	9.8	10.8	9.3

* Karaman: Konya, Aksehir, Kayseri. **Zulkadrive: Kirsehir, Maras. *** Rum-i Kadim: Amsya, Tokat, Canik. **** Rum-i Hadis: Trebizond, Kemah, Malatya

Source: Calculations from Ömer L. Barkan. 'Contribution à l'étude de la conjoncture demographique'. This table, which enables us to measure the demographic trends in the sixteenth century, needs to be completed with the statistics relating to the province of Diyarbekir (census of 1520–35 only): Muslims 354,300; Christians 59,700; Jews 1,400. Ömer Lutfi Barkan. 'Essai sur les données des registres de recensement dans l'empire ottoman au XVe et XVIe siècle' in Journal of the Economic and Social History of the Orient, No. 1, 1958 (p. 211).

Table 5.2: (continued)

Male population of some Anatolian Provinces in 1831 by Religion (thousands)

Community	Muslims	Christians	Armenians	Jew	Gypsies	Total
Number	1,842	237	15	2	7	2,102
Percentage share	87.6	11.3	0.7	0.1	0.3	100.0

* Incomplete census based on the Anatolian provinces of Sivas, Adana, Trebizond, Kars and Cildir

Source: Kemal Karpat, *Ottoman Population, 1830–1914: Demographic and Social Characteristics*, Madison, 1985

Table 5.3: Land Transfers with and without Litigation in Anatolia by Religion, Sixteenth and Seventeenth Centuries

Ankara

	Without Litigation				With Litigation			
	1592–1600		1688–1691		1592–1600		1688–1691	
	Seller	Buyer	Seller	Buyer	Plaintiff	Accused	Plaintiff	Accused
Muslims	91	91	77	74	98	91	95	85
Christians	7	7	23	26	2	8	5	15
Jews	2	2	-	-	-	1	-	-
Total	100	100	100	100	100	100	100	100

Kayseri

	Without Litigation				With Litigation			
	1590–1600		1689–1692		1586–1610		1689–1692	
	Seller	Buyer	Seller	Buyer	Plaintiff	Accused	Plaintiff	Accused
Muslims	74	68	85	77	68	72	81	93
Christians	26	32	15	23	32	28	19	7
Jews	-	-	-	-	-	-	-	-
Total	100	100	100	100	100	100	100	100

Source: Suraiya Faroqhi, *Towns and Townsmen of Ottoman Anatolia*, Cambridge, 1984.

Table 5.4: Ottoman Population by Religion and Province (in thousands)

a - Census of 1881/1882–1893

Province	Muslims	Greeks	Armenians	Others	Jews	Total
Istanbul*	425	188	152	13	45	823
Edirne**	224	229	16	71	14	554
Çatalca	15	36	1	6	1	59
Biga	99	15	2	1	2	119
Hüdavendigar	1,133	133	58	6	3	1,333
Aydin*	1,119	197	14	3	22	1,355
Izmit	133	24	37	1	0	196
Kastamonu	929	15	3	0	0	947
Ankara	736	35	68	9	0	848
Konya	877	57	10	0	0	944
Adana	341	6	45	4	0	396
Trebizond	857	155	42	2	0	1,056
Elaziz	300	1	73	8	0	382
Sivas	767	38	117	5	0	926
Diyarbekir	290	1	47	31	1	370
Erzerum	446	3	101	9	0	559
Bitlis	167	0	101	9	0	277
Van	60	0	60	0	0	120
Aleppo***	397	4	41	22	2	466
Total	9,315	1,136	987	199	91	11,728

* Not including 131,000 foreigners in Istanbul and 56,000 in Aydin. ** Sanjaks of Edirne, Gelibolu, Kirkkilise and Tekirdagi. *** Anatolian part only.

Table 5.4: (continued)

b - Census 1906/1907

Province	Muslims	Greeks	Armenians	Others	Jews	Total
Istanbul*	432	177	71	9	48	737
Edirne**	335	291	25	79	22	752
Çatalca	23	44	1	8	2	78
Biga	141	38	2	1	3	185
Hüdavendigar	1,431	166	80	8	4	1,689
Aydin*	1,332	285	19	2	33	1,670
Izmit	201	36	51	2	0	290
Kastamonu	1088	23	10	0	0	1,121
Ankara	1012	42	98	5	1	1,158
Konya	1,146	87	15	1	0	1,249
Adana	436	11	50	7	0	504
Trebizond	1,072	215	51	2	0	1,340
Elaziz	391	1	74	8	0	473
Sivas	973	67	147	7	0	1,194
Diyarbekir	316	1	52	23	1	393
Erzerum	552	6	116	2	0	675
Bitlis	198	0	95	5	0	298
Van	55	0	59	0	0	114
Aleppo***	441	5	58	19	2	525
Total	11,571	1,496	1,077	187	116	14,447

* Not including 129,000 foreigners in Istanbul and 57,000 in Aydin. ** Sanjaks of Edirne, Gelibolu, Kirkkilise and Tekirdagi. *** Anatolian part only.

Table 5.4: (continued)

b - Ottoman Population in 1914

Province	Muslims	Greeks	Armenians	Others	Jews	Total
Istanbul	560	205	83	9	52	910
Edirne	360	225	20	4	23	631
Çatalca	20	37	1	1	2	60
Kale-i Sultaniye	150	9	3	1	4	166
Hüdavendigar	474	75	61	3	4	616
Kutahhya	303	9	4	1	0	317
Karesi	360	98	9	7	0	473
Karahisar-i Sahip	278	1	7	0	0	286
Aydin	1,249	299	20	5	35	1,609
Mentese	189	20	0	1	2	211
Izmit	227	40	56	2	0	325
Kastamonu	737	21	9	0	0	767
Bolu	399	5	3	1	0	409
Kayseri	184	27	50	2	0	263
Eskisehir	141	3	9	0	1	153
Ankara	877	20	52	6	1	956
Konya	751	25	13	0	0	789
Antalya	236	12	1	1	0	249
Nigde	227	58	5	1	0	291
Icil	102	3	0	0	0	105
Adana	342	9	53	8	0	411
Trebizond	921	162	39	1	0	1,123
Canik	266	99	27	1	0	393
Elaziz	446	1	80	11	0	538
Sivas	940	75	147	7	0	1,169
Diyarbekir	492	2	66	58	2	620
Erzerum	673	5	134	3	0	815
Bitlis	310	0	118	10	0	438
Van	179	0	68	11	1	259
Maras	153	0	32	7	0	192
Urfa	149	0	17	4	1	171
Aleppo*	244	7	20	12	1	284
Total	12,941	1,549	1,204	176	128	15,997

* Anatolian part only.

Sources: Calculated from Karpat, *Ottoman Population* and Vital Cuinet, *La Turquie d'Asie*, Paris, 1896.

Table 5.5: Annual Rate of Population Growth in the Ottoman Empire (present-day Turkey only) by Religion, 1881–1906, 1906–14

Periode	Muslims	Greeks	Armenians	Other Christians	Jews	Non-Muslims	Total
1881–1906*	12.0	15.3	4.8	-3.4	14.0	9.8	11.6
1906–1914	14.0	4.4	13.9	-7.6	11.2	7.5	12.7
1881–1914*	12.6	11.9	7.6	-4.7	13.1	9.1	11.9

* For the calculation of this rate the year 1888 has been taken as the reference year.

Source: as Table 5.4

Table 5.6: Percentage of non-Muslims in the Ottoman Empire (present-day Turkey only), 1881, 1906, 1914

Region	1881	1906	1914
Istanbul	48.4	41.4	38.4
European Turkey	61.0	56.9	45.0
Anatolia	16.0	16.3	16.6
Total	20.6	19.9	19.1

Source: as Table 5.4

Table 5.7: School attendance in the *Vilayat* of Izmir, Muslim and non-Muslim, end-Nineteenth Century

| | Primary Education | | Secondary Education | |
	Rate of Attendance	Girls/ 100 Boys	Rate of Scooling	Girls/ 100 Boys
Muslims	17.8	0	5.7	5
Non-Muslims	98.0	53	61.6	59

* Mainly Greek Orthodox

Source: Cuinet, *La Turquie d'Asie*

Table 5.8: Estimates of Armenian Victims of the Deportation of 1915. Thousands

Source	Toynbee*	Source	Lepsius**
Armenian population before the deportation	1,600–2,000	Armenian population before the deportation	1,845
Refugees in Aleppo, Damascus, Deir al-Zor	486	Refugees up to the edge of the Arabian desert	150–200
Refugees in other parts of Turkey	300	Muslim converts in Turkey	200
Refugees in Russian Caucasus	183	Refugees in Russian Caucasus and Alexandria	244
Armenians in the districts conquered by the Russians	12		
Refugees in Salma (Persia)	9		
Total refugees	990	Total refugees and Islamicized	594–644
Not deported from Istanbul and Izmir	150	Not deported from Istanbul and Izmir	205
Total survivors	1,140	Total survivors	799–849
Total victims	460–860	Total victims	996–1,046
Average	660	Average	1,021

Sources: * Arnold Toynbee, in *The Treatment of the Armenians in the Ottoman Empire*, London 1916.
** Johannès Lepsius, *Archivès du génocide des Arméniens*.

Table 5.8: (continued)

	Gürün*	MacCarthy**
Armenian population before the deportation***	1,300	1,465
Emigrants in Arab countries	225	225
in Iran	50	50
in France 1931	35	30
in USA, Canada	35	35
in Russia	420	400
in Bulgaria	15	20
in Greece, Cyprus	45	48
Other destinations	50	3
Total emigrants after the war	875	811
Armenians in Turkey 1927 / in Turkey****	124	70
Total survivors	999	881
Total victims	301	584
Armenians deported in 1916	703	

Sources: * Kamuran Gürün, *The Armenian File: The Myth of Innocence Exposed*, New York, 1985.
** Justin MacCarthy, *Muslims and Minorities: The Population of Ottoman Anatolia at the End of the Empire*, New York, 1983.
*** Excluding Istanbul and European Turkey (104,000 before 1914).
**** Mainly in Istanbul.

Table 5.9: Population of the Republic of Turkey by Religion, 1914–91.
(in thousands)

Year	1914	1927	1935	1945	1955	1965	1991
Muslims	12,941	13,290	15,851	18,511	23,810	31,139	56,860
Greeks	1,549	110	125	104	87	76	8
Armenians	1,204	77	61	60	60	64	67
Other Christians	176	71	41	38	62	74	50
Jews	128	82	79	77	46	38	20
Total	15,997	13,630	16,157	18,790	24,065	31,391	57,005
Percentage of non-Muslims	19.1	2.5	1.9	1.5	1.1	0.8	0.2
Greeks of Hellenic nationality	n.d.	26	18	14	12	10	n.d.

Sources: from 1914 to 1965, Ottoman and Turkish censuses and statistical abstracts; 1991, Norman Horner, *A Guide to Christian Churches in the Middle East*, Mission focus, n. d.; Jews, personal communication to the authors.

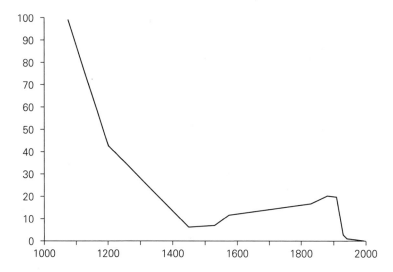

Figure 5.1: Percentage of non-Muslims in Turkey, 1071 to date

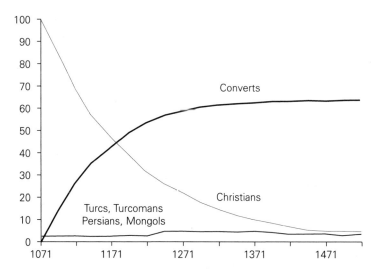

* Assuming that one out of seven non-Muslims converted in each generation

Figure 5.2: Conversions to Islam in Anatolia, 1071–1520*

CHAPTER SIX

Islam under Christian Domination:
The French Empire in North Africa

And I, listening sadly to all these things, asked myself what could be the future of a country delivered to such men and where this succession of violence and injustice would finally end, if not with a revolt by the indigenous people and the ruin of the Europeans.[Alexis de Tocqueville, *Notes sur l'Algérie*, Paris, 1841]

What, I wondered, if the French of Algeria had freed the system, progressively granted Muslim representation and at the same time slackened the link with the metropolitan country? That would be the beginning of Utopia.[Pierre Nora, *Les Français d'Algérie*, Paris, 1961]

North Africa was French for 130 years, much less time than the Crusaders, whose expedition to the Levant originated in France, held on in the Holy Land. Although there were, of course, real differences between the two episodes it is instructive to compare them.

Among the differences there was, first of all, distance. Before the compass was adopted from Arab navigators, Jerusalem was, for the Europeans, at the end of the known world, on the borders of the land of Gog and Magog. Algiers, on the other hand, was closer to Toulon than Paris. When the steamship, the telegraph and aviation were introduced the western Mediterranean was reduced to the dimensions of a lake. The colonial Maghreb was thus tightly linked to the metropolitan country, while the Latin kingdoms of the East were from the beginning cut off from the imperial centre. Relations between international forces had dramatically changed. During the European Middle Ages, the Crusaders set out to attack a land where a brilliant culture was still in evidence; by contrast, attacking a weak outlying province of the Ottoman Empire, the Algiers expedition occurred at the peak of French power. In the Levant the Franks had believed that they would find an ally in Arab Christianity; setting out for the Maghreb, the French navy knew that Christianity had been extinguished there seven centuries earlier.

Nevertheless, there were profound similarities between the Crusades and the colonial conquest of the Maghreb. Both started as military adventures but became, almost by accident, settlement projects. In each case, the call of distant lands spread out from France and extended rapidly to the neighbouring countries, bringing together a sort of Euro–Catholic coalition against Islam. Above all, demography was the common characteristic of the two episodes. The Crusaders and the *pieds-noirs* always remained in an extreme minority and, in the enclaves of Acre or Bab el-Oued, the descendants of the first immigrants were still, several generations later, foreigners unable to mix with the local population. In both the Latin states of the East and in the Maghreb, a total rejection of Arab–Muslim culture prevented the European transplant from taking root.

This dual failure tempts us to search for the causes, if only to help us evaluate the fate of the Jewish state in the East – the third attempt to colonize an Arab land, and one whose history is today still being written today before our eyes. This concern is shared by Israeli scholars, who have done excellent studies on the Crusades[1] and colonial North Africa.[2] Was the bankruptcy of the French project in North Africa written into its very nature, or was it the result of an accumulation of repeated errors – the violence and injustice which, only ten years after the landing at Algiers, de Tocqueville had the vision to realize would lead to the call for retreat? Later, numerous observers became alarmed at the political and demographic realities of the colony and predicted a bleak future for it.

Until the very end, however, even the most pessimistic could not have imagined the extent and speed of the retreat. Even when the outcome of the war launched against the French in 1954 was still uncertain, it was believed that only 250,000 French from Algeria would opt to return definitively to France,[3] and that all the others would be determined to stay, or indecisive. In reality, barely a tenth remained.

The Dream of Rechristianization

The French landing at Algiers in 1830 was not the first European invasion of North Africa after the Muslim conquest. In 1497, in the enthusiasm of the Reconquista, the Spanish had pursued the 'infidels' to their own land and built a protectorate in the Kingdom of Tlemcen. It survived for three centuries; but the French found no trace of it other than an intermediate society of 'renegades' and Mozarabs.[4] Had Christopher Columbus not, five years earlier, discovered by chance on the other side of the Atlantic a people who were even more infidel the memory of this push into the land of Islam might have survived and Spain's military energy would undoubtedly have been diverted to North Africa. The French colonization was of much shorter duration, but it left a deeper impression. While Spain was confined to the coast, France penetrated the depths of the Sahara, implanted a new language in a foreign population, moved over to Tunisia in 1881 and then Morocco in 1912. This was a unique enterprise in the history of French colonialism. It mobilized more than 1 million people and enormous material resources – more than Christian Europe had ever assembled to gain a footing in the Muslim Mediterranean.

Large-scale expeditions of this kind must be sustained by a grand idea and the objective the French minister of war, Clermont-Tonnerre, set for himself in order to overcome the reticence of King Charles X was nothing less than the return of Africa to the bosom of Christendom.[5] To the Muslim inhabitants of Algeria on the other hand, the French expedition was presented as a temporary occupation whose sole aim was to drive out the Ottomans and return the country to its legitimate masters, the Arabs. A proclamation drawn up in Arabic and distributed on the arrival of the troops, stated that the French had not come to take possession of the town. Anticipating with some brilliance, but not without duplicity, similar promises made by Louis Bonaparte to the Emir Abd al-Qadir in 1855 and Lawrence of Arabia; to the Sherif of Mecca in 1916, Clermont-Tonnerre understood that Arab nationalist feelings could smoulder under Turkish power.

'Even when victorious [after the taking of Algiers], French policy remained in the framework of that of the Spanish; nobody believed that the hinterland could be of any interest for the new invaders.'[6] Realism quickly replaced the plan to bring back Christianity and the occupation was extended as circumstances dictated the change to colonization. At first uniquely military, French, and destined only for Algeria, the settlement became civilian and European and then extended to neighbouring countries. The consolidation of the diverse components of this growing society, which remained a minority despite its demographic vitality, became a constant preoccupation of the colonial administration. The laws it proclaimed and the measures it took, slowly fashioned a unique society; but this was a foreign body confronting Muslim society which allowed itself to be drawn into the fatal spiral of separation.

The idea of rechrisianization faded away after the July Revolution in 1830 when Louis Bonaparte came to the throne. Holding pronounced secular views, often openly anti-clerical, colonial officers and civil servants banned missionary activities, prohibited religious proselytizing and were opposed to conversions. paradoxically, under the Third Republic the administration became less strongly anti-clerical and closed its eyes from 1881 to the activity of the missions provided that they were discreet and confined themselves to the hinterland.[7] But the missionaries were not very successful: 100 years later, there were less than a thousand converts[8] scattered in remote Kabylian villages. Known in Algerian dialect as *m'tourni* (from the French word for 'turned'), the converts were rejected by Muslims and Europeans alike and were never able to create a bridge between the two societies.

Nostalgic ideas of rechristianization were once again expressed during the celebrations of the centenary of the taking of Algiers in 1930:

> If Republican France does not have the wisdom to patronize Christianity openly and fully in North Africa in order to allow the missionaries to bring Muslims to the Gospel with official support, it is not necessary to come from the line of the Prophets to announce that despite the impressive amount of capital that it has poured into these lands for 100 years and the great works that it has accomplished, despite the education it has distributed widely to the Berber and Arab tribes, despite even the extensive French settlement, it cannot be sure of retaining indefinitely the Moroccan, Algerian and Tunisian empires.[9]

Mixed marriages were also rare and thus unable to help with a rapprochement: of 100,000 marriages celebrated by Europeans in Algeria between 1830 and 1877, there were barely more than 120 where the bride was Muslim. As one observer noted: 'In any year, at most one or two regular unions are registered between Muslim men and Europeans! It is not simply an exception, it is a demo-graphic curiosity ... Among Europeans and Muslim women the unions are even less numerous.'[10] The rejection was mutual. No one was ready to give their daughters in marriage: neither the Europeans, whose population had an excess of males, nor the Muslims for whom Islamic law continued to govern personal status and under which it was forbidden for a father to allow his daughter to marry a Christian or a Jew who had not previously converted.

Religion and the absence of intermarriage were not the only forces that kept the two societies apart. Ignorance of the language of the colonized was almost universal among the *pieds-noirs*. The officers in 1830 and the first settlers had learned Arabic and showed an interest in the culture of North Africa – at the time Oriental studies enjoyed considerable prestige in France where Silvestre de Sacy had, in 1810, produced his *Grammaire Arabe*. But once it became commonplace to cross the Mediterranean, once a complex colonial society with all its hierarchies was established, and once many new arrivals, especially Spanish and Italian, had first to learn French in order to be accepted, the ordinary process of ostracism was set in motion. Separate quarters were built and the symbiosis of the different European communities quickly replaced the timid approaches made between the early settlers and the Muslims. By the turn of the century, the settlers and their children had given up learning Arabic.[11]

The Making of a Colonial Society

The census statistics reflect colonial society in the making in two ways. It was not until the sixth census, taken in 1856, that the majority of indigenous people were counted. Before then only the French, the indigenous Jews and the first foreigners from Europe were included. The Muslim population featured in the statistical annuals rather as a compulsory appendix. Looking through one at random, that of 1878,[12] we find ten pages with a wealth of detail on the movements of the French population and of other European nationalities, but only a few lines on the Muslims. The census of 1856, brief as it was, revealed the extent of the disequilibrium between the indigenous population and the settlers; less than 100,000 French as against 2.3 million Muslims.[13] Such an imbalance was untenable. In order to end it, the French population needed reinforcement, either by the integration of indigenous people, whether Muslims or Jews, or by the immigration and naturalization of foreigners, or by an appeal to those of French origin.[14]

Would there have been other ways, besides conversion, of integrating the Muslim population without forcing them to give up their religion? A fairer system of education for the Algerians, who were generally kept illiterate at the very time that France's great educational reform was taking place under the Third Republic, would undoubtedly have helped by extending knowledge of French; but it would also have fundamentally changed colonial relations. In 1880, out of 49,610 pupils attending government primary schools in Algiers, Oran and Constantine, there were only 2,702 Muslims (5 per cent), of whom only 335 were girls; 210 pupils attended the Arab–French schools and 2,687 the Muslim schools.[15] France might also have turned to the Berber-speaking people – who were believed to practise a more syncretic Islam and who, 150 years later, were to defend the French language in the streets of Algiers and Tizi-Ouzou – to reduce social polarization. Yet no such policy was adopted.

Another method might have been to equalize legal status; but the indigenous Muslims remained subjects and not French citizens. They could have only achieved citizenship by giving up the personal status laws which in Islam regulate marriage, divorce and inheritance in particular – an act tantamount to repudiating a part of their religious beliefs and traditions. However, the issue never arose since the settlers were adamantly opposed to granting them nationality. The Registrar-General's offices systematically blocked individual requests by Muslims for the right of citizenship[16] and until 1940 permitted barely 40 naturalizations per year.

Forty years after the invasion the colonial administration turned towards the other Algerian community, the Jews, who were divided from the Muslims by their religious beliefs but not their way of life. 'A considerable number of Israelites there live exactly the same life as the Arabs, armed and dressed like them, riding their horse in the same way and making war as necessary just like them,' wrote the French Consul in Sousse in 1845. 'These Jews are so well blended into the rest of the population that it is impossible to distinguish them.'[17] Initially the privilege of French nationality was granted to individuals by the Senatus Consult of 1865, then to the whole body of indigenous Jews by the Crémieux Decree of 1870 which applied throughout the colonial era, except in 1943 under Vichy. Since Jews regarded individual naturalization as a renunciation of their customs only about 100 claimed it before 1870, but they welcomed the Crémieux Decree which did not link repudiation of this kind to the grant of civil and political rights. The French population of Algeria – 122,000 citizens in 1866 – was automatically increased by 44,000 four years later.[18]

The Crémieux Decree created genuine citizens, profoundly changed the behaviour of Algerian Jews and finally integrated them into the conquering society. The compulsory education that was introduced for all French citizens under the Third Republic was probably the most potent factor to remove the Jewish community from proximity to Islam, causing it to slowly give up its marriage and dress traditions, its way of life and even the use of the Arabic language.

However, the addition of indigenous Jews to a group that was a small minority made little impression on the imbalance of the population. The law of automatic naturalization of 1889 had very different implications. It stated that any child born in France, or in Algeria to a foreigner born in France or in Algeria, was French by birth. Moreover, it made it easier for other foreigners to obtain French nationality subject to certain residence conditions.[19] Conceived in order to give France a population boost vis-à-vis Germany after the loss of Alsace and Lorraine, the measure applied equally to Algeria.

Before 1899 European immigrants – especially the Spanish (75 per cent), Italians (20 per cent) and Maltese (3 per cent) – had entered Algeria at such a rate that in the census of 1886 they were equal in number to French. The pressure of numbers and competition over social status had, moreover, revived distrust towards the foreigner, which even surpassed that towards the indigenous people.[20] The Spanish were the primary target because of their high birth rate and sustained immigration in the region of Oran, close to their own country. It was alleged that they intended to use their demographic strength to bring about a partition of the colony to the benefit of Spain. The Spanish, closely followed by the Italians and Maltese, had on average 6.6 children while the French had 4. Only the Germans had less. Indeed, if the average birth rate among Europeans in Algeria, 29 per thousand, was reasonable it was solely because it was very high among the Spanish and Italians (36 per thousand) – among the French it had fallen to 22 per thousand.[21]

Seen as competition rather than reinforcement, the generalized naturalization of these foreigners was badly received. For example, the author of a book published in 1889, *Péril étranger en Algérie*, wrote 'The naturalized citizen is the forerunner, the trail-blazer and the protector of the foreigner ... The Italian or Spanish worker has become a much more dangerous plague than drought or an invasion of locusts.'[22] But in its own way the colony was preparing for the naturalizations. Mixed marriages united a large number of French and foreigners. In 1884, about one-quarter of the marriages between Europeans were across nationality, as against 16 per cent in the period 1830–81. 'The tendency of different people to join together, far from decreasing is becoming stronger each year,' noted a contemporary.[23] The French school, which had been closed to Algerians, opened up more and more to the children of foreigners in order to break down barriers.

Twenty years later, the French community had added 200,000 naturalized citizens to its number as a result of the law of 1889. This success was achieved with the consent of the Spanish government, which authorized its citizens to acquire French nationality hence losing 150,000 of its own nationals – about 1 per cent of the population, mostly impoverished peasants and unemployed workers.[24] Only a short time before their naturalization the fecundity of these new French had aroused fears. Now they happily took their place as 'neo-Latins'[25] and stopped being a cause of concern. The problem of foreigners thus fell into oblivion. At the time of Algerian independence, only 50,000 Europeans (1 in 15) had not wanted or obtained French nationality (see Table 6.1 and Figure 6.1).

The integration of indigenous Jews and Europeans of foreign origin brought into being a nation whose diverse components melted together into one society. Before it disappeared, it could boast 1 million people (984,000 in 1954), a symbolic threshold for the minorities in the Arab and Turkish Muslim world. In the face of the majority religion, this new society, a product of both French and cosmopolitan Mediterranean culture, enhanced its legitimacy by claiming affiliation with the Roman Empire. Several centuries after the triumph of Islam it dreamed that it would renew the lost tradition of an Africa that was Latin and Christian. Jacques Berque has eloquently depicted this invocation of the spirits:

> Competing with the Arab in the search for origins, it [colonialism] tended to overflow with historical grandeur. After the Islamization of the 'dark centuries', it revived Christian Africa ... This rivalry at all levels, which set the North African against the neo-Latin, brought Augustine and Cyprian to the rescue of Foucauld in order to confront the horsemen of Oqba.'[26]

The Algerian alchemy – the *pieds-noirs* astonishingly described themselves as 'Algerians' – was unsuccessful in both Tunisia and Morocco. In these two countries France did not entertain the same imperial ambition. Furthermore, other European countries were careful to contain French expansion in the region. The cementing of the various non-Muslim sections of the population around the

French nucleus was thus more difficult, partly because Italy and Great Britain were less flexible than Spain and showed themselves reluctant to lose their nationals or Crown subjects originally from Malta and Gibraltar. The Crémieux Decree and the law of 1889 did not extend to Tunisia and Morocco, where foreigners of European origin and indigenous Jews could only become French citizens by individual procedure. Consequently, the Jews of those countries retained their national traditions, as did the majority of foreigners who had not become French.

In Morocco, the division of the land into two zones of protection – French in the South and Spanish in the north and extreme south (Ifni and Tarfaya) – as well as an international zone (Tangiers), reinforced the segmentation of the foreign communities. In 1951, for example, virtually all the 270,000 French lived in the southern zone which had only attracted 50,000 foreigners, mainly Spanish. Almost three-quarters of the latter had preferred the north or Tangiers.

Soldiers, Settlers and Labourers Face a Muslim Population

The French expeditionary corps – 30,000 men at the time Algiers was taken, 100,000 when Field-Marshal Bugeaud took command of it some time later – remained for 40 years the sole master of Algeria. Bugeaud was bent on conquering the whole of Algeria and opening it to colonization and in 1840 declared before the French parliament: 'We need a large invasion of Africa like that achieved by the Franks and the Goths.' He took possession of the coasts before approaching the Sahara. Like the Arabs who invaded a thousand years before them, in the Bedouin tradition, the expeditionary corps ensured its supplies by making raids. But unlike the Arabs, who came from far-off provinces with few people, and who controlled the land long before they managed to Islamize and Arabize it, the French could be confident because their country was close to hand and had a large population.

In the immediate wake of the army, French civilians (especially traders) began to gather in Algiers. However, the idea began to develop that one day agriculture would take over from the army and the administration in the interior of the country. The agrarian initiative was left to large settlers who, little by little, appropriated and equipped estates of several thousand hectares, and to Spanish labourers who encroached on the land of their Arab neighbours in order to expand the meagre plots granted free of charge by the French administration. The joint possession of villages, which characterized the Arab system of land ownership, facilitated expropriation.

In 1839, an insurrection of the tribes had almost brought an end to the conquest. Subsequently, Muslim revolts could spring up anywhere, in the same way that they did in Palestine at the time of the 1936 uprising. The French military administration, which relied on the armed settlers, began to conceive a new way of occupying the territory. Since its own resources were insufficient to control the country efficiently, it appealed to the civilian population and opened the flood-gates of immigration. Giving up the idea of increasing the number of under-populated large estates which marked the beginning of the colonization, it encouraged the creation of densely populated European villages on land confiscated from the tribes, then incited the inhabitants to constitute themselves into armed legions. 'The fighting army,' Demontès observed later,

> ... must be followed by a kind of colonizing legion, composed of young, vigorous men who are armed and disciplined: they would populate the villages, cultivate the land and establish families ... They would occupy the villages which could, when needed, resist the attacks of the indigenous people, that is to say they would be fortified villages and heavily populated ... In place of the extreme individualism of recent times, there must exist between them the feelings of social solidarity which bind together all the members of a collective in the face of a real and continuing danger.[27]

The tangle of military and agricultural activities, the imprint of socialist and associationist ideas, especially after the 1848 revolution in France, curiously foreshadowed the organization of the kibbutz in Palestine a century later. The civilian contribution was not only a help but an essential device in the face of an enemy who could levy unlimited fighting men from its population and have recourse, in the name of Islamic solidarity, to the greater human and military resources of Morocco, which was still a sovereign power. Like the kibbutz too,[28] these 'fortified villages' were more of a myth in the collective memory of the *pieds-noirs* than the foundation of the Algerian colonial economy.

The European civilian colony was small and at the mercy of tropical diseases and the attacks of the tribes. Whereas life expectancy continued to increase in France, the mortality rate in Algeria reached a level worthy of the dark ages; more than 50 per thousand until 1855. The birth rate, despite an improvement between 1830 and 1851, was not sufficient to compensate.[29] The systematically negative natural rate of growth which marked the first decades of settlement (-13 per thousand between 1830 and 1856) would, without external support, have doomed the colony to certain death. It is an irony of history that misfortunes in the metropolitan country, especially the revolutions and war, enabled the French colony to survive. The 1848 revolution sent to Algeria 60,000 victims of the political and economic situation, Parisian workers who had been ruined or were unemployed, citizens who were often anxious to have access to a property which France denied them. 'For one reason or another, all those who went to settle in Algeria had a failed life behind them.'[30] In 1860, after visiting Algeria, Napoleon III had envisaged the creation of an Arab kingdom under French tutelage and slowed down the colonization considerably by protecting the collective lands of the tribes through the Senatus Consult of 1863.[31] The plan for an 'Arab kingdom' in Algeria led to a temporary pause in the immigration before it crumbled. Colonization resumed in the wake of the Franco–German war of 1870 and the Paris Commune. People from Alsace and Lorraine who had been dispossessed of their land, *communards* who were transported from their towns, all flowed onto the lands of the rebellious tribes which were sequestered in 1871 – more than 450,000 hectares in Kabylia alone, of which 100,000 hectares were immediately allotted to immigrants from Alsace and Lorraine.[32]

These migrations were the most important in the French history of Algeria. After reaching almost 15,000 arrivals net each year (that is, a rate of 42 per thousand), they progressively slowed down and even flowed in the reverse direction during the two world wars. These trends frustrated the policy of increasing the density of the population from the European village fabric. To the military administration, the creation of a dense European settlement in the hinterland and not only on the coast, had been an obsessive preoccupation, the way to avoid the mistake made by Spain in its occupation of Tlemcen. However, the large European peasantry envisaged by the founding fathers never materialized. Colonial agriculture moved with giant steps toward large landowners who had little need for labourers. 'From the second generation of settlers, three or four plots joined together into a single productive unit. Small ownership evolved into medium or large, and the settlement villages were depopulated.'[33] In about 1930, 34,000 European proprietors owned 2.3 million hectares – an average of 67 hectares to each European proprietor as against 5.5 in the case of Muslims.

The Europeans gradually deserted the countryside for the towns, especially the largest, Algiers and Oran (see Table 6.2). In 1886, for the first time, their rate of urbanization reached 50 per cent. Many of the refugees of the war and the Paris Commune quickly moved from the countryside and were not replaced, for new arrivals also settled in the towns – and continued to do so. On the eve of independence, two out of three French were town-dwellers, half of them in Algiers or Oran.

In the twentieth century, the decline of Europeans in the rural areas – 30,000 people spread over the area – attracted the attention of only a few observers. Charles-André Julien, for example, was already noting in 1931 the failure of the European settlement in the heart of the country, stirring up an armed rising in the colony.[34] And in 1937 two statisticians, who avoided the political implication of their observations, pointed out that 'the town represents a refuge for the European population who, as a result of diverse circumstances – especially of an economic nature – show a tendency to desert the countryside.'[35] The classic factors of rural migration were certainly present: poor educational facilities in the countryside and the attraction of the towns. But equally, perhaps, there was the urge of a minority to stick together, like the Franks of the Latin kingdoms 700 years earlier. Several other Christian communities in the Arab Muslim world would feel at one moment or another the disadvantage of being widely dispersed, among them the Christians of Syria who at about the same period as the European settlers in Algeria began to concentrate in the towns as did, a little later, the Copts of Egypt.

It was at this time that Muslim population growth in the Maghreb took off. By the simple fact that it celebrated its centenary in 1930, the new European thrust had lasted longer than the first Latin kingdom of Jerusalem. However, while the colony celebrated the anniversary of the taking of Algiers with pomp and ceremony and while, in a climate of fervour where the Crusades were invoked, the Church was renewing at Carthage a tradition of councils that had been lost since Roman times, the statistics began to show an irresistible growth of the Muslim population. Remarking on the situation, a newspaper published in Tunis wrote: 'The Crusade is beginning again: so the posters or the uniform donned by thousands of European children proclaim. The Muslims also thought of the Crusades during which so much blood was shed, and so many men were returned to barbarism.'[36]

Perhaps these Muslims, whose imminent extinction had been

predicted at the end of the nineteenth century, were already confident of their numerical strength. 'My well-considered opinion,' wrote a doctor in the 1880s, 'is that far from increasing, the indigenous population will continually diminish, to the extent that we can predict its complete disappearance from here in one or two centuries. How can we accept that the Muslims are a vigorous group when they regularly count more deaths than births?'[37] In 1925, while the techniques of predicting population growth were being refined, the American demographer Raymond Pearl fell victim to a similar myopia. He predicted that the Algerian Muslims would number 5.4 million by 1980.[38] The figure counted in that year was in fact 18.6 million, about 70 per cent higher than Pearl's estimate. At around the same time, talented writers used seductive phrases to express what the scholars predicted. For example, Henri de Montherlant: 'The misery of Islam, its lack of worth, its lack of talent, its aborted and lost soul, it is clearly the poor defeated race. A dying race, that is being ended by contact with us, is crying silently and with no strength.'[39]

Still moderate after the First World War, the Muslim birth rate soon increased rapidly: 35 per thousand in 1935 according to official figures, in reality 42 per thousand.[40] Not only was the European birth rate overtaken but also a falling death began to reverse the hierarchy of population growth (see Table 6.3). Figures suggesting that the natural rate of increase of the Muslims would be less than half that of the Europeans had, in the 1920s, been reassuring;[41] by the 1930s there was concern that the relationship would be reversed. The growth rate of the Muslims was by then 2.4 times higher than that of the Europeans, at a time when immigration from Europe was dwindling and the settlers were deserting the rural areas.

The colony arrogantly ignored the evidence. It 'could not recognize in the increasing upward curve after 1930 and even more after 1935, the revenge of the Oriental multitude who would thus submerge the colonial power.'[42] However, scholars and politicians who studied the figures understood: 'Such a demographic situation poses problems in the economic sector – *and I add, the political one* – that will become more and more difficult to resolve in the future. Will France be defeated – demographically speaking – by its conquest?'[43] The population scare now spread like wildfire.

Barely a decade elapsed between Pearl's projection and an anxious report presented to an audience of international demographers in 1937. In his *Régression relative des Européens en Algérie*, Mesnard expressed the concern of the comfortably off in the face of the 'inferior races', well before Vogt[44] and other prophets of doom:

> This phenomenon [of falling birth rate] does not spare the 'European' people who are in contact with the semi-civilized populations, whether they are numerically dominant or not. Whether it is in the United States (Negroes), in New Zealand (Maoris) or even in South Africa where the most lively of the European colonies in the world exists, the most civilized population sees itself decreasing as a proportion of the total population …This natural phenomenon is easily explained by the fact that the races which we call inferior are at this moment fully benefiting from the material advantages of our civilization, while we are poisoned by its excesses (socialism, materialism, etc.) Thus, far from a European wave drowning the world, as might have been thought a short time ago, this wave is recoiling before another which is much stronger … In what concerns us personally, apart from the insignificant case of New Caledonia, our only area of colonization is in North Africa.[45]

The 1930s was a decade of great ruptures, demographic as well as political. The real questions were for the first time being addressed without complacency, but they remained unanswered. Thus a bill proposed by Maurice Violette in 1930 and picked up again by the government of Léon Blum in 1936, would have granted the immediate right to vote to 21,000 Muslims of the 'Frenchified elite' in the same way as to the 203,000 French of Algeria. The Muslim population would through this measure have progressively acquired citizenship rights. Although this was a relatively modest plan, it was vehemently rejected by the settlers whose mayors threatened to resign. In order to justify this rejection, reference was once more made to the history of the Romans 'whose empire was immediately compromised by the accession of all the subject peoples to citizenship and whose national character was finally ruined when this right was granted to everyone by Antonin Caracalla'.[46]

The French Front Populaire in 1936 created a mechanism that might have transformed the status of the Algerian Muslims and bring them gradually to the age of political majority. The school could have become the centre of a new Algerian policy. By winning over the Muslim youth on a large scale, it would have increased the numbers eligible for citizenship under the terms of the Violette bill. In 1929, 6 per cent of the population of primary school age attended school, in 1944 the figure 8.8 per cent. By 1954, at the beginning of the Algerian war, it had increased to no more than 15.4 per cent. If the French language had been taught more widely while there was still time, the barriers to cultural understanding might have been raised; but paradoxically, it was not until after Algerian independence that the use of French spread among the people.[47] In the end, such an action would undoubtedly have changed the course of Algerian demography, which has shown itself sensitive to levels of education, especially among women.

Seen from France, there was still nothing alarming about the European settlement in North Africa. The 'new parts'[48] – Tunisia and Morocco which were opened much later to colonization – made up for what Algeria was no longer able to provide. By allowing the process to continue, these two countries enabled the Europeans to assert their presence temporarily. Extended to the whole of the Maghreb, colonialism thus re-established an entity that had been forgotten since the time of the Umayyads.[49]

With differences in the legal framework, Algerian history was repeated in Tunisia and Morocco. Though dominated by town-dwellers – almost three-quarters of the European population of the two protectorates – European settlement also controlled the country-side. Concerned about the advances of the Italians and distrustful of the intentions of their government, the French administration encouraged the settlers to occupy the land. In Tunisia rural settlement was at first neglected. It began to take off towards the turn of the century and after the First World War it increased again. From 1910 to 1929 271,000 hectares were assigned to 1,400 settlers. In Morocco in the 1930s, 3 million hectares of good land were divided almost equally between the *felahin* (800,000 hectares) and the settlers (722,000 hectares), the remainder belonging to the Treasury of the sultan or the local communities.[50] Thus, in the Maghreb by 1930 one-third of the cultivated area had passed into the hands of the Europeans. This huge agricultural holding followed a logic that was more political – to ensure the permanence of the Western presence – than economic. 'This base on the land,' writes Laraoui, 'was regarded as a political necessity and thus the old Romanizing ideology continued to influence minds.'[51]

Rivalling in appearance Algeria in its colonial heyday, the non-Muslim population of the protectorates was almost 1 million: more than 300,000 in Tunisia in 1956 and almost 700,000 in Morocco in 1951, respectively 11 and 7 per cent of the total population, as against nearly 14 per cent in Algeria (see Tables 6.4 and 6.5; Figures 6.2 and 6.3). These statistics include the indigenous Jews. But neither the law nor the structure of colonial society justified this grouping, for the Jews had nothing in common with the settlers except that they were not Muslim. In these countries, where the Europeans had established more superficial roots than in Algeria, and where foreigners and indigenous Jews were less 'French', the two groups were an artificial entity. The colonial system itself, a simple protectorate, had not benefited from the strong survival instinct that existed in Algeria. 'Not many years ago the French population of Morocco became conscious of its social reality. From the beginning it had only been a sort of appendix to the central power', a journalist with no illusions wrote in 1926.[52]

In the view of one of its members, the Moroccan Jewish community 'remained largely unacquainted with the attractions of the West, attached to the values of traditional Judaism and faithful in its hopes; when the time came, it was ready to emigrate en masse to Israel, ignoring considerations of political reality, obeying Messianic and spiritual urges and so realizing a millenarian dream.'[53] The distance that had been maintained between the French and the Moroccan Jews became obvious later when they settled in Israel and Algerian Jews chose to settle in France.

Islam, the Sole Religion

The end of the story can be read in numerous memoirs. After the Evian Agreements of 1962 which ended the Algerian war, nearly all the *pieds-noirs* went to France. In the patriotic fervour, these families became known as 'repatriates' although they had been born overseas and, in the case of more than half, came from an ancestor who had set out from Spain or Italy.

On the eve of the double shock of independence and the creation of the state of Israel, 2 million non-Muslims – Christians of European origin and indigenous Jews – lived in the Maghreb. This presence, which it was believed would remain for ever, has now virtually disappeared. The 100,000 Europeans who currently live in the region are not, except in rare cases, survivors of the former colony, but foreigners, mainly immigrants, whose status differs in no way from those of any other foreign nationals.[54]

The tragedy kind of a different kind that was played out in the Eastern Mediterranean fifty years earlier, ending in the disappearance of the 3 million Christian Greeks and Armenians of Turkey had something in common with this episode. In the Ottoman Empire, as in the colonial Maghreb, the People of the Book enjoyed a special status. That it was conceded by Islam in the first case and imposed by a Christian metropolitan country in the second, was irrelevant: a statutory difference divided both from the majority of the population. Perhaps it was because these communities constituted an exception in their beliefs and behaviour that they lost their place in the nation-state which seeks uniformity.

The Jews themselves, who had survived the first disappearance of the Christianity that was indigenous to the Maghreb in the thirteenth century, did not survive the second disappearance of a Christianity that was, this time, of foreign origin. Today only a few families remain, and many of these are in the process of leaving. The destiny of the Jewish community was sealed by the two last large invasions from Europe – the first local, in the Maghreb, and the second further away, in Palestine. By completely integrating the Jewish community of Algeria into the colony, the French occupation forced it to share its final fate – exodus.[55] Israel, for its part, could only endow itself with a solid demographic base by drawing on the rich human resources of the two other countries of the Maghreb. In Morocco, for example, the different Israeli–Arab conflicts marked the erosion of the Jewish community: from 265,000 in 1948, the Jewish population declined to 222,000 in 1951 after the creation of Israel, to 160,000 in 1960 after the Suez crisis, and to only 31,000 in 1971 after the 1967 war.

Now that the demographic presence of Europe has ended, what remains of its cultural presence of, to use Jacques Berque's phrase, the 'Latinity reintroduced into North Africa during the colonial era'?[56] If we judge by language, progress is remarkable. When France abandoned the Maghreb, it left 24 million Muslims, of which 2 million were French-speaking. Today, the figures belie a widely-held impression that French is in retreat in the Maghreb.[57] In Algeria, for example, where there are frequent debates on bilingualism and Arabization, only 31 per cent of the generations educated before independence were French-speaking, while among the generations which attended school after 1962 under the Algerian Republic, 72 per cent are French-speaking.[58] From independence to the present, the increase of education in French has multiplied the number of French-speakers twice as much as population growth has done: it is the result of a political will rather than a mechanism of the birth-rate.[59]

Because the schools remained bilingual despite some vicissitudes, and to a small degree because of population growth, the French-speaking population today amounts to 23 million people out of a North African population of 60 million.[60] After France itself, Algeria is the most important of the French-speaking countries of the world (see Table 6.6). 'All those who in the past have launched France into its colonial adventures would be surprised by the results. They dreamed of an empire but we have harvested something much better – a French-speaking world', Jean Bourgeois-Pichat wrote recently.[61] The Frank settlement of the Holy Land is today discredited and the Spanish in the Maghreb, forgotten. But the French colonization of the Ifriqiyya has ended in a paradoxical symmetry; 2 million North Africans in France have succeeded the 2 million French in the Maghreb. The demographic and cultural bases exist for this exchange to be continued.

Table 6.1: Population of Algeria by Religion and Nationality, 1833–1987
(in thousands)

Year	French	Foreigners	Christians	Jews	Muslims	Total
1833	4	4	8	40	1,952	2,000
1836	6	9	15	41	1,945	2,000
1841	17	21	37	41	1,922	2,000
1845	46	49	95	42	1,891	2,028
1851	66	65	131	42	2,324	2,497
1856	93	67	159	43	2,307	2,509
1861	112	81	193	43	2,733	2,969
1866	122	96	218	44	2,652	2,914
1872	130	116	245	45	2,125	2,415
1876	141	155	297	48	2,463	2,808
1881	178	181	360	53	2,843	3,255
1886	204	203	407	58	3,287	3,752
1891	252	216	468	63	3,577	4,108
1896	299	212	510	68	3,783	4,362
1901	341	218	559	75	4,089	4,723
1906	433	166	599	81	4,478	5,158
1911	473	189	662	90	4,741	5,493
1921	503	189	692	99	4,923	5,715
1926	553	176	729	105	5,151	5,984
1931	623	148	772	110	5,588	6,470
1936	704	127	831	116	6,201	7,147
1948	746	46	792	130	7,679	8,601
1954	796	50	846	138	8,449	9,433
1966	65	16	81	3	12,018	12,102
1977	53	13	65	2	16,881	16,948
1987	40	9	49	1	22,989	23,039

Sources: Censuses from the colonial period and from independent Algeria.
Jacques Taïeb, 'Les Juifs du Maghreb au XIXieme siècle, Aperçus de Démographie Historique et Répartition Géographique', *Population,* No. 2, Paris, 1992;
Encyclopedia Judaica, 'Algeria'.

Table 6.2: European Urban Population Concentration in Algeria, 1866–1954 (in thousands)

Year	1866	1886	1906	1926	1931	1936	1948	1954
Algiers	52.0	80.8	134.5	193.2	214.5	230.2	247.7	276.6
Oran	31.0	56.1	89.0	126.5	131.8	155.6	174.0	181.6
Constantine	14.0	19.9	26.0	41.5	48.2	50.5	37.2	40.7
Bône	11.1	20.7	30.0	31.1	37.2	45.0	44.5	46.1
Sidi Bel Abbès	6.2	14.5	19.4	28.0	27.7	30.3	28.3	31.9
Mostaganem	6.5	5.9	10.7	12.9	12.8	17.6	18.0	19.2
Tlemcen	7.1	8.3	11.9	11.6	11.7	12.6	12.9	11.8
Philippeville	10.8	17.4	15.9	20.8	23.2	32.8	27.5	28.3
Sétif	3.4	3.7	6.3	8.9	9.9	8.2	8.4	7.9
Total	142.1	227.3	343.7	474.5	517.0	582.8	598.5	644.1
Europeans	218.0	464.8	680.3	833.4	881.6	946.0	922.3	984.0

Sources: Censuses from the colonial period

Table 6.3: Birth, Death and Natural Increase Rates in Algeria, 1922–35 (per thousand)

Year	1922	1926	1930	1935
Birth rate				
Europeans	28	25	25	21
Muslims	25	28	30	35
Ratio (%)	89	112	120	167
Death rate				
Europeans	19	16	15	14
Muslims	21	16	14	18
Ratio (%)	111	100	93	129
Rate of natural increase				
Europeans	9	9	10	7
Muslims	4	12	16	17
Ratio (%)	44	133	160	243

Source: Uncorrected statistics of the colonial Registry-General

Table 6.4: Population of Tunisia by Religion and Nationality, 1881–1984 (in thousands)

Year	French	Foreigners	Christians	Jews	Muslims	Total
1881	1	18	19	25	1,476	1,520
1886	4	26	29	27	1,520	1,577
1891	10	33	43	29	1,566	1,638
1896	16	66	82	32	1,612	1,726
1901	24	87	111	35	1,661	1,806
1906	35	94	129	38	1,710	1,877
1911	50	126	176	41	1,722	1,939
1921	55	102	156	48	1,889	2,094
1926	71	102	173	54	1,932	2,160
1931	91	104	195	56	2,087	2,338
1936	108	105	213	60	2,336	2,608
1946	144	96	240	71	2,898	3,209
1956	180	75	255	58	3,470	3,783
1966	17	16	33	8	4,501	4,541
1975	12	9	21	5	5,605	5,631
1984	7	6	13	3	7,001	7,017

Sources: Censuses and estimates of the Tunisian protectorate and after independence; Taïeb, 'Les Juifs du Maghreb'; *Encyclopedia Judaica,* 'Tunisia'.

Table 6.5: Population of Morocco by Religion and Nationality, 1912–82 (in thousands)

Year	French	Foreigners	Christians	Jews	Muslims	Total
1912	2	2	4	115	4,881	5,000
1921	52	77	128	116	4,716	4,960
1926	67	83	150	142	5,339	5,631
1931	117	106	223	152	5,833	6,207
1936	137	124	260	191	6,773	7,223
1947	233	168	401	224	8,036	8,660
1951	267	181	449	222	8,529	9,200
1960	172	132	304	160	11,163	11,626
1971	48	37	85	31	15,263	15,379
1982	27	20	47	15	20,358	20,420

Sources: Censuses and estimates from the French and Spanish protectorates of the international zone of Tangier and of independent Morocco; Taïeb, 'Les Juifs du Maghreb'; *Encyclopedia Judaica,* 'Morocco'.

Table 6.6: French-speaking Population of the Maghreb at Independence and Today (in thousands)

Country	At Independence	Today
Algeria (1962)	1,400	12,800
Morocco (1956)	430	6.700
Tunisia (1956)	470	3,400
Total	2,300	22,900

Source: Authors' calculations from census statistics

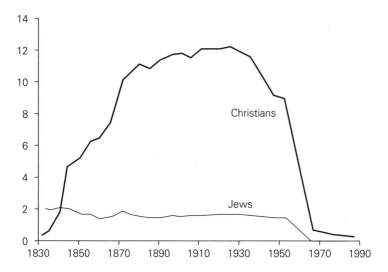

Figure 6.1: Percentage of Christians and Jews in Algeria, 1833–1987

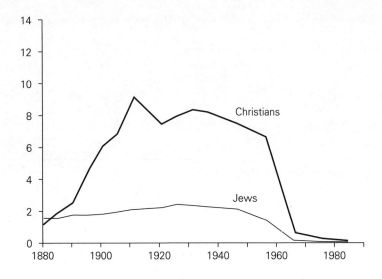

Figure 6.2: Percentage of Christians and Jews in Tunisia, 1881–1984

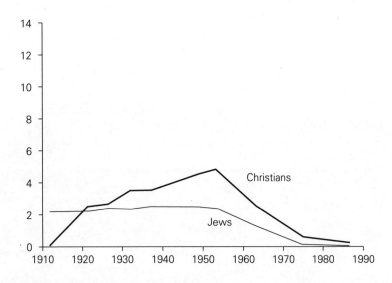

Figure 6.3: Percentage of Christians and Jews in Morocco, 1912–82

CHAPTER SEVEN

Israel and the Palestinian Population Explosion

The character of a state is conditioned in the first place by its demographic composition, the standard of living and unity of its population.[Abba Eban, Israeli minister of foreign affairs (1966–74), 25 August 1967.[1]]

Without high, constantly growing, Jewish immigration to Israel, without a significant increase in the rate of Jewish births in the country, we are condemned to become a minority, even if the threats of the Arab dictators to exterminate Israel are thwarted by our national army. To ignore this danger is tantamount to saying *après moi le déluge*. [David Ben Gurion, prime minister of Israel (1948–63), 17 November 1967.[2]]

The Mediterranean has always been both a place of refuge and a thoroughfare. After the Arabs many people settled on its southern shores – Franks, Turks, Mongols, French again, this time accompanied by Italians and Spaniards, then Jews. However the European migrants, who had been reticent about adopting the language or religion of their hosts and cutting their links with their native land, eventually returned to their own continent. The Asian invaders are today barely distinguishable from their hosts. What then will become of the Jews who arrived in the Near East both from Europe and from the rest of the Arab world, and who had no native land? It is clearly too soon to predict the outcome, for the Zionist project which began in the early twentieth century will continue for a long time.

Nationalism Creates Demography

Theodor Herzl, the founding father of Zionism and author of *The Jewish State*, initially pursued his dream of creating a Jewish homeland in Palestine by approaching the protector of the Holy Places, the

Ottoman sultan Abdülhamid. He had preconceived ideas about the sultan, whose uncle had granted the privileges of a quasi-state to the Christian subjects of Mount Lebanon[3] and imagined that the Ottomans would be easily persuaded to relinquish another part of their authority. However, the small Jewish community of Palestine was not comparable in either size or political significance with the Maronites. It was descended partly from a few hundred families who had never left the area and who were joined in the sixteenth century by a branch of the great migration that took place after the Spanish Reconquista. In 1852 there were only 13,000 Jews in Palestine, barely 4 per cent of the population of the districts of Jerusalem, Acre and Nablus, although another more dynamic wave of immigration was already looming. In the last quarter of the nineteenth century, a first group of Jewish settlers arrived in Palestine despite the re-Islamization policies of Abdulhamid and his as a ruler with an iron will. In far-off Istanbul it was not possible to observe the extent of such population movements, and little importance was attached to the transactions which progressively transferred the land from the Arabs to the Jews.

Even before the first Zionist congress held in Basle in 1897, the Jewish population of the three *sanjaks* of Jerusalem, Acre and Nablus had begun to increase as a result both of immigration and natural reproduction – a high birth rate and a falling death rate (see Table 7.1). As the foreign element grew, these three Ottoman districts became Palestine – a Roman name which had not been used either for administrative or indeed current purposes since the Abbasid period,[4] and a name that was to became synonymous with the country's tumultuous political future. Between 1850 and 1914, 84,300 Jews[5] crossed the Mediterranean – 44,000 of them after 1897 – in order to acquire legally and peacefully a region that the Crusaders had only been able to penetrate by military force.

However, many of these early migrants moved on – some because they had only intended to make a pilgrimage, others because they were disappointed by the Promised Land. 'Re-emigration', which is a cause of such concern to the leaders of Israel today, was already a common practice. David Ben Gurion, the president of the first Israeli government estimated that eight out of ten of the Jewish immigrants to Palestine before the British mandate (1919–48) had returned to Europe or set sail for America in the weeks or months immediately after their arrival – in the same way as many Soviet Jews a century later. In the end, 33,000 immigrants settled in Palestine before the First World War, many acquiring Ottoman nationality. By this time the country had 602,000 Muslims, 81,000 Christians alongside 60,000 Jews, of whom 39,000 were Ottomans.[6]

The arrival during this period of the first two contingents of Jews, a founding act of Zionist colonization, was of political rather than demographic importance and had little impact on the religious composition of the population. Far from being the human desert imagined by those who set out for Zion, Palestine was in fact inhabited by a significant Arab population and its confessional mosaic was similar to that of other areas of the Ottoman Empire. The Jewish presence was less pronounced there than in Iraq and Yemen, but more than in the rest of Syria.

The partition of the defeated Ottoman Empire was, as we have seen, accompanied by the brutal extinction of Christianity in Anatolia and its slow erosion in the Levant. Throughout the old empire the Muslim population had asserted its demographic strength except in Palestine where it was progressively turned into a minority. If the Young Turks, who governed the Ottoman Empire during the war, had chosen to fight with the Triple Entente rather than the Triple Alliance, or if they had remained neutral, would they have allowed an 'infidel' and nationalist colonization to take root in the third holy city of Islam, at the very time when they were trying to limit the expansion of Christianity? Almost certainly not; the repression which they let loose on the Jews of Palestine in 1914–18 leaves little room for doubt. They showed no signs of applying double standards and moved with equal enthusiasm to root out Armenian and Greek nationalism, to neutralize Arab nationalism and to check the rise of Jewish nationalism. Zionism was banished in the same way as all non-Turkish and non-Muslim centrifugal movements. The mass deportation of Jews and their flight to Egypt probably lost the Jewish population of Palestine 40 per cent of its total strength during the war.

In the Balfour Declaration of 1917, the British crown promised to the Zionist movement the creation of a Jewish national homeland in Palestine, although at the time it had been granted no prerogative in the region. The pledge was honoured, enabling the 59,000 Jews resident there in 1918 to become the 650,000 Israeli citizens of the Hebrew state at its birth on 14 May 1948. Throughout this period, the British government performed a constant balancing act. From one White Paper to another (1922 and 1939), it attempted the nearly impossible task of mediation between conflicting Arab and Jewish nationalisms. Between the Arab majority and the Jewish minority, London took decisions with the help of the Bible – but inspired by Pontius Pilate rather than Solomon.

The rapid increase of the Jewish population owed very little to natural growth and almost everything to immigration. On the eve of the Nazi holocaust the Jews, persecuted in Europe, found the doors closed to immigrants in the New World. But the intense activity of the Zionist movement, together with the benevolence of the mandatory power, enabled more than 500,000 refugees to enter Palestine. Although they did not force the indigenous population to leave, the arrival en masse of this immigrant population created the extreme tension which eventually brought about the flight of the Arab population.

From Hernán Cortes who burnt his ships in order to settle his men for eternity, to the Boers who buried in the Transvaal their past as Dutch outcasts by inventing a language, history is full of examples of a small group of immigrants who created a state. Indeed, the Arabs and the Turks did precisely this; however the creation of the Jewish state differed in two ways. The Arabs who conquered the Near East and then the Maghreb, and the Turks who seized Anatolia, were never numerous and did not want to remain a closed group. On the contrary, they first infiltrated and modified local institutions then mixed with the indigenous people until, in the end, they were indistinguishable. Today the Anatolians call themselves Turks and the North Africans Arabs. This is not what happened in Palestine where the immigrants replaced the former inhabitants, although not without resistance.

Much has been written about 'the willingness of the large Arab landowners to sell their land to Zionist organizations … In addition these purchases involved very lucrative land speculation … That is, the Zionists paid a high price for their holy land.'[7] But the Palestinians were not all large landowners and they did not all accumulate profits. A national feeling awakened both against the seizure of power by the British and the appropriation of land by the Jews. Peasants and humble town dwellers rose up in protest; but the riots of 1920–21 and the revolt of 1936–39 did not reverse either the British mandate or the wave of migration. Nor did the politics of the large feudal lords to whom the people left the political initiative.

Aside from the visible forms of protest in which it engaged, the population responded with a change in its demographic behaviour.

In a way that was unusual for the time and the place, the British administration scrupulously recorded each year the birth rates and death rates of the two populations (see Table 7.2). These embodied certain classic characteristics of differential population growth – a higher natural growth among the Arabs than among the new arrivals, despite the higher mortality rate among the former. However, the figures can only be fully understood by comparing Palestine to less threatened neighbouring Arab countries. Such a comparison shows that from the time of the mandate, no doubt unconsciously, the Palestinians used the large family as a political weapon. In order to redress the balance which immigration was tilting in favour of the Jews, their birth rate ran constantly ahead of any level known in the world. At its lowest in 1942, it reached 45 per thousand and at its height it was 60 per thousand.[8] With an average birth rate of 55 per thousand, that is eight to nine children to each woman, this was certainly a world record for the period. By comparison, the high fertility rates of the Arab–Muslim region seem insignificant: in the same period the birth rate reached 44 per thousand among the Muslims of Egypt (1944–8) and 40 per thousand in Syria. Even in Algeria, where future struggles would be sustained by a high birth rate, the levels were lower (42 per thousand between 1926 and 1929 among the Muslims). Thus demographically Palestine stood out from its neighbours, both during this period and for a long time afterwards – between 1985 and 1995 the birth rate in Gaza and the West Bank remained constantly high (see chapter 8).[9]

In 1995 the population of the State of Israel was 5.5 million consisting of 4.7 million Jews and 850,000 Arabs who are Israeli citizens. In addition there were 2.2 million Arabs in the occupied or autonomous territories (Gaza, the West Bank, Jerusalem and the Golan Heights).[10] Given present – and foreseeable – birth rates, Arabs could outnumber Jews in this region before the year 2010. Until the 1967 war, the Law of Return[11] compensated for the different birth rates. Indeed a balance of migration of 1 million people between 1949 and 1967 enabled the Jews to maintain their share in the Israeli population at 88 per cent.

The post-1967 occupation initiated a new disequilibrium immediately reducing the proportion of Jews within the new borders to 64 per cent. In subsequent years continuing Jewish immigration on the one hand, and Palestinian emigration to the Gulf on the other hand, once again ameliorated the impact of differential birth rates. However, these two migratory movements dried up in the 1980s with the onset of an economic crisis in Israel and a fall in oil prices which led the Gulf states to cut back on employment. The question of differential growth rates then moved into the political arena. Beyond a belief in one God, the Israelis and their Palestinian adversaries found themselves in agreement on only one point; they both recognized the demographic dimension of their conflict and placed the stakes in the occupied territories.

Whether 'hawks' or 'doves', all Israeli politicians have attempted to imitate the trumpet call to Jericho. The most intransigent believed that military subjugation of the land would bring security. A few hawks floated even more radical solutions to guarantee the future, such as the huge exchange of the Arabs of Israel and the occupied territories against the few Jews who remained in Arab countries proposed by Rabbi Kahane just before his violent death.[12] Amounting to a mass expulsion of Palestinians this would have been an extremely unequal exchange – a repeat of the exchange of Greeks and Turks in 1923. But the thinking of this armed Savonarola crowned a long tradition. Honourable personalities, sometimes socialist, had already recommended 'creating a Palestine, at the very least a western Palestine without Arabs ... and there is no other way than to transfer all the Arabs to the neighbouring countries, to transfer them out of here. We must not leave a single village, nor a single tribe.'[13]

In return, the doves proclaimed far and wide that an Israel which swallowed up too much land outside its 1948 borders would sooner or later suffer demographically. The minimalists among them were even prepared to return all the occupied territories except Jerusalem in order to rediscover their original purity and preserve the spirit of the family, which extolled the predominance of the Jewish element and the harmonious functioning of a democratic game which would not be disturbed by the intractability of the Arab opposition. They accepted a return to the area of the 1948 borders, with a few changes, which today has a population 85 per cent Jewish. However, deep down, this little Israel was slowly sickening with another illness: the spatial enclosure of the Jewish majority by a Palestinian minority which was backed by its Arab neighbours.

The Israeli Arabs: a Growing Nucleus

From the instant it came into existence, the State of Israel was plunged into war with its neighbours. By the time the fighting ended between 600,000 and 840,000 Palestinians had left their homes.[14] Only 156,000 escaped the exodus. Their history might have been very short had the repression described so passionately in 1968 by Nathan Weinstock, an Israeli of the far left, been successful: 'The agrarian policy pursued by the Israeli authorities since 1948 towards the Arab minority,' he observed, 'can be summed up in two words: "systematic plunder." All imaginable methods – the promulgation of new laws, improper interpretation of old legal arrangements, military tyranny – were used to achieve this end. Out of the 110,000 hectares belonging to Arab peasants in 1948, 70,000 hectares of the best land were confiscated or expropriated by various procedures and 34,000 villagers were dispossessed.'[15]

However, history decided otherwise. Known as 'Israeli Arabs', these forgotten people have joined other groups with a dual appellation which brings together people who were enemies: 'Ottoman Greeks', 'Turkish Armenians' and 'Arab Jews'. This uncomfortable position means that Israeli Arabs are distrusted on both sides. Among other Arabs they were suspect for not having chosen exile, and even more so after they were granted Israeli nationality. More generally, they have rarely been of interest to journalists whose attention has been focused on events further afield: the Arab–Israeli wars, the Palestinian diaspora in Jordan and Lebanon and its methods of struggle around the world, the uprising in the occupied territories and finally the Oslo and Washington peace accord between Israel and the PLO. Among Jews they are a potential 'enemy within' despite the fact that they have in many ways been loyal citizens:

> The behaviour of the Arabs, confided one of them, does not justify the repressive measures used against them. Neither the sovereignty of the State of Israel, the public institutions nor even its power have ever been questioned. The Arabs of Israel have remained almost totally calm since they became citizens of the State of Israel. More than three-quarters of the Arab votes go to Zionist parties: MAPAI, MAPAM, Akhdoth Haavoda, Herut, and even to the Jewish religious parties. The MAKI (Communist Party) which openly defends Arab interests, only received one-fifth of the votes. The final irony was the extension of military rule to the Arabs, which was achieved with the help of the Arabs in parliament.[16]

The fact that they are ostracized in this way has, paradoxically, favoured the survival of Israeli Arabs as a group. In the first place, their Israeli passport – a travel document that cannot be used in Arab countries[17] – has prevented them from emigrating. Thus, while they have been deprived of a share in the riches of the Gulf, their ranks have not been reduced. This absence of migration since 1948 demonstrates the extent to which the Israeli Arabs have settled down and contrasts in a startling way with the continuous flow that has produced a diaspora of 3.5 million Palestinians in 1995.[18] In the second place their policy of keeping their heads down has favoured their demography. Their natural growth far exceeds that of the Jews although it does not match the level of other Palestinians. To the credit of the efficient health system in Israel, the life expectancy of Israeli Arabs (74.3 years) is close to that of the Jews (76.7 years) – and the highest of all Arabs. At the same time their crude death rate (3.4 per thousand) is half that of the Jews,[19] whose age distribution is characterized by a higher proportion of older people – a long-term advantage, for this distribution changes slowly.

For a long time, and reflecting deep social needs, fertility followed parallel trends among Israeli Arabs (with a significant difference between Christians and Muslims)[20] and in the West Bank and Gaza. After 1970, however, the trend diverged and among the Israeli Arabs, especially Christians, fertility levels suddenly fell: a change that conforms to the normal pattern brought about by a decline in the rate of mortality and a higher level of education.[21] The difference between Arab Christians and Muslims here stems from the longer-standing influence exerted over the former by Western lifestyles which lead them to restrict the size of their families from an earlier stage. Among the Arabs the Christians have also been the group most interested in birth control – a difference expressed in the first instance by less frequent and less early marriages. Permanent celibacy was already the fate of 15 per cent of Christian women belonging to the generation born under the mandate and today affects more than 20 per cent of them. A convergence is, however, now taking place in the age of marriage, with Muslim women marrying almost as late as Christians. Contraceptive practices similarly divide Christians from Muslims. A study carried out in the early 1980s in the little village of Shefaram in Galilee has shows that the ideal family size – three or four children – was almost the same among Christians, Muslims and Druzes. Actual behaviour, however, was more dif-ferentiated: 40 per cent of Christian women, as against 25 per cent of Muslim and Druze women, used a form of contraception aimed at the definitive ending of procreation.[22] Since 1986 there has been a second notable change in the general trend and the birth rate among the Israeli Arabs, especially Muslims, is again rising – from 33.8 per thousand in 1986 to 37.9 in 1995 – even though there has

been no change in the factors which should have continued to make
it fall.

Let us stop to consider for a moment this heterogeneity. Statistics
always instil a political vision of society. In Israel, differences of
religion, origin and status are underlined. In the same way that
separate tables provide data for Jews of European origin and others,
largely consisting of Arab Jews, Israeli Arabs are classified according
to their different communities. In one sense Israel has simply
renewed the Ottoman practice of counting Christians and Muslims
separately. But to single out the Druzes among the Muslims is new,
and so too is the distinction introduced by Israeli statisticians between
the sedentary and the small nomadic population (less than 38,000).
Ethnic origin is sometimes retained, as with the Circassians (3,000
people) who are Muslims originating from the Caucasus but long
since Arabized. Druzes and Circassians are admitted to military
service in Israel, unlike other Muslims and Christians. The desire to
mitigate the bipolarization of Arabs and Jews in favour of a more
diversified body perhaps motivates the statisticians, but the desire to
separate the Christians may also be a factor.

The granting of 'a special status to the Christian communities in
order to distinguish them from the Muslim majority and so prevent
the formation of an Arab organization at the national level,'[23] at the
suggestion of the MAPAI Labour Party, derived its inspiration from
the Lebanese civil war which, looked at from Israel, was simply a
struggle between the different confessions. But this was to forget
that the Christians were among the first to protest against the Jewish
immigration and that they are always at the head of the nationalist
movements. It is no coincidence that the Palestinians appointed not
only a woman but a Christian, Hanan Ashrawi, to lead their team in
the November 1991 peace talks in Madrid.

Occupation of the Land of Israel

Throughout the long history of the non-Muslim minorities in the
Arab and Turkish Mediterranean, whether Christians or Jews, there
have been periods when they tended to concentrate their communities, mostly in the towns, for economic reasons and for reasons
of security. The short history of the State of Israel is, in a sense,
a remarkable example of this pattern, for never before has a minority
population gathered together simultaneously from the four corners
of the region. Almost all the Arab and Turkish Jews, from Baghdad

to South Morocco, from Yemen to Istanbul, arrived in Israel within a decade of its creation. Today they form 52 per cent of the country's population[24] (see Table 7.3). Their predilection for urban life has, however, often passed unnoticed. Viewed from this perspective the pioneering kibbutz movement was little more than a rallying call. The reality is that, in 1995, 66 per cent of Israeli Jews lived on 12 per cent of the land, mainly in the urban districts of the centre – Tel Aviv, Jerusalem, Rehovot, Petah-Tiqwa, Ramla and Ashkelon – where they are in a large majority (98 per cent).

As soon as one leaves these towns the Arab world feels very close, whether in terms of distance (since the region is so small) or diversity of religions. Even within its recognized borders, Israel has allowed Arab demography a free rein in the frontier areas. Not only is the Jewish population there less of a majority (79 per cent in the Negev) or already a minority (49 per cent in Galilee)[25] and growing more slowly than the Arab population, but it is also unevenly distributed over the territory: 70 per cent of the Jews of the north (Galilee, Haifa, Sharon) are grouped in ten localities of 20,000 inhabitants or more; 75 per cent of the Arabs in all other localities, those of less than 20,000 inhabitants. Because these villages and hamlets are more dispersed than the towns, the Arabs dominate the interior of the country.[26] Backing onto Lebanon, the seven districts of the north include almost all Israel's 850,000 non-Jews:[27] 82 per cent of Israeli Arabs live between Natanya (20 kilometres from Tel Aviv) and Safad on the Lebanese border.

For security reasons, the Israeli authorities once wanted to prevent such an Arab concentration. In practice what has evolved is the reverse of their intention: a demographic compartmentalization. In 1976, alerted by this disequilibrium, the government called for the 'Judaization of the Galilee'. Linking the growing political activity of the Arabs to their population increase, the Koening Report called for a disguised Arab exodus 'by the encouragement and increase of their difficulties in finding work in Israel and by the intensification of the police presence in the Arab sectors aiming at intimidation,'[28] which would be followed by a return of the Jews. The latter had to be persuaded to stop disdaining the *Gelil ha goyim*, the 'Galilee of many nations' as it was called in the Bible by virtue of the multitude of non-Jewish inhabitants there, Aramains and Phoenicians. The report therefore proposed to colonize 6,000 hectares of good land which would be confiscated from the Arabs. However, various internal and international pressures, especially the 'Levantinization' of the mind among the Jewish population that the founding fathers had so dreaded, blocked the plan. Between 1983 and 1993 the population of Galilee increased by 236,000 inhabitants of which 122,000, more than half, were Arab.

What of the future? Before looking into a crystal ball, we should consider the history of population forecasts and projections. In Israel as elsewhere, demographic projections are both an efficient system of calculating the future supply of population and a reflection of collective psychology. Hypotheses about future patterns of fertility and migration determine the result; but such hypotheses are generally formulated either in a moment of general optimism or in a period of uncertainty. When Israel celebrated its tenth anniversary in 1958, two years after the victory in the Sinai, the mood was positive. Reassured by the military defeat of President Naser, migrants arrived en masse. Jewish fertility, which was so low in Europe and America, was boosted by the arrival of Jews from the Arab world and demographic projections took this into account. It was, therefore, anticipated that the Jewish population would grow so rapidly that it would push the Arab population from 11.1 per cent in 1958 to 10.4 per cent in 1970.[29]

Ten years later the 1967 war enlarged the territory of the State of Israel and the demographers had to begin all over again. They were careful not to include the entire population of the occupied territories in their new calculations, but they did incorporate two new Arab groups into the Israeli population – those of the old town of Jerusalem, taken from the Jordanians, and those of the Golan Heights, taken from Syria – well before the formal annexation of these two areas in 1980 and 1981. The immediate result of this statistical redefinition was to raise the overall proportion of Arabs to 14.1 per cent, and the longer-term effect was to integrate their much higher fertility rate. When an Israeli demographer unveiled the new future the reversal of prospects was striking: by 1993 Arabs would make up 20.6 per cent of the population, that is more than one inhabitant in five.[30] Even within the same unit of study, that is the recognized borders of Israel, for which the 1958 projection had estimated an Arab population of 9 per cent by 1993, the new projection put the proportion at 17 per cent – that is almost double.[31]

In the period after the 1967 war a debate began between the 'territorialists' – those for whom the occupied territories, although inhabited by Arabs, would guarantee the superiority of Israel and therefore peace – and the defenders of the 'demographic majority'

– those for whom the quest for a population as Jewish as possible must remain the priority. This debate influenced a study of the population by Dov Friedlander and Calvin Goldsheider undertaken at the very time that President Sadat was taking a large step towards peace.[32] The authors produced various scenarios, in the framework of a strong hypothesis – a greater Israel that would annex all the occupied territories – and a weak hypothesis – a smaller Israel that would annex only East Jerusalem and the Golan Heights. Even in the latter scenario, the prospect of Arab population growth was inescapable: from 18.2 per cent in 1990 to 21.2 per cent in 2010. Twenty years had changed the rosy expectation of a withering of the Arab community into the certain knowledge that Israel was carrying a millstone around its neck. While Menachem Begin was in the midst of negotiations at Camp David, the statisticians were sending an implicit message that the territorial gains should be abandoned. The realism of the scholars and the gloom of the supporters of Greater Israel now began to permeate the discussions. 'The demographic facts of life in Israel and these areas [the occupied territories]' states one commentary on the Camp David Accords, 'precluded the possibility of annexation or incorporation of Gaza and the West Bank into the State of Israel.'[33]

At the end of the 1980s Israeli officials thought that inward and outward migration would reach an equilibrium.[34] Arrivals had slowed down immediately after the occupation of Lebanon – Operation 'Peace in Galilee' – in 1982 and by 1985 re-emigration exceeded them.[35] Some years later, however, the collapse of Communism, in Ethiopia and especially in eastern Europe, unlocked other doors. In 1990, 181,000 immigrants (Falashas and above all Russians) landed in Israel and 151,000 during 1991[36] – almost as many as in the whole of the previous 18 years (1972–89). A year later the figures were severely cut to 43,000 immigrants in 1992, 43,000 in 1993 and about 45,000 in 1994.

The future of this new wave of migration is unclear: will it continue? at what level? and until when? Will the number who effectively settle there continue to be a third as in the previous decade? And will their fertility remain as low as it was in their native Russia? In their last published projections,[37] Israeli demographers took into account the new migration trends and estimated that between 500,000 and 800,000 Jews from the former Soviet Union might settle before 1995. But a comparison between their forecast and what has actually happened clearly indicates that the flow of immigrants fell short of the demographers' least optimistic assumption by one-third.

In 2001, the Arab population of 'smaller' Israel will finally reach 1 million,[38] and so represent between 16 and 17 per cent of the population, that is to say appreciably more than today despite Jewish immigration. Furthermore, during the first decade of the next century the Palestinians will become the majority in the larger body formed by Israel and the occupied or autonomous territories. Whatever the rhythm and volume of new immigration, it will barely change this.[39] However, the geographical distribution of the population is, as we have noted, uneven. By prolonging the projections until the centenary of Israel in 2048, a horizon which is very conjectural for the demographer but close in the scale of the life of a country, we can see a deepening of distortions which already loom (see Table 7.4). Given the hypothesis that an authoritative distribution of the new immigrants will not alter the imbalances that already exist, the whole of the north (5,100 km^2) – Galilee, the district of Haifa and the sub-district of Sharon – will once more become the biblical 'land of many nations' in which the Arab population will be slightly larger than the Jewish. In the Negev, whose desert stretches over more than half of Israel (12,800 km^2), the Arabs could be almost a majority. In the centre, over less than 3,000 km^2, the conurbations of Tel Aviv and Jerusalem as well as the areas immediately behind would alone retain the homogeneity dreamed of by the founding fathers, with only 6 per cent Arabs.

During the Crusades, these very same regions were of crucial importance to the Franks. Only a few years after their conquest of Jerusalem and the creation of a Latin kingdom in an area close to that of central Israel, the Franks had to guarantee its security by controlling two buffer zones – Galilee in the north and the Negev in the south. The comparison must stop here, for by contrast to the Frank kingdoms of the Levant or the French rule in Algeria, within the borders of Israel there is an immigrant majority which dictates its law to an indigenous minority, the two being separated by a fundamental distinction of identity.

But the demography of Israel is now inscribed in two other, larger circles – that defined by the boundaries of Palestine under the mandate and that formed by the whole Near Eastern, or Arab–Muslim bloc. In the first circle, the demographic game has already been played and its political implications duly taken into account with the Israel/PLO peace agreement; in the second this is even more true. It is, however, here that the new settler community will have to be accepted. War enabled it to live in isolation, but peace will demand intercourse. The Israelis will therefore have to discover the resource of their Arab citizens. The mixed population of the regions in which the Arabs form a growing proportion, on the borders of the neighbouring states, could make them into either buffer zones or thoroughfares. The future will show whether the policies adopted by the State of Israel will fashion them into a bridge that will link the Jewish minority of the Levant to the rest of the confessional mosaic of the East.

Table 7.1: Rate of Population Growth in Palestine by Religion, 1860–1949. (per thousand)

Year	Muslims	Christians	Jews	Total
1860	10.4	16.4	7.4	10.8
1882	10.8	21.7	21.1	12.2
1895	12.3	15.8	32.6	13.5
1905	23.7	17.7	87.1	26.8
1914	-15.2	-35.0	-9.5	-16.7
1918	12.1	19.7	119.6	23.2
1922	21.5	22.2	69.1	28.2
1931	24.7	37.8	156.2	54.6
1936	25.5	24.2	57.5	34.6
1939	30.5	29.8	39.2	33.1
1946	-196.7	-156.9	173.4	-31.6
1949	30.9	3.0	53.7	43.7

Source: Ottoman and British census data.

Table 7.2: Birth and Death Rates by Religion, 1924–1996 (per thousand)

Year	Birth rate				Death rate			
	Muslims	Druze	Christians	Jews	Muslims	Druze	Christians	Jews
1924	55.5	39.0	40.4	38.3	29.9	19.3	16.8	12.6
1925	54.7	59.3	37.2	33.2	31.2	32.5	18.8	15.1
1926	60.2	55.0	40.0	36.0	28.6	34.9	17.9	12.1
1927	56.1	50.3	38.9	35.1	33.0	28.1	20.1	13.4
1928	60.9	45.6	40.4	35.4	35.1	21.0	18.9	12.1
1929	57.7	43.7	37.9	34.1	31.7	26.7	17.9	11.8
1930	60.3	45.0	39.0	33.4	27.9	19.2	16.2	9.6
1931	60.3	51.7	39.0	32.7	29.6	16.5	15.7	9.7
1932	49.0	43.7	36.4	29.2	26.3	22.3	15.9	9.7
1933	49.8	47.0	36.0	29.2	24.1	17.6	14.0	9.3
1934	46.6	41.8	33.5	30.0	26.7	31.0	16.2	9.5
1935	52.6	42.8	34.4	30.6	23.5	21.0	13.9	8.5
1936	53.1	51.0	36.2	29.7	20.0	20.1	12.6	8.8
1937	49.8	44.1	33.6	26.5	24.9	22.8	14.0	7.7
1938	47.2	42.4	34.4	26.3	18.7	16.8	12.5	8.1
1939	46.4	40.9	31.3	23.0	17.4	17.6	11.5	7.6
1940	47.4	50.8	31.1	23.7	24.7	18.1	12.2	8.2
1941	49.2	44.5	29.1	20.7	21.4	21.4	11.1	7.9
1942	45.2	35.1	27.8	22.7	19.9	18.4	12.1	8.6
1943	52.4	49.0	32.6	29.0	19.0	13.1	11.6	7.7
1944	53.7	44.6	31.0	30.2	17.3	17.5	10.1	7.1
1945	54.2	45.0	32.7	30.3	16.7	12.9	9.9	6.7

Table 7.2: (continued0

Year	Birth rate				Death rate			
	Muslims	Druze	Christians	Jews	Muslims	Druze	Christians	Jews
1946	54.2	47.0	33.3	29.1	15.9	17.0	9.1	6.4
1947				30.0				6.2
1948				26.3				6.7
1949				30.0				6.8
1950		43.2*		33.0		9.5*		6.5
1951		46.5*		32.7		8.8*		6.4
1952		45.6*		31.6		11.5*		6.8
1953	53.1	54.0	32.5	30.2	10.4	8.8	8.3	6.3
1954	48.8	48.0	33.6	27.3	9.8	9.2	9.4	6.4
1955	50.1	44.5	34.8	27.2	9.1	9.3	7.0	5.8
1956	51.7	47.1	33.8	26.7	9.8	8.7	8.1	6.3
1957	46.3	48.0	34.4	25.9	8.0	8.2	7.3	5.9
1962	51.7	46.7	34.9	22.5	6.4	6.8	6.9	5.8
1967	51.0	43.6	30.4	22.5	6.1	5.3	5.9	6.7
1972	49.5	42.7	26.9	24.3	5.8	5.3	7.0	7.3
1975	46.3		25.6	25.0	5.6		6.7	7.4
1976	47.0		25.5	25.1	4.9		6.3	7.1
1977	44.6	41.8	24.6	23.6	5.0	5.0	6.4	7.2
1978	42.6		23.7	22.3	4.7		6.0	7.2
1979	42.1		23.1	22.0	4.3		6.2	7.1
1980	38.9	39.2	22.1	22.0	4.2	4.4	6.1	7.2
1981	37.3	36.1	20.0	21.4	3.9	4.0	5.7	7.1

Table 7.2: (continued0

Year	Birth rate				Death rate			
	Muslims	Druze	Christians	Jews	Muslims	Druze	Christians	Jews
1982	37.3	36.0	20.3	21.8	3.8	4.0	5.9	7.4
1983	36.6	35.8	20.3	22.0	3.7	4.5	5.9	7.5
1984	36.0	32.7	19.2	21.6	3.7	3.6	5.8	7.3
1985	34.8	31.6	18.3	21.6	3.7	3.4	5.2	7.2
1986	33.8	30.8	22.0	21.2	3.4	3.4	5.6	7.5
1987	34.4	30.5	22.3	20.5	3.4	3.6	5.3	7.3
1988	35.5	30.5	22.1	20.2	3.5	3.1	5.4	7.2
1989	36.2	30.8	22.8	19.7	3.3	3.6	5.4	7.0
1990	36.8	31.0	22.2	19.4	3.2	3.4	4.8	6.8
1991	37.4	29.1	19.9	18.6	3.2	3.5	4.4	6.9
1992	37.0	30.5	18.9	18.7	3.4	3.6	4.6	7.2
1993	37.5	30.3	18.5	18.5	3.1	3.6	4.3	6.9
1994	37.1	29.2	18.7	18.4	3.0	4.0	4.3	6.9
1995	37.9	28.8	16.7	18.1	3.0	4.0	4.3	7.1
1996**	37.3	27.9	16.1	18.3	2.9	4.0	4.3	7.0

* Total non-Jews

** First six months

Sources: For the Mandate period, Justin McCarthy, *The Population of Palestine*, New York, Columbia University Press, 1990. From 1948, Central Bureau of Statistics, *Statistical Abstracts of Israel*, Jerusalem, 1950–94. For 1996, Central Bureau of Statistics, *Monthly Bulletin of Statistics*, Jerusalem, October 1996

Table 7.3: Jewish Population of the Arab Countries and Turkey c. 1948 and Immigration to Israel, 1948–86 (in thousands)

Country	Jews in 1948	1948–1951	1952–1960	1961–1964	1965–1971	1972–1979	Total
Turkey 1945	77.0	34.5	6.9	4.8	9.3	3.1	60.4
Syria 1948	31.0	2.7	1.9	1.3	0.9	0.8	8.5
Lebanon1948	5.2	0.2	0.8	0.2	2.1	0.6	4.0
Jordan 1948	0.2						0.1
Iraq 1947	120.0	123.3	3.0	0.5	1.6	0.9	129.4
North Yemen 1948	46.0	45.0	0.8	0.5	0.1		46.4
South Yemen 1948	5.0	3.3	0.4	0.2	0.3		4.2
Saudi Arabia 1948	0.2	0.2					0.2
Egypt 1947	67.0	8.8	17.5	1.2	1.7	0.5	30.0
Libya 1948	38.0	31.0	2.1	0.3	2.1	0.2	35.8
Tunisia 1946	74.0	13.3	23.6	3.8	7.8	2.1	52.2
Algeria 1941	130.0	3.8	3.4	9.7	3.2	2.1	23.7
Morocco 1948	265.0	28.3	95.9	100.4	30.2	7.8	265.7
Sub-total	858.6	294.4	156.3	122.9	59.3	18.1	660.6
Total immigrants		686.7	294.5	228.0	197.8	267.6	1250.3

Sources: Central Bureau of Statistics, *Immigration to Israel – 1986*, Jerusalem, 1987; Population censuses, *Encyclopedia Judaica*

Table 7.4: Arab and Jewish Population of Israel from 1948 and Projected to 2048. (in thousands)

Year	1948	1961	1972	1983	1990	1995	2000	2005	2010	2015	2020	2025	2030	2035	2040	2045	2048
North																	
Jews	228	602	780	937	1,089	1,273	1,308	1,339	1,367	1,391	1,412	1,430	1,446	1,458	1,468	1,475	1,478
Arabs	128	208	320	465	583	687	782	876	969	1,059	1,145	1,225	1,300	1,368	1,430	1,485	1,509
Centre																	
Jews	471	1,252	1,734	2,182	2,594	3,085	3,221	3,352	3477	3,597	3,711	3,820	3,924	4,023	4,116	4,206	4,248
Arabs	15	21	25	39	54	67	80	96	117	130	148	168	189	211	233	257	269
South																	
Jews	1	79	171	231	264	304	308	311	313	315	315	315	314	312	310	307	306
Arabs	13	18	30	44	72	88	104	121	139	158	178	198	219	239	260	281	291
Total																	
Jews	700	1,933	2,685	3,350	3,947	4,663	4,838	5,003	5,158	5,303	5,439	5,566	5,683	5,793	5,894	5,988	6,032
Arabs	156	247	375	548	708	842	966	1,093	1,221	1,347	1,471	1,592	1,708	1,819	1,924	2,023	2,069

North: districts of Galilee, Haifa, sub-district of Sharon.
Centre: districts of Jerusalem, Tel-Aviv and of the centre excluding Sharon, sub-district of Ashkelon.
South: sub-district of Beer Sheva

Table 7.4: Arab and Jewish Population of Israel from 1948 and Projected to 2048. Percentage of Arabs. (continued)

Year	1948	1961	1972	1983	1990	1995	2000	2005	2010	2015	2020	2025	2030	2035	2040	2045	2048
North	36.0	25.7	29.1	33.2	34.9	35.0	37.4	39.6	41.5	43.2	44.8	46.1	47.3	48.4	49.4	50.2	50.5
Centre	3.1	1.6	1.4	1.8	2.0	2.1	2.4	2.8	3.1	3.5	3.8	4.2	4.6	5.0	5.4	5.8	6.0
South	92.9	18.6	14.9	16.0	21.4	22.4	25.2	28.0	30.8	33.5	36.1	38.6	41.1	43.4	45.6	47.7	48.8
Total	18.2	11.3	12.3	14.1	15.2	15.3	16.6	17.9	19.2	20.3	21.3	22.2	23.1	23.9	24.6	25.3	25.5

North: districts of Galilee, Haifa, sub-district of Sharon.
Centre: districts of Jerusalem, Tel-Aviv and of the centre excluding Sharon, sub-district of Ashkelon.
South: sub-district of Beer Sheva

Sources: projection of total population: to 2005, Central Bureau of Statistics, *Monthly Bulletin of Statistics*, supplement, October 1991 (excluding East Jerusalem and Golan for the Arabs).

For 2010–2048, extrapolation of the trend of compound rates of growth for the period 1990–2005.

For regional populations, Central Bureau of Statistics, *Statistical Abstract of Israel*, Jerusalem, 1991, extrapolation of proportional changes.

CHAPTER EIGHT

Arab Christianity in The Twentieth Century: Decline or Eclipse?

The history of Arabism is made up of continuous links forming a tight chain. If one considers that the bond of the Arabic language and culture across these countries is closer than in any other area of the world, and that religious tolerance was born, has prospered and still exists between different religions in the neighbouring countries, one will be persuaded that my phrase 'the Egyptians are Arabs' expresses these affinities. [Makram Obeid, a militant Copt of the Wafd Party[1]]

The Ottoman Empire favoured Christian and Jewish demography; but the colonial interlude and, even more so, independence had quite the opposite effect. Under the pressures set in motion by the creation of Israel, Jews almost disappeared from Arab countries. There was, however, no sudden political turning point for Eastern Christianity, which experienced neither the massacres nor the expulsions that wiped out Christianity in Turkey. On the contrary, the relative decline of the Eastern Christian population after the First World War has been the result of a slow, silent, process: a convergence of mortality rates, a re-arrangement of fertility rates, and emigration – general features of a differential demography that are still with us.

The Decline of Christian Communities

Two facts inhibit a proper comparison of the situation of Christian communities before and after the collapse of the Ottoman Empire. The first is the re-organization of the political map of the Middle East by the mandatory powers after the First World War and as a result of the 1948 war between Israel and its neighbours. Of all the Arab states that have a Christian community today, only Egypt retains more or less the same borders that it had a century ago. Egyptian census data thus allows us to follow the progress of the three religions since 1882. To the east of Suez, however, Ottoman administrative divisions, which had in many places corresponded to ethnic–linguistic or religious divisions, were replaced after 1918 by borders which reflected the military and economic interests of the mandatory powers rather than social and political realities.

Although the new borders do not correspond to the old it is still possible, thanks to the very detailed Ottoman censuses taken at intervals between 1881 and 1914, to reconstruct the population of the period into the current division between national states (see Table 8.1). This invaluable material, and the detailed panorama of society that can be derived from it, was for almost three-quarters of a century kept under lock and key. Recently unearthed and analysed by the Turkish scholar Kemal Karpat,[2] it corrects the picture that has hitherto been diffused in the literature by European observers, often very considerably. Members of the diplomatic service and scholarly societies knew of the existence of these Ottoman surveys but they had no idea of their precise contents. Furthermore, whether as a result of their personal sympathies, or simply because they could acquire information more easily from the Christian elite, they were often inclined to overestimate the importance of the Christian community.[3]

The Ottoman statistics are the last to provide a picture of the distribution of the population by communities. Among the former Arab lands of the Ottoman Empire, only Egypt and Jordan have maintained the practice of counting the population according to their religion (see Table 8.2). Iraq and Syria continued to collect such statistics until the 1960s when the secular ideology of the ruling Ba'th Party required that all reference to religion be eliminated. In Lebanon, where religion is the principal criterion in the allocation of political roles and administrative duties, the census itself has been prohibited since the end of the French mandate (1943) because the trends the figures would reveal have become an issue. Finally, although Israel has always been meticulous about recording the religious identity of its nationals, it has not kept this kind of detail for the occupied territories since 1967.

The early part of the twentieth century was a golden age for Arab Christians. They felt firmly established and, eager to pursue progress,[4] they helped to promote the new idea of an Arab nation. The death of the Ottoman Empire had sealed the fate of an organized Muslim community (*umma islamiyya*), which had for a long time kept the Christians in the ambivalent status of *dhimmi*, a community that was under juridical subjection yet at the same time enjoyed economic and cultural pre-eminence. The *khatt-i sherif* of 1839 and the Tanzimat of 1856 and 1867 had established statutory equality. But these reforms, which were soon abolished by Sultan Abdül-hamid, went against their original intention and caused tensions. In the vacuum of a world which had to be recreated, two main successors appeared – Turkish nationalism and Islamic fundamentalism. Neither promised a particularly sunny future for Arab Christianity.

In the face of nascent Turkish nationalism, which excluded the Arab territories of the empire from its plans for renewal, and Islamic fundamentalism which excluded non-Muslims, in the years after the First World War the Christian intellectuals of the Levant proposed alternatives. Some – like Suleiman Boustani, a minister and member of the Ottoman Diet – were 'Ottomanists' who retained their attachment to the 'sick man', and called for its restoration[5] – a position which at the end of the twentieth century, rife with disillusion over the nation-state in the Near East, is beginning to find new favour among intellectuals from the region.[6] Centrifugal nationalisms, Lebanese, Assyrian and so on, also acquired some followers. But there were in addition, among Christians as well as Muslims, people who proclaimed an identity based on their common language; Arabism was born in the two communities simultaneously. 'O sons of the Arabs, glorify the Arabic language and you will live! Under tents, Arabs were kings; now in your castles will you be slaves?' wrote the Christian author Butros Boustani (1819–83).

At this point the economic opportunities and the idea of modernity that Eastern Christians drew from their links with Europe did not compromise their relations with the Muslim environment. French and British intrusion into the affairs of the region had not assumed the magnitude that it did under the mandates. This rather favourable situation benefited Christian demography and during this period Christians made up a larger proportion of the population than at any time since the Crusades: 26.4 per cent in the Near East (Syria, Palestine and Lebanon in 1914) and 8 per cent in Egypt. In Iraq where, 500 years earlier, the intolerance of the Mongols had definitively marginalized Christians they were only 2.2 per cent of the population. But whereas in Iraq the proportion of Christians grew slowly until 1960 (to 3.1 per cent), in the other countries it dwindled – to 10.1 per cent in the Near East as a whole (Lebanon,

Syria, Israel and Jordan) in 1990 and 5.8 per cent in Egypt. This decline was the result not of violence but of the free play of demographic forces (see Table 8.3).

Religion And Mortality Rates

In Egypt,[7] at the beginning of the century and earlier,[8] Christians enjoyed better conditions of health than Muslims. In 1900, both in the Delta and in Upper Egypt, the regions with the most Christians were those with the lowest infant mortality (see Table 8.4). This correspondence may, of course, simply indicate that Christians lived in regions where the mortality rate was moderate for all, including Muslims. But from 1944 the statistics give mortality rates by religion, demonstrating a higher rate among Muslims that persisted in independent Egypt (see Table 8.5).[9] Over time, however, the difference between the communities was reduced. By 1920 the regional correlation had already disappeared and, as very high mortality rates fell overall, the advantage of the Christians over the Muslims diminished, apparently disappearing during the 1970s.[10]

In the case of Palestine more detailed information is available [11] thanks to the statistical series kept by the Registry Office under the British mandate and continued by Israel after 1948. In the years before the creation of Israel, the life expectancy of Christians was almost 10 years greater than that of Muslims and Druze.[12] The Christians undoubtedly had a geographical advantage, being firmly established in the towns: 75 per cent of Jews and Christians were town-dwellers in 1931 compared to less than 30 per cent of the Muslims and Druze.[13] In addition, the Christians had a sociological advantage: the number of children aged 5 to 14 years receiving a primary education was already 90 per cent in 1943, as against 25 per cent among Muslims.[14] The Israeli statistics show that, while infant mortality in the two communities has fallen considerably,[15] to this day the Muslims have not quite caught up with the Christians (see Table 8.6). The gap, however, is now less than 4.5 years whereas it exceeded 9 years in the period 1970–74.

In the 1960s, Lebanon showed much greater inequalities than the rest of the region, with the level of infant mortality among the Muslims about 50 per cent higher than that among Christians (see Table 8.7). The social and geographical factors behind the differential growth were also more varied. A pertinent example is the Lebanese Shi'a, who in recent years have mobilized under the banner of the 'disinherited of the earth'.[16] But this it is not only because Shi'ism has always been an Islam in revolt. With a large peasant class dispossessed by the local feudalism of the south and the Beqa'a valley, the Shi'i community showed all the characteristics of underdevelopment that the other communities were spared – a restrictive tribalism, low income, a high level of illiteracy, and a regional base isolated from the main lines of communication. The polite claims of the working class, organized in trade unions, were echoed more spontaneously, in the uproar of the Shi'i campaign in the countryside: for example, in the uprising by the tobacco planters in the South in 1973. On the other hand, in Beirut at the beginning of the 1980s, the civil war which divided Christians and Muslims placed identical existential constraints in their way, making them apparently indistinguishable. An inquiry into the state of health of the population of Beirut in 1984 demonstrated that similar behaviour by the two communities in matters of health[17] could explain a similar level of infant and juvenile mortality. Around 1980, between 50 and 60 per thousand of new-born children died before the age of five years, irrespective of religion.[18]

In the case of Iraq, Jordan and Syria there are no statistics to show differences in mortality according to religion.

Reactions to the Western Family Model

In the Ottoman period it is probable that Christians had a higher birth rate than Muslims.[19] However, in the twentieth century the situation has been reversed. Among Muslims the birth rate has increased as a result of a consolidation of the family: divorce, which formerly displaced one-third of Muslim women at the peak of their reproductive years,[20] has become less common. Simultaneously the Christians started to limit their births.

Egypt

In Egypt in the 1940s the birth rate of Muslims exceeded that of Christians by 30 per cent and the gap has remained remarkably constant until the present day (see Table 8.8).[21] The only exception has been the period 1954–58, the beginning of the Naser era, when the birth rate collapsed among Christians but was maintained among Muslims. One reason for this could, of course, be that the political change brought about by the 1952 revolution was sufficiently radical to disorganize the administration and that the registration of births was disrupted rather than the birth rate itself. However, there is no reason why this should be the case for one group and not others. A better explanation is that events sometimes affect the birth-rate by raising collective anxieties, and while Naserism did not threaten Muslims as a community, it caused Christians to halt their reproduction: one of a number of signs that they felt insecure.

From 1805 until the revolution of 1952 which overthrew the dynasty of Muhammad Ali, a climate of harmony had prevailed between the two communities in Egypt. The Copts had helped to build independence by supporting the Urabi revolt in 1882 and supplying cadres and militants to Sa'ad Zaghlul's Wafd Party.[22] But they had reservations about the 1952 revolution, many of whose leaders, the Free Officers, sympathized with the Muslim Brotherhood, or like the future president Anwar al-Sadat, had even been members of the organization. Furthermore, the republic very soon limited their power. As a secular state it suppressed the religious tribunals, thus subjecting Christians to a civil law influenced by the Muslim *shari'a*. Being egalitarian, it promoted the fight against illiteracy while imposing the study of the Qur'an on all pupils in the state schools. Finally, when it became socialist under the presidency of Gamal Abd al-Naser, Egypt enacted nationalization laws (in 1964) and an agrarian reform which destroyed a class of businessmen and landowners with a large Christian component.[23]

The unhappy situation of the Christians prompted a massive 'return' to Lebanon of Syrian Christians, some of whom had been in Egypt since the seventeenth century. The Copts, who had lived along the Nile throughout their history, chose another form of community withdrawal: they abandoned the regions where they were weakest to gather in Cairo and in the Upper Egyptian towns of Minya, Asyut and Beni-Suef where larger communities offered a feeling of security. A generation later, these same provincial towns have become centres of Islamic activism and religious exclusion. Gripped by a level of religious fear unknown in Egypt since the reign of Baybars seven centuries ago, the Copts have been driven by sackings of their churches and businesses to group in specific districts or to go into exile.

The birth-rate among the Copts began to fall before that of the Muslims, and before modern contraception existed. When new contraceptive devices did become available, the differential between the two populations was maintained but did not increase. It is probable that the Copts were less inclined to adopt contraception than Muslims. On 26 March 1964, ten years ahead of other Arab countries except Bourguiba's Tunisia, Naser defied tradition by stating in the National Assembly that he favoured a policy of birth control. But the Coptic hierarchy which, like other Christian churches, believed that contraception violated various divine commandments, did not welcome the move. In addition, their strong misgivings as a minority strengthened their reticence: 'We already share the difficulties of all the minorities of the world,' declared one Coptic dignitary, 'must we increase them by reducing our size? By encouraging birth control we are hurrying towards racial suicide.'[24]

Whether the Egyptian statistics tell the truth about the Copts is a hotly debated question. How, some critics have asked, can their population be no more than 3 million in a country which, in languages other than Arabic, carries their name? In Arabic Egypt is called Misr, which formerly signified 'capital' or 'borders'. But in all other languages its name shows a clear etymological relationship discovered by Volney, a scholarly traveller of the eighteenth century: 'They claim that the name of the Copts comes from the town of Coptos where they retreated, it is said, at the time of the persecutions by the Greeks; but I believe that its origin is more natural and more ancient. The Arabic term *qoubti* (a Copt) seems to me an evident alteration of the Greek *ai-goupti-os* (an Egyptian).'[25] Apart from the name, Egypt is profoundly influenced by the culture of these first inhabitants who are proud of their Pharaonic ancestry; is it reasonable to believe, therefore, that Copts are only between 5 and 6 per cent of the population?

In a book which is otherwise well documented we find the following unsubstantiated statement about the Copts, one that accepts the idea of falsified statistics uncritically: 'The 1976 census evaluated them at two and a half million people, which is undoubtedly too low. The reality is certainly closer to 7 or 8 million.'[26] Christian Cannuyer, in his recent book on the Copts, similarly distances itself from a century of census work in Egypt:

The question of their number is impossible to resolve. In the 1986 census they account for 8 per cent of the Egyptians [that is, almost 3,300,000],[27] which is better than the 6.3 per cent in the 1976 census, but remains a *noqta*, a 'joke': the more or less systematic manipulation by Muslim officials and the holding back of information on the part of the Copts, renders this figure [for 1986] barely credible. On the basis of its baptism registers the Church claims 11 million faithful, but this time the estimate seems to be far-fetched. As a half-way hypothesis, the number of 7 to 8 million Copts is put forward.[28]

The Western press, which has difficulty acknowledging that a minority is a minority, often accepts these over-estimates. The propensity for numerical inflation is not, however, new: 'These figures seem to be a little far-fetched,'[29] pointed out Pierre Rondot, commenting on the estimates of Father Idlibi who believed that Egypt had 3 million Christians in 1952.

However, if there has been under-estimation in the official statistics, it has been remarkably consistent over the years. Since 1882 the censuses have shown a perfectly regular decline in the Coptic population. Furthermore, political regimes in the twentieth century have been rather fickle in their attitude to the Copts. Had they wanted to manipulate the figures, some administrations would have over-estimated and others under-estimated their numbers. The British mandatory authority, for example, would have had an interest in magnifying the size of the community on which it occasionally relied – notably for recruiting its officials. Today, on the other hand, there might be a tendency on the part of the Copts themselves to suppress their religion wherever they fear the appearance of Islamic fundamentalism. If the figures were false, we should therefore expect a break between the trends they depict before and after the regime of Naser. But there is no such break.

There is further evidence to support the reliability of the official figures: the statistics of the Registrar General, which record a lower birth rate among the Copts, and the censuses which record a slower growth of their community, are perfectly coherent. If the Copt community today consisted of 11 rather than 3 million people, their 90,000 births per annum would correspond to a birth rate of 11 per thousand instead of 30 per thousand. Such a low rate would be quite incompatible with maintaining the proportion of Copts in the population. It is of course possible that some Copts hide their religion and it is also possible that a confusion over names leads census takers to sometimes enter the Muslim religion on their returns. But how would this dissimulation affect, with the same frequency and over such a long period, two independent operations – the periodic census of the population and the registration of births performed at almost the same time as baptism, an eminently religious act?

The slow decline of the Copts of Egypt, from 8 to 6 per cent of the population in just a century, is not in fact the result of any statistical plot but simply the demographic consequence of the social advances of their community.[30] Examples abound, not only in the East, of communities making a demographic overbid, as though a minority must come numerically as close as possible to the majority in order to merit attention. The *pieds-noirs* in Algeria, the Greeks and the Armenians in Turkey, the Assyro–Chaldeans in Iraq all overestimated their size – and in doing so drank from a poisoned chalice.

The Palestinians

Whereas in Egypt differences in the birth rate by religion were quite small, among the Palestinians there was a marked contrast between communities. The creation of the State of Israel was a rupture in the history of the Palestinian people, and given its radical impact on their geographical distribution it is not difficult to imagine that it affected their reproduction as well. But the upheaval also affected the statistics, in such a way that the demographic indicators reflect both the population change and the effects of the administrative changeover. Before 1948 the British records entered the births of the whole population of Palestine. After 1948 the Israeli administration continued to gather statistics according to religion;[31] but these only related to the small number of Palestinians of Israeli nationality (18 per cent in 1948, 15 per cent in 1995) and, after 1967, those from the occupied territories (29 per cent).

Despite the ruptures this exceptionally long series provides us with some certainties. First, for at least 70 years Christian families in Palestine have been much smaller than Druze families, which in turn have been smaller than other Muslim families. Under the mandate, religion had a strong influence on family norms; on average Christian women had five children and Muslim eight. Under the Israeli administration, the gap first widened and then narrowed. At the beginning of the 1970s, the total fertility rate among Muslims increased to nine children per woman,[32] as if the large family provided a refuge for Muslims but not for Christians whose fertility dropped.

At the same time, the misfortunes experienced by the population of the West Bank and Gaza and their consequent politicization frustrated what demographers had believed to be a law. Here the population simultaneously held three records which were *a priori* incompatible: their level of education,[33] urbanization (100 per cent in Gaza) and their fertility (see Table 8.9). In most other situations, where community and political tensions are less acute, progress in primary education and a lowering of fertility go together. Both arise from changing family roles, especially the status of children: when children joined the working population at a young age this favoured a large number of offspring; by contrast the cost of a prolonged education generally discourages parents from having many children.

In the occupied territories, however, UNRWA accepted partial responsibility for education expenses and thus helped to relieve the economic burden that unproductive children represent. But it is not for this reason that the large family is still as highly valued in the West Bank and Gaza as it was formerly in the countryside. The eight or nine children born to Palestinian woman here represent a political act rather than an economic resource.[34] By contrast, Palestinian women of Israeli nationality have two or three times fewer children, depending on whether they are Muslim or Christian. Never before, and in no other place, have the differences between groups been so marked; but the determinant of differential fertility in this exceptional case is political status rather than religion. Thus Gaza, a camp city in a constant state of insecurity, stands at the head of the fertility stakes. In 1989, when the Intifada had been in progress for more than a year and the secularism of the PLO was being challenged by the Islamism of HAMAS, the fertility rate reached a peak, with an average of 9.5 children recorded for Gazan women. The West Bank, which despite everything retains some of the characteristics of a structured society, comes next. Last in line are the Israeli Arabs among whom the second generation, who have now reached childbearing age, tend to adopt the behaviour of the society of which they have inadvertently become a part.

It is impossible to ignore the link between fertility and politics in this pattern. The diverging fertility trends since 1980 observed among Palestinian communities are partly a demographic response to politics. Around this date the Islamic Resistance Movement, Harakat al-Muqawama al-Islamiyya, more commonly known under its acronym HAMAS (courage) was formed. In one of its first tracts, this movement, which proved attractive to the youth of Gaza and the West Bank, claimed the primacy of Islam in the struggle for Palestine: 'The PLO has adopted the idea of the secular state which completely contradicts the idea of religion. The Islamism of Palestine is part of our religion. The day the PLO adopts Islam as a way of life, we will become its soldiers.'[35] Perhaps by omission, the Christians were thus *ipso facto* excluded from the defence of the national cause despite the eminence of their political and intellectual representatives.

Palestinian Christians are increasingly choosing individual success as their goal. The Muslim population of Gaza and the West Bank on one hand, and the Israeli Arabs on the other both place their hopes in the family. But while the former have opted for a large family group the latter, and especially the Christians among them, have preferred to concentrate on the social promotion of their children – which very clearly means a small family.

Lebanon

In Lebanon, both Islam and Christianity are more diverse than in Egypt or Palestine. On the eve of the civil war of 1975, a relatively high fertility rate was still current among the Maronites (see Table 8.10). It seemed that not only was the spirit of the mountain still alive among them, but that they also feared becoming a minority in a country where, constitutionally, they held both a majority in parliament and the presidency of the state. The 1926 electoral law had set out a fixed division of parliamentary seats according to confession,[36] and the national pact of 1943 – a verbal agreement between the Maronite politician Beshara al-Khuri and the Sunni Riad al-Solh – had reserved the presidency of the republic to a Maronite, the post of prime minister to a Sunni and the presidency of the Chamber of Deputies to a Shi'a. This division of powers was inspired by the distribution of the population shown in the 1922 and 1932 censuses[37] and was maintained until 1989 when an agreement negotiated in dramatic circumstances in Taif between the survivors of the last Lebanese parliament, elected in 1973, revised some of the provisions of the old national pact in the interests of re-establishing confessional harmony. Under the Taif agreement, the distribution of high offices remained unchanged and the presidency was still reserved to a Christian. But parliamentary equality was granted to the Muslims[38] and, ironically, given a conference venue in the heart of Wahhabi Arabia, the arrangements were confirmed in writing for the first time.

While politics had kept the confessional allocations static, the demography of the various religious communities had been moving for a long time. There was certainly a widespread awareness of this on-going redistribution, which in 1960 pushed President Chehab to introduce parity between Muslims and Christians in public office,[39] but it remained unspoken. This is why, after 1932, no population count was undertaken in Lebanon although the census – which was perceived as an anti-constitutional act – was never prohibited in writing any more than the national pact itself was committed to paper.

By 1960 the proportion of Christians in the population had certainly decreased, and their birth rate continued to fall in subsequent years.[40] By the mid-1980s, with a total fertility rate of 2.1 children per woman,[41] the Lebanese Christians, despite their proximity to areas where fertility among certain populations is presently at a peak – until recently the Lebanese in Jabal Amel, and above all the Palestinians in Gaza and the West Bank – were the first Arab population to achieve a demographic transition, the effects of which were accentuated by emigration.

Nevertheless, the Christians today still form about 40–45 per cent of the Lebanese population.[42] The straightened circumstances of Christian communities in neighbouring countries have, paradoxically, strengthened their position in Lebanon. In the 1950s and 1960s a large migration of Syrian, Egyptian and Iraqi nationals, mainly Christians, took place to Beirut, a city they apparently perceived as a haven. Many were subsequently naturalized and there can be no doubt that they were warmly welcomed by Christian politicians, as an impassioned statement made by president-elect Bashir Jumayyil on the very day of his assassination, 14 September 1982, demonstrates:

> Lebanon is a homeland for all Christians, for others than ourselves if they want to come. We must protect it. We want to be present for ever in this East. We have a country where we can live with our heads held high without someone coming to order us 'go to the left!' as in the time of the Turks. We refuse to live in dhimmitude.[43]

Even President Fouad Chehab (1958–64), perhaps the only Lebanese statesman to remain above his confessional clientele and, though a Christian, to fight for the social promotion of the Muslims also favoured Christian population growth through naturalization.[44]

The Greek Orthodox of Lebanon, like their Palestinian co-religionists,[45] but unlike the Maronites, soon followed the demographic patterns prevalent in the north of the Mediterranean. This might appear paradoxical for, being the spiritual heirs of Byzantium – and its quarrels with Rome – they are the most 'Oriental' of the Christians of the Levant and have the closest relationship with their

Muslim neighbours. At the time of the Crusades they had remained loyal to the local Muslim governments and, because they were not suspected of any allegiance to the Franks, they had no need to isolate themselves behind a mountain range but could flourish in the coastal regions beside the Sunnis. Together with the Sunnis they formed the first nucleus of coastal towns, starting with Beirut, which developed in the middle of the nineteenth century because of their access to Europe. From Beirut, Aleppo, Damascus, Latakia and Jaffa they controlled the commercial routes throughout the Ottoman Empire. The break up of the empire and the creation of Greater Lebanon in 1920 went some way to reducing their political and economic prerogatives[46] and the pre-eminent Christian community to the East of Suez suddenly became the second of the Christian communities and the fourth of the confessions in the young state. When the new borders cut them off from their co-religionists and commercial partners in Palestine (in 1948) and Syria (in 1952), they had to redirect their activity and it was to the Western world that they gravitated.

The history of the Greek Catholics was close to that of the Orthodox, from whom they had split.[47] Like the Orthodox, the Greek Catholics clustered in Beirut as well as on the route linking Damascus to the Mediterranean,[48] and in demographic terms there was little difference between them. Calmly accepting their minority status, these two communities are widely represented in the intelligentsia and among the business bourgeoisie. Rather than playing the numbers game (which they cannot win), they attempt to maintain the advantage of holding a high position. Greek catholic women have a role in society as well as in the family and female children are heirs: for this reason a small family is preferable for this group.

Among the Muslim groups reproductive behaviour also divides neatly.[49] The Lebanese Sunnis are townspeople with no roots in the mountains[50] and are to the Shi'a what the Orthodox are to the Maronites. From 1970 they have displayed clear signs of Malthusianism. Consequently, two generations after those in Istanbul,[51] they were some way ahead of the Sunni Muslims in the rest of the world.[52] A minority like any other group in Lebanon, their community drew confidence from belonging to a large majority within Islam. Thus freed from the obsession with numbers, it adopted some of the values of the pre-war multi-confessional society which was then dominated by the Christian relationship with the West.[53]

In the time of the Fatimids, the Shi'a had been the majority

Muslim community but they were later persecuted by the Mamluks who drove them back to the Jabal Amel and the Beqaʻa. Volney, writing at the end of the eighteenth century, found their numbers much reduced and believed that they would probably become an extinct group:

> At this time there are no more than 500 Metawali [Shiʻi] families who have taken refuge in the Anti-Lebanon and the Lebanon of the Maronites; and henceforth banned from their native land it is likely that they will ultimately vanish and take with them the very name of the nation.[54]

Volney was a remarkably perceptive observer and many of his predictions have proved correct. He was, however, wrong about the future of the Shiʻa in Lebanon whose demographic recovery began in the mid-twentieth century and has continued until recently. While Lebanon as a whole has the lowest fertility rate in the Arab world, the rural Shiʻa remained an exception to the general trend until the mid-1980s. In 1984 young wives in the south of the country had 4.5 children by the time they were 30, while those aged 50 had eight.[55]

Shiʻi expansion in the urban areas began in the years before the 1975–90 war when they left their poor, feudal enclaves in the south and the Beqaʻa and settled in the suburbs of Beirut. Before the proclamation of Greater Lebanon there were almost no Shiʻa in the capital – as few as 80 in 1895 and 1,500 in 1920.[56] In 1950 their community was still modest in size – 28,000 people, that is 6 per cent of the population.[57] In 1975, they were estimated to be 316,000,[58] that is 29 per cent of the population of Greater Beirut. The military and economic destruction that came soon after this date added to the exodus.

Under the pressure of war, both Maronite and Shiʻi groups fled from the mountains to Beirut. Both constructed new suburbs rather than live in the centre of the city which was left to the old owners, Greek Orthodox in the east and Sunnis in the west. But although there were superficial similarities in the movement of these two groups into the city they were in fact very different. The Maronites simply consolidated and extended a base that had been established for several generations. For the Shiʻa retreating before the Israeli occupying force, the town was a new discovery. A few were able to set up home in sometimes luxurious apartments abandoned by their owners (often Christian), but most were forced to construct the poverty belt that became the southern suburbs. Their migration took no more than ten years and overturned the social make-up of the west of the capital – a change that will, without doubt, be seen by history as one of the greatest in the Lebanese population.

The Lebanese statistics reveal some hidden facts of differential demography. The manner in which Eastern Christianity has been marginalized in modern times arises in one way or another from its proximity to Western Christianity. Previously this proximity was political; it is now cultural. Maronites, Greek Catholics and Orthodox were not merely content to adopt as a norm – admittedly with a delay – the small family size found in the West; they have followed the same methods and adopted the same values. At the beginning of the 1970s, after the fashion of the French in the last century but in the age of the contraceptive pill, the Christians of Lebanon controlled their fertility by natural methods which did not clash with the moral rules laid down by the pope.[59] Muslim women, whether Sunni or Shi'a, were at the time more familiar with modern contraceptive methods despite their much higher fertility.

The status of the Christian minorities under the Ottomans had allowed them the exercise – sometimes the near monopoly – of certain economic positions. Membership in the Christian community had early on given them access to those societies with the most substantial material progress. These societies maintained close contact with the Christians of the East, notably through the Catholic and Protestant schools and universities,[60] whose first achievement was the birth of a Christian elite. However, this created, at the very foundation of the societies of the Levant, an educational inequality which was decisive in the confessional dialogue for the simple reason that it set into motion the demographic process that was to transform the equilibrium between the different communities. The service industries and urbanization, a comfortable social position, school education, for women as well as men – these factors associated with an early demographic transition were combined among the Christians rather than the Muslims. However, at different times they produced quite opposite results: in the Ottoman period Christian population growth accelerated, in the twentieth century it slowed down.

Migration and the Search for Co-Religionists

Historically, the Eastern Christians have been, above all, a people who belonged to a land, even if that land was a town – a characteristic that has, without any doubt, protected them for more than a thousand years. Until the middle of the nineteenth century they effectively experienced no movement at all, with the exception of the Syrians who had settled in Cairo or Alexandria a century earlier. With the Syrio–Lebanese emigration from 1860, and the push from the towns in the Fertile Crescent and from the Nile Valley, this long-standing pattern changed: today it is mobility which maintains the dynamism of Eastern Christian communities.

To look first at Egypt, a country divided into two parts by its capital, Cairo. Christians disappeared from the rural areas of Lower Egypt a long time ago and now they make up only 1.5 per cent of the population of the Delta (excluding Alexandria). Even in Alexandria itself, the confessional mosaic which Lawrence Durrell depicted so vividly in his *Alexandrian Quartet* has now faded.[61] The city's non-Muslim inhabitants fell from 26 to 6 per cent of the population between 1927 and 1986, and also lost their diversity. Besides the Jews, whose numbers fell from 24,690 in 1937 to 64 in 1986, many foreigners have left Alexandria, and this Mediterranean metropolis, which had nearly 100,000 foreigners among its 700,000 inhabitants on the eve of the Second World War,[62] has now been transformed into a gigantic locality of almost 3 million inhabitants in which foreigners are no more than a small nucleus of 10,000 people.[63] Port Said and Isma'ilia, two towns which were created as a result of the construction of the Suez Canal,[64] have for 75 years been progressively deserted by Christians who made up 25 per cent of their population on the eve of the First World War but are today barely 4 per cent. In fact Isma'ilia not only saw the birth of the Suez Canal Company, of which it was the seat, but also of modern Islamism – it was there in 1928 that Hasan al-Banna founded the Association of Muslim Brothers. This trend was soon widespread in the Arab world,[65] and professed as constant principles the struggle for the restoration of Islamic law, the *shari'a*, and the building of a Muslim economy freed from the 'Crusaders', that is to say its foreign controllers. The Suez Canal, a offending symbol of all this, became one of the first arenas of Islamic activism.

To the south of Cairo Christians are better established. Here they form one-tenth of the population and, like the Muslims, have maintained a solid rural base – 70 per cent of the Muslims of Upper Egypt[66] and 63 per cent of the Christians live in the countryside (see Table 8.11). It is already a long time since its proportion was slightly higher in the towns.[67] In Middle Egypt, where the Coptic presence is strong, a change is nevertheless occurring. The proportion of Christians in the population is decreasing and their community is becoming increasingly urbanized. This double change is particularly noticeable in the four provinces where the Copts are more numerous – Asyut, Minya, Sohag and Qena. The relative decline first showed in the 1960 census; but the migration of the Copts from the Nile Valley accelerated noticeably when the Islamic movements enlarged their network and some of their sympathizers entered the top administration.[68] The campuses where the new preachers of Islam were most popular, in addition to the universities of Cairo, were Asyut, Minya and Sohag. The Tanzim al-Jihad (Organization of the Holy War), created in 1975 in Alexandria, quickly travelled up the Nile in order to engage in a series of attacks against the property of Copts in Middle Egypt – places of worship and trade or private houses.

At the cross-roads of the two Egypts, on the outskirts of the capital, the provinces of Giza and Kaliubia stand out. As recipients of the migration from Middle and Lower Egypt, they are the only regions of the country where the share of Christians in the population has increased. Offering to the Copts the security of numbers, and market opportunities that suit their economic dynamism, the huge metropolis and its suburbs has already brought together 28 per cent of the Copts (21 per cent of the Muslims). In the very long term, will Cairo became their real sanctuary?

The erosion of the Christian communities in Syria has been more abrupt and has a different origin. From 1948 to 1960, the last year for which we have statistics of the distribution of the population by religion, their proportion in the total dropped from 14.1 to 7.9 per cent (see Table 8.12).[69] Only in Damascus and the province of Hassakeh, and as a result of migration, did their rate of growth exceed zero with Christians moving from the rest of Syria in former case and from Turkey in the latter. Elsewhere their numbers have, in absolute terms, declined. However, unlike Egypt, the decline of the Christian population in Syria has not been accompanied by their geographical concentration. Those Syrian Christians who left their land for the most part settled in neither Damascus nor Aleppo – the main areas for trade, public service and culture – but in Beirut, Paris, Milan, Detroit and Australia.

As elsewhere, the explanation for this movement lies in politics. After independence in 1943, Syria embarked on one of those periods of political instability which on so many occasions in Turkish and Arab history have affected the religious minorities. For some fifteen years the country experienced one coup d'état after another. Nor

were the Christians of Syria, who were largely of the Orthodox or
Catholic Greek rite, reassured by politicians such as Husni al-Za'im,
one of Syria's many short-lived presidents who held power in 1949
and who derived his inspiration from the thought and political action
of Atatürk. In this uncertain atmosphere most successful members
of the Christian bourgeoisie of Aleppo and Damascus took their
capital and set off for Beirut within a few years of independence.

As much as the creation of Greater Lebanon in 1920 on lands
that were claimed by Syria, the exodus of people and wealth explains
why a persistent resentment towards Lebanon has been the only
constant political feature among successive Syrian rulers. The Ba'thist
coup of 1963 brought comparative stability although, until the ascent
to power of Hafez Asad in 1970, intra-party disputes brought several
changes of government and the regime's ideological outlook accord-
ingly swung from relatively conservative to radical. The Syrian Ba'th
Party, which first aimed to restrict the Muslim Brothers, did not in
itself worry the Christians.[70] It was officially secular and included
Christians among its founding members, one of whom, Michel
Aflaq,[71] wrote: 'We consider Arabism to be the body of which the
soul is Islam.'[72] Before long, however, power in the Ba'th party –
and consequently in the Syrian state – became concentrated in the
hands of Alawis, an ultra schismatic branch of Islam.[73] Above the
sometimes deadly quarrels, the minorities of the Near East know
how to find a chance solidarity in the face of the only majority in
the region, Sunni Islam.

Iraq is the only country where Christianity has not declined, at
least until 1965, the date of the last census to provide details of
religion. Nevertheless, the two decades that followed the Second
World War saw a radical change in the geographical distribution of
the Christian community. In less than 20 years half of the Christians
left the provinces of Niniva (Mosul) and Dohuk for the capital
where, by 1965, 51 per cent of the country's Christians were grouped
together (see Table 8.13). Perhaps the north of the country where
Christians had lived for centuries no longer offered them economic
opportunities or perhaps coexistence with the Kurds become
impossible. In the period between the two world wars, the Nestorian
Assyrians, who make up about 10 per cent of the Assyrian population
of Iraq, suffered the hostility of both the Turks and other Iraqis. In
1914–18 they had sided with the Russians and the Allies against the
Ottomans and later, under the British Mandate, had given strong
support to the imperial power in its attempt to maintain order in the

face of frequent Kurdish and Shiʻi uprisings. When independence came to Iraq in 1930, they were suddenly answerable to the new powers. Massacred by the Kurdish irregulars in 1933, with the support of the Iraqi military[74] but the disapproval of King Faysal, they took the path of exile. The Chaldeans, who constitute 90 per cent of the Assyrian population, did not suffer the same fate; nevertheless they left this insecure area and settled in Baghdad.

Between 1975 and 1990, many regions of the world welcomed Lebanese migrants in search of a respite from the protracted civil war, temporary for some, of longer duration for others, perhaps for ever. Wars often produce such an exodus, but almost always towards the nearest place of refuge. During the harshest of the battles, particularly before the intervention of the Syrian army in 1976, numerous families did find temporary asylum in Damascus. However, the refugees very quickly departed to more distant places and in a more organized fashion and their exodus never assumed the appearance, sadly familiar today, of the chaotic withdrawal of people in retreat. The Lebanese could respond to political and economic insecurity by settling overseas because their fathers and their fathers' fathers had led the way. The flight from Lebanon was, in short, a sort of rediscovery of history, a simple speeding up – however strongly – of a tradition of migration which had existed for more than a century.[75] Before the civil war, Lebanon was already one of the rare countries in the world whose people, whether or not they held Lebanese nationality, were as numerous outside the country's borders as they were within.

The departure of the first contingents of emigrants coincided with the first inter-communal war in the history of modern Lebanon, in 1860 (see Chapter 5). A demonstration of both the population pressure in the mountain and the search for larger trading areas than the Levant,[76] emigration soon began to create intercontinental networks. The process continued until 1975, interrupted only by the crisis of 1929 and the two world wars (see Table 8.16). Compared to much Arab emigration in the twentieth century, which responded to a demand for labour overseas and was a rejection of misery at home, Lebanese emigration before 1975 had, above all, been entre-preneurial in character. For this reason it sustained its momentum in the two great periods of prosperity before the First World War and under the governments of presidents Chehab (1958–64) and Helou (1964–70).[77]

What was the religious composition of the emigration and how did it change the confessional distribution of the population that remained in the country?[78] Leaving a world where identity is determined by membership in a religious group, the migrants settled in secular lands whose statistics relegated religion to the private domain and are of no help in answering this question. Furthermore, for reasons we have already touched upon, the Lebanese administration abandoned the census in 1932 and so there is no precise data from this source either. We do know, however, from the Lebanese series that up to 1932 the Christians formed 85 per cent of the diaspora (see Table 8.17)[79] and that among them the Maronites were the majority, though the Greek Orthodox and Catholics clearly had the strongest propensity to leave. This trend continued at least until independence, and probably until the advent of the rentier economies in the Gulf: the large Lebanese communities which were established in this period in the Americas, Egypt or Oceania were predominantly Christian, while those in West Africa were initially Shi'a. Although the economic position of the Christians remaining in Lebanon was strengthened, this was due to the capital invested by relatives in America. Their population was declining, however, both directly through the effects of migration, and indirectly through a falling of the birth rate which was now enhanced by affluence.[80]

The 1950s and 1960s was a period of exceptional population redistribution. While there was continued emigration overseas, still largely Christian, three immigration trends changed the religious equilibrium in Lebanon. The Lebanese who left Egypt at the time of the Free Officers' revolution, as well as the Syrians who left their country in the period of uncertainty after nationalization, were predominantly Christian. By contrast, the large majority of Palestinians who were forced out into the neighbouring countries in 1948 and again in 1967 were Muslim.[81] At the beginning of the 1970s, they would have numbered about 350,000.[82] The immigration of 280,000 Syrian non-skilled workers in the same period[83] also added, though temporarily, to the Muslim population.

Two new developments, one regional and one national, changed the direction of Lebanese emigration in the following years. The first was the rise in oil prices. The decision of the Gulf princes to invest, or to spend, a substantial part of the revenues at home created one of the largest markets for migrant labour in the world, the third after the United States and Western Europe. Being as short of manpower and technical skills as they were well supplied with capital, the countries of the Gulf appealed for both. A branch of the Palestinian diaspora had settled in Kuwait and Saudi Arabia after 1948, and Palestinians were now the first to arrive in the new Eldorado. At the end of the 1960s, however, they were followed by other Arabs, Egyptians, Syrians and Lebanese – to mention only the multi-confessional countries.

The second development to accelerate Lebanese emigration was the disruption of security, the collapse of the economy, and finally of social structures and even community solidarity which marked the 15 years of civil war. From 1975 a reign of terror was established in Beirut; in 1984 the Lebanese pound collapsed after the country had lost both the assets of the PLO and the remittances from migrants in the Gulf; [84] and in 1988 intra-confessional conflict began among the Shi'a to be followed in 1989 by the battles within the Maronite community. With all these reverses, emigration returned to the high levels of the early part of the century.

The change was not only quantitative. The rush to the Gulf, the earlier emigration, very largely involved the Muslim population. Yet, once again, there are no reliable statistics from which to construct a confessional balance-sheet, not because of the secularism of the host countries in which Islam is the state religion, but the sparsity of their population statistics. [85]

The civil war in Lebanon reactivated not only the tradition of emigration, but also old community solidarities. Between 1860 and 1975 the national construction of Lesser then Greater Lebanon, however imperfect, did its work. Little by little a mixed population grew in each *caza*, if not in each village, [86] to the point that nearly everyone could boast of neighbours who belonged to another confession. The first ten years of the war practically swept away this century of apprenticeship in communal life. Isolating itself between the Qadisha and the Nahr al-Kalb, a small Christian enclave has been cleared of all Muslim elements and the pre-1860 community boundaries have been rediscovered with very few changes. A comparable process has taken place in the Shuf, where the mountain is now almost completely Druze, and in the central and northern Beqa'a, where Shi'i Islam rules practically undivided. Seeking refuge near to their own, the people have quite naturally rediscovered the cradle of their families; in other words, they have retraced, in the opposite direction, the migratory paths which led them in the past to the melting pots which even small villages had become.

But there is one development that the war has not prevented – the polarization of Beirut. Probably, the capital and its suburbs today contain three-quarters of the Lebanese population. In the confined space of an agglomeration that was formerly shared between two masters, Sunni and Greek Orthodox, all the communities of Lebanon are now found – for the first time in proportion to their actual importance. They have never before been so physically close. If the barriers that were erected during the fighting continue to fall, Beirut will become the confessional melting-pot that the mountain refused to be.

Table 8.1: Correspondence between the National Boundaries today and the Ottoman *Vilayat* in the Fertile Cresent

Countries in 1995	Ottoman Division 1881–1893
Iraq	Vilayat of Baghdad (whole). Vilayat of Mosul (whole). Vilayat of Basra (except Kuwait).
Israel	Vilayat of Beirut: sanjak of Acre. Mutasarrifiya of Jerusalem: caza of Jaffa
Jordan and Palestine	Vilayat of Beirut: sanjak of Balqa Mutasarrifiya of Jerusalem: cazas of Jerusalem, Hebron, Gaza Vilayat of Damascus: sanjak of Ma'an**
Lebanon	Vilayat of Beirut: sanjak of Beirut, cazas of Tripoli and Akkar. Vilayat of Damascus: cazas of Hasbaya, Rachaya, Ba'albek, Beqa'a. Mutasarrifiya of Mount Lebanon.
Syria	Vilayat of Beirut: sanjak of Latakia, cazas of Safita and Qala'at el-Husn. Vilayat of Aleppo: sanjak of Aleppo. Vilayat of Damascus: cazas of Damascus and Douma Sanjak of Deir Ezzor.

* The Census of 1881–93 does not provide details for the vilaya of Basra.

** No census was taken in the sanjak of Ma'an and the mutasarrifiya of Mount Lebanon. We have used the figures of V. Cuinet, *Syrie, Liban et Palestine: Géographie Administrative, Statistique et Raisonnée,* Paris, 1896.

Table 8.2: Christian Populations in the Arab East, 1894–1986

A *Total size*

Year	Egypt	Iraq	Jordan	Syria	Palestine*	Lebanon
1894		31,775	39,269	176,828	42,871	418,702
1907	913,592					
1914		32,493	49,520	134,546	69,456	502,101
1917	1,026,107					
1922					71,464	335,668
1927	1,181,910					
1931					88,907	
1932						392,544
1937	1,304,000					
1943						544,822
1945				414,907		
1946					145,063	
1947	1,501,635	156,258				
1948				436,510		
1949					93,000	
1950			49,475			
1956						769,558
1960	1,905,182			361,064		
1961			82,174		96,355	
1965		248,737				
1966	2,018,562					
1972					76,502	
1975						998,000
1976	2,285,620					
1979			153,182			
1983					99,525	
1986	2,829,349					

Table 8.2: (continued)

B. *Percentage of total population*

Year	Egypt	Iraq	Jordan	Syria	Palestine*	Lebanon
1894		2.16	8.96	10.88	13.30	60.47
1907	8.14					
1914		2.16	9.06	10.13	11.26	57.64
1917	8.07					
1922					9.50	55.11
1927	8.34					
1931					8.60	
1932						49.90
1937	8.19					
1943						52.07
1945				14.07		
1946					7.59	
1947	7.92	3.24				
1948				14.07		
1949					5.26	
1950			8.25			
1956						54.66
1960	7.33			7.91		
1961			6.89		3.23	
1965		3.09				
1966	6.74					
1972					2.04	
1975						42.90
1976	6.24					
1979			4.23			
1983					2.10	
1986	5.87					

* Palestine of the British mandate and present day Israel, West Bank and Gaza.
Other countries according to their current borders.

Table 8.3: Infant Mortality Rate among Christians in Egypt, 1902–34 (per thousand)

Region	1902–1909	1910–1919	1920–1929	1930–1934
Delta 1	261	231	186	178
Delta 2	232	214	198	179
Valley 1	337	320	289	257
Valley 2	292	304	274	235

1: Provinces where Christians represent less than 10% of total population.
2: Provinces where Christians represent more than 10% of total population.

Table 8.4: Crude Death Rate in Egypt by Religion, 1944–1980 (per thousand)

Period	Muslims	Christians	Excess Muslim death rate (per cent)
1944–1948	25.2	18.1	39.5
1949–1953	19.5	15.0	30.4
1954–1958	17.8	10.3	72.7
1959–1960	17.0	11.9	42.1
1974	13.3	12.4	7.3
1980	10.3	10.6	-2.7

Sources: Registrar General and Censuses of Egypt.

Table 8.5: Infant Mortality Rate among Muslims and Christians in Israel, 1955–89 (per thousand)

Period	Christians	Muslims	Muslim gap (years)	Excess Muslim death rate (per cent)
1955–1959	46.1	60.6	-	31.5
1960–1964	42.1	46.4	5.4	10.1
1965–1969	32.9	43.8	7.1	32.9
1970–1974	29.5	40.4	9.1	36.9
1975–1979	20.9	32.1	8.8	53.9
1980–1984	17.8	23.0	6.2	28.8
1985–1989	12.1	17.3	4.6	43.4

Source: *Statistical Abstract of Israel,* 1990.

Table 8.6: Infant Mortality Rate among Christians and Muslims in Lebanon, 1971

Age of mother	Per thousand		Excess Muslim death rate (per cent)
	Christians	Muslims	
20–24	31.1	66.6	114.0
25–29	35.3	36.1	2.3
30–34	39.4	71.2	81.0
35–39	68.0	95.3	40.1
40–44	61.7	87.3	41.5
45–49	91.0	147.4	62.0

Source: *al-Usra fi Lubnan* (The Family in Lebanon). Lebanese Family Planning Association, Beirut, 1974. 2 vol.

Table 8.7: Crude Birth Rate in Egypt by Religion, 1944–80

Period	Crude Birth Rate (per thousand)		Excess Muslim birth rate (per cent)
	Muslims	Christians	
1944–1948	43.7	33.8	29.4
1949–1953	44.8	33.3	34.5
1954–1958	42.5	24.6	73.0
1959–1960	43.8	31.4	39.5
1974	37.9	29.0	30.5
1980	38.9	30.8	26.0

Sources: Registry General and population censuses (non-corrected statistics).

Table 8.8: Fertility Rate of Palestinians by Religion, 1925–90

Period	Total Fertility Rate Children per woman			Excess Fertility Rate of Muslim Women Per Cent
	Christians	Druze	Muslims	
All Palestinians				
1925–1929	5.83	7.62	8.69	49
1930–1934	5.52	6.88	7.98	45
1935–1939	5.10	6.64	7.47	46
1940–1944	4.55	6.72	7.44	64
Israeli Arabs				
1955–1959	4.62	7.08	8.13	76
1960–1964	4.67	7.79	9.33	100
1965–1969	4.26	7.30	9.22	117
1970–1974	3.42	7.14	8.57	151
1975–1979	3.13	6.91	7.25	132
1980–1984	2.37	5.41	5.51	132
1985–1989	2.49	4.19	4.70	88

Occupied Territories

Period	West Bank	Gaza
1986–1969	7.63	7.74
1970–1974	7.92	8.38
1975–1979	7.96	9.01
1980–1984	7.13	8.25
1985–1990	7.23	8.71

Source: 1932–1944: McCarthy, *The Population of Palestine*; 1955–1990: Statistical Abstract of Israel, vol. 41, Jerusalem, 1990.

Table 8.9: Fertility by Religion in Lebanon, 1971

| | Christians | | | Muslims | |
	Maronites	Others	Sunnites	Shi'ites	Druzes
Age Specific Fertility Rate in 1970, per thousand married women					
15–19	158	158	380	300	300
20–24	343	400	378	443	316
25–29	350	252	355	463	300
30–34	202	198	324	360	154
35–39	113	68	230	281	150
40–44	65	19	74	172	56
Average final number of children per women					
Children per Married women aged 45–49	5.20	5.14	6.91	8.49	5.33
Total Fertility Rate	3.81	3.33	5.18	6.58	3.56
Contraceptive methods (per cent)					
Pill	10	12	20	17	15
Withdrawal	10	32	20	10	33

Source: J. Chamie, *Religion and Fertility. Arab Christian–Muslim Differentials* Cambridge, 1981.

Table 8.10: Population of Egypt by Religion and Province, 1986

Mohafazat	Muslims	Christians	Others
Cairo	5,436,780	565,101	5,409
Alexandria	2,713,749	182,294	416
Port-Said	377,730	16,095	16
Suez	311,011	13,786	55
Damietta	738,079	1,751	16
Dakahlia	3,457,715	35,304	187
Sharquia	3,369,380	41,333	711
Kalyubia	2,417,819	89,948	21
Kafr Sheikh	1,784,454	11,266	29
Gharbia	2,815,099	47,722	174
Menufia	2,182,246	40,707	81
Behera	3,205,880	44,792	57
Isma'ilia	525,667	15,546	10
Giza	3,534,542	148,098	180
Beni-Suef	1,359,842	79,046	31
Fayum	1,487,569	54,466	223
Minia	2,160,359	480,592	85
Asyut	1,810,739	395,588	88
Sohag	2,141,482	307,343	55
Qena	2,091,479	153,860	53
Aswan	751,691	41,678	10
Red Sea	81,369	3,547	0
Wadi al-Gadid	109,391	1,751	0
Matruh	155,561	1,551	0
North Sinai	168,990	652	6
South Sinai	24,708	217	0
Total	45,213,331	2,774,034	7,913

Source: Population census

Table 8.11: Population of Syria by Religion and Province, 1948 and 1960

| | Administrative Estimate 1948 | | | | 1960 Census | | | |
	Muslims	Christians	Jews	Total	Muslims	Christians	Jews	Total
Total	2,588,436	436,510	32,510	3,057,456	4,198,464	361,064	5,067	4,565,121
Damascus city					481,838	45,641	2,392	529,963
Damascus	560,486	75,122	15, 862	651,470	431,510	23,839	7	455,396
Homs	178,915	49,026	0	227,941	318,420	61,975	0	380,471
Hama	149,732	21,034	0	170,766	288,815	24,283	0	313,101
Latakia	391,253	82,500	1	473 ,754	470,598	44,967	0	515,568
Aleppo	777,877	128,627	14,468	920,972	1,153,267	87,210	1,852	1,242,547
Hassakeh	104,128	45,744	2,074	151,946	250,339	58,262	816	309,494
Deir Ezzor	228,640	4597	85	233,322	348,842	3,118	0	351,977
Suweida	80,773	8,826	10	89,609	86,902	5,109	0	92,011
Dera'a	116,632	21,034	10	137,676	156,263	6,660	0	162,923

Table 8.12: Population of Iraq by Religion and Province, 1947 and 1965

	1947				1965			
	Muslims	Christians	Jews	Total	Muslims	Christians	Jews	Total
Baghdad	702,316	37,059	77,542	816,917	1915,619	127,140	2,616	2,045,375
Niniva and Dohuk	507,422	77,386	10,345	595,153	819,538	69,014	49	888,601
Muthanna and Qadissiya	377,007	285	825	378,117	542,573	604	51	543,228
Dhi Qar	370,281	939	652	371,872	496,998	1,835	17	498,850
Basra	349,302	8,868	10,537	368,707	653,290	15,929	260	669,479
Maysan	301,477	3,401	2,131	307,009	342,833	2,615	19	345,467
Kirkuk	274,124	7,808	4,042	285,974	459,634	13,960	32	473,626
Karbela	274,210	15	39	274,264	339,832	22	0	339,854
Diyala	268,531	839	2,851	272,221	396150	1,207	6	397,363
Babel	259,129	212	1,865	261,206	447,501	657	10	448,168
Irbil	228615	8,051	3,109	239,775	347,515	8,731	47	356,293
Sulaymaniya	223,562	566	2,271	226,399	397,337	2,402	29	399,768
Wasit	224,241	340	349	224,930	333,647	664	20	334,331
Anbar	180,991	10,489	1,442	192,922	303,029	3,958	25	307,012
Total	4,541,208	156,258	118,000	4,815,466	7,795,496	248,737	3,182	8,047,415

Table 8.13: Population of Jordan by Religion and District, 1950, 1961, 1979

District	1950		1961		1979	
	Muslims	Christians	Muslims	Christians	Muslims	Christians
Balqa	212,734	30,364	464,279	47,057	1,228,385	68,344
Amman			390,510	41,792	1,089,025	61,676
Balqa			73,769	5,265	139,360	6,668
Ajlun Irbid	223,343	12,278	262,728	11,166	587,991	13,769
Karek	95,896	6,652	63,953	3,257	119,480	4,591
Ma'an	18,552	181	46,406	503	71,802	2,016
Total	550,525	49,475	837,366	61,983	2,007,658	88,720

Table 8.14: Population of the West Bank and Gaza by Religion and Region, 1961, 1972, 1990

Region	1961		1972		1990	
	Muslims	Christians	Muslims	Christians	Muslims	Christians
Jerusalem	301,648	42,618	74,400	11,800	131,700	14,600
Rest of the West Bank	457,731	3,237	622,557	4,403	948,250	6,750
Gaza*			595,900		895,400	

* No census was taken in Gaza under the Egyptian administration.

Sources: 1961, census of Jordan; 1972-1990, Israeli statistics.

Table 8.15: Lebanese Emigration, 1860–1987

Period	Annual Number	Average Rate (per cent)
1860–1899	3,000	0.8
1900–1913	15,000	3.4
1914–1918	0	0.0
1919–1938	4,400	0.6
1939–1945	0	0.0
1946–1958	3,500	0.3
1959–1962	14,700	0.8
1963–1972	5,200	0.3
1975–1979	53,200	2.0
1980–1983	33,000	1.1
1984–1987	68,400	2.3

Sources: 1860–1958: Elie Safa. *L'Emigration Libanaise*, Beirut, 1960; 1959–1972: Y. Courbage and P. Fargues, 'La Situation Démographique au Liban', vol. II, Libraire Orientale,1974; 1975–1987: B. Labaki, 'L'émigration externe'. *Maghreb-Machrek,* no. 125, Paris, 1989.

Note: 1860–1958 = emigration (definitive departures); 1958–1987 = net emigration (departures less arrivals)

Table 8.16: Lebanese Population in Lebanon and in the Diaspora, 1932 Census

Community	Absolute Numbers in 1932		Propensity to emigrate (per cent)	Contribution to the Diaspora (per cent)
	In Lebanon	Outside		
Maronite	227,800	123,397	35	49
Greek Orthodox	77,312	57,031	42	22
Greek Catholic	46,709	29,627	39	12
Protestant	6,869	2,931	30	1
Armenian	31,992	2,424	7	1
Other Christians	6,264	434	6	0
Total Christians	396,946	215,844	35	85
Sunnis	178,130	17,205	9	7
Shi'a	155,035	10,910	7	4
Druze	53,334	8,750	14	3
Total Muslims	386,499	36,865	9	14
Jews and others	9,981	1,677	14	1
Total	793,426	254,386	24	100

Source: E. de Vaumas, 'La Répartition confessionnelle au Liban et l'equilibre de l'État libanais', *Revue de Géographie Alpine*, vol XLIII/III, Grenoble, 1955.

Table 8.17: Estimated Number of Eastern Christians by Rite and by Country, 1995 (in thousands)

Church	Egypt*	Lebanon	Syria	Iraq	Jordan	Israel	Palestine	Turkey	Total Middle East
Copt (all rites)	3,289.9	1.9	0.0	1.8	1.2	0.8	2.8	0.0	3,298.0
Greek Orthodox	4.4	294.8	503.0	0.8	81.4	33.0	41.6	13.9	972.9
Maronite	2.5	490.9	28.0	0.0	0.0	7.3	0.3	0.0	529.0
Greek Catholic	4.7	255.2	111.8	0.7	22.1	43.9	4.4	0.0	442.8
Armenian Apostolic	7.6	196.4	111.8	25.0	3.5	1.3	2.9	68.3	416.8
Chaldean Catholic	0.5	4.9	6.7	390.3	0.0	0.0	0.0	6.8	409.2
Jacobite	0.2	14.7	89.4	37.2	2.2	0.1	2.5	39.9	186.2
Latin	3.8	2.9	11.1	5.2	34.9	13.2	15.2	5.7	92.0
Protestant	20.9	20.2	20.1	5.8	4.4	4.5	4.8	5.2	85.9
Syrian Catholic	1.3	19.7	22.4	55.5	0.0	0.1	0.5	1.7	101.2
Nestorian	0.0	4.9	16.8	87.7	0.0	0.0	0.9	0.0	110.3
Armenian Catholic	0.6	19.7	24.6	5.5	0.4	0.1	0.3	5.1	56.3
Total Christian	3,336.6	1,326.2	945.7	615.5	150.1	104.3	76.2	146.6	6,701.0
Percentage of Population	5.7	43.8	6.4	2.9	4.2	2.1	3.8	0.2	4.0

* Total number of Christians extrapolated from 1986 census

Source: Authors' calculations from statistics in Norman A. Horner, *A Guide to Christian Churches*.

Notes

Chapter 1

1 Quoted in Antoine Fattal, *Le Statut légal des non-musulmans en pays d'Islam*, Beirut, 1958.

2 S. D. Goitein estimates that the Jews represented 1 per cent of the population in the whole of the region. 'Jewish Society and Institutions under Islam', *Journal of World History*, XI, 1968.

3 Zoroastrianism, the religion of the Sasanian state, was widespread in the Iranian plateau but practised little in Mesopotamia.

4 'Yemen', *The Catholic Encyclopedia*, New York, 1967.

5 This is a much discussed text since it did not oblige the Najranis to pay the *jizya*. See Fattal, *Le Statut légal*.

6 Phillip K. Hitti, *History of the Arabs (from the Earliest Times to the Present)*, 5th ed., London, 1953.

7 Direct information on the population was not collected until the advent of the Ottoman empire.

8 Josiah Cox Russell, 'The Population of Medieval Egypt', *Medieval Demography*, New York, 1987.

9 Some authors have suggested a figure twice as large as that of Russell, but less convincingly. See for example, Michael W. Dols, *The Black Death in the Middle East*, Princeton, 1977.

10 Alfred J. Butler, *The Arab Conquest of Egypt and the Last Thirty Years of the Roman Dominion*, Oxford, 1902.

11 Josiah Cox Russell, 'Late Ancient and Medieval Population', *Transactions of the American Philosophical Society*, 48/III, 1958.

12 Bernard Lewis, *The Jews of Islam*, London, 1985.

13 The text and the spirit of this treaty have been the subject of much controversy. Was it a contract giving 'protection', like that to many other Christian and Jewish tribes, or was it a pact between two equal partners?

14 Fattal, *Le Statut légal*.

15 'Bahrain' in *Encyclopedia Judaïca*, Jerusalem, 1971.

16 'Aden', ibid.

17 T. W. Arnold, *The Preaching of Islam. A History of the Propagation of the Muslim Faith*, London, 1896.

18 Hitti, *History of the Arabs.*

19 Cox Russell, 'Late Ancient and Medieval Population'

20 Quoted in Arnold, *The Preaching of Islam.*

21 Eliyahu Ashtor, *Histoire des prix et des salaires dans l'Orient médiéval*, Paris, 1969.

22 Ibid.

23 Cox Russell, 'Late Ancient and Medieval Population'.

24 A. S. Tritton, 'Nasara', *Encyclopédie de L'Islam. Dictionnaire géographique, ethnographique et biographique des peuples musulmans*, 37, Leiden, 1928.

25 800,000 according to H. H. Howorth (*History of the Mongols*, London, 1927) a figure which says more about traumatic memories of the experience than it does about demographic reality.

26 Aziz S. Atiya, *A History of Eastern Christianity*, London, 1968.

27 So called because of their scepticism of the virginity of Mary.

28 Henri Lammens, *La Syrie. Précis historique*, 2 vols, Beirut, 1921, and Hitti, *History of the Arabs.*

29 J. Sauvaget, *Les Monuments historiques de Damas*, Beirut, 1932.

30 Lammens, *La Syrie.*

31 Quoted by Fattal, *Le Statut légal.*

32 Lammens, *La Syrie.*

33 Hitti, *History of the Arabs.*

34 Contrary to expectation, and widely-held opinion, polygamy in its Arab–Muslim form effectively moderates fertility – a phenomenon that has been confirmed by twentieth-centruy demographers.

35 Ashtor, *Histoire des prix.*

36 Figure reported by Patriarch al-Duwayhi (1630–1704) quoted in Atiya, *A History.*

37 The Maronite Sulaiman Frangieh used this name for his militia during the Lebanese civil war (1975–90).

38 Fattal, *Le Statut légal.*

39 Shi'ism, the main division in Islam, is itself divided into branches. See Henri Laoust, *Les Schismes dans l'Islam*, Paris, 1965; Yann Richard, *L'Islam chiite*, Paris, 1991.

40 Lammens, *La Syrie.*

41 Ashtor, *Histoire des prix.*

42 Cox Russell, 'Late Ancient and Medieval Population'.

43 This estimate is based on the registers of conscription; A. N. Poliak, 'The Demographic Evolution of the Middle East: Population Trends since 1348', *Palestine and the Middle East*, X, 5, 1938.

44 Up to one-third of the population according to Dols, *The Black Death.*

45 'Syria' in *Encyclopedia Judaïca.*

46 Atiya, *History of Eastern Christianity*

47 Text kept by Tabari (310 AH, 923 AD), quoted by Fattal, *Le Statut légal.*

48 Figure 1.1. shows the progress of Islam in Egypt indicated by the statements of the *jizya* as and a much slower alternative which corresponds to the hypothesis of Daniel C. Dennett Jr., *Conversion and the Poll Tax in Early Islam*, Cambridge Mass., 1950.

49   Atiya, *History of Eastern Christianity* and 'The Copts' in *Encyclopédia de l'Islam*, new ed., Paris, 1979.

50   E. L. Butcher, *Story of the Church of Egypt*, London, 1897, quoted by Aziz S. Atiya in 'The Copts'.

51   Tritton, 'Nasara'.

52   Atiya, *A History of Eastern Christianity*.

53   The word means 'sea' in fact, but comes from the huge size of the Nile.

54   al-Maqrizi, *Description topographique et historique de l'Egypte*, Paris, 1895.

55   M. Clerget, *Le Caire*, Cairo, 1934.

56   Amin Maalouf has revived the memory of this extraordinary traveller in *Leo the African*, London, 1986.

57   Some contemporary Islamist movements quote as an authority Ibn Taymiyya, a thinker of the Mamluk period.

58   Atiya, *A History of Eastern Christianity*.

59   'Egypt' in *Encyclopedia Judaïca*.

60   Lewis, *The Jews of Islam*.

61   'Egypt', *Encyclopedia Judaïca*.

62   *Chronique de Michel le Syrien*, quoted in Georges C. Anawati, 'Factors and Effects of Arabization and Islamization in Medieval Egypt and Syria', in Speros Vryonis (ed.), *Islam and Cultural Change in the Middle Ages*, Wiesbaden, 1975.

63   Maxime Rodinson, *Mohammed*, London, 1971.

64   Arnold, *The Preaching of Islam*.

65   Dennett Jr, *Conversion and the Poll Tax*.

66   Relying on the existence of chronicles that describe numerous conversions under Caliph 'Umar II and the lack of such documents for the previous period, Dennett Jr, (ibid) and Nehemia Levtzion, 'Toward a Comparative Study of Islamization' in Nehemia Levtzion (ed.), *Conversion to Islam*, New York, 1979, believe on the contrary that there were no significant conversions in Egypt at the very beginning of Islam. The fiscal data would seem to us to provide more conclusive evidence than accounts which are necessarily anecdotal.

67   Dominique Sourdel, 'Iraq', *Encyclopédie de l'Islam*.

68   Levtzion, 'Toward a Comparative Study of Islamization.'

69   Henri Lammens, *La Syrie*.

70   Asking why Islamization was never complete in Egypt, Anawati ('Arabization and Islamization in Medieval Egypt and Syria') suggested that there was a residual group of both Christians and Jews for whom deep-felt conviction overrode the social and material advantages of conversion.

71   Some Arab historians attribute this convention to Umar I.

72   Jules Michelet, *Histoire de France*, vol. I, Paris, 1876.

73   The expression comes from Henri Lammens.

74   Qur'an, III/28, IV/144, V/57, IX/23, LX/13.

75   Ibn Khaldun: the Muqaddimah, 3 vols translated by F. Rosenthal, London, 1958.

76   Arnold, *The Preaching of Islam*.

77   Gérard de Nerval, *Le Voyage en Orient*, Paris, 1980.

Chapter 2

1 Charles Courtois, *Les Vandales et l'Afrique*, quoted by Abdallah Laraoui, *The History of the Maghrib: An Interpretive Essay*. Princeton, NJ, 1977.

2 From Donat, a dissident bishop of Carthage (313–55).

3 Laraoui, *The History of the Maghrib*.

4 Emile-Félix Gautier, *L'Islamisation de l'Afrique du Nord. Les siècles obscurs du Maghreb*, Paris, 1927.

5 G. Drague, *Esquisse d'histoire religieuse du Maroc. Confréries et Zaouïas*, Cahiers de l'Afrique et de l'Asie, no.2, Paris, 1951.

6 Ibn Khaldun, *Histoire des Berbères*.

7 1.9 million according to Cox Russell, *Late Ancient and Medieval Population*, Marcel Reinhard, André Armengaud and Jacques Dupaquier consider this to be a low estimate; *Histoire générale de la population mondiale*, Paris, Montchrestien, 1968.

8 According to S. D. Goitein, 'Jewish Society and Institutions under Islam', *Journal of World History*, XI, 1968.

9 Haïm Zafrani, *Mille ans de vie juive au Maroc (histoire, culture, religion et magie)*, Paris, 1983.

10 Al-Bayan, *Histoire de l'Afrique et de l'Espagne* (compilation dating from the end of the thirteenth century), translated by E. Fagnan, Algiers, 1901.

11 Laraoui, *The History of the Maghrib*.

12 As is demonstrated today by Kabyle (Berber-speaking Algerians) reticence towards Islamic activism and hasty Arabization.

13 Nehemia Levtzion, 'Toward a Comparative Study of Islamization,' in Levtzion (ed.), *Conversion to Islam*.

14 Mohammed Arkoun makes an important qualification, recalling the independence that the ulema retained at first vis-à-vis power, particularly under the Abbasid caliphate which witnessed a real secularization of thought: 'Din, Dawla, Duniya,' *L'Islam, morale et politique*, Paris, 1986.

15 Ibn Khaldun, *Al-Muqaddima*, trans. Georges-Henri Bousquet, *Les Textes sociologique de la Mouqaddima*, Paris, 1965.

16 Ibn Khaldun, *Histoires des Berbères*.

17 See for example, M. Shaban: 'The most spectacular conversions occurred in North Africa. Numerous Berbers were converted and 12,000 of them were recruited into the Arab army.' 'Conversion to Early Islam,' in Levtzion, *Conversion to Islam*.

18 Gautier, *L'Islamisation de l'Afrique du Nord*.

19 On Kharijism, which in North Africa survives only in the Mzab and Djerba, as well as in Oman and Zanzibar, see for example Henri Laoust, *Les Schismes dans l'Islam*, Paris, 1965.

20 Laraoui, *The History of the Maghrib*.

21 Gautier, *L'Islamisation de l'Afrique du Nord*. Fernand Braudel also takes up this idea of a forgotten atavism, *La Méditerranée*, Paris, 1986.

22 Ibn Khaldun, *Histoires des Berbères*.

23 Gautier, *L'Islamisation de l'Afrique du Nord*.

24 Lewis, *The Jews of Islam*.

25 On the legal status of the *dhimmi* and the question of intermarriage, see

for example the 'Nasara' in *Encyclopédie de l'Islam*.

26   Ibn Khaldun, *Histoire des Berbères*.

27   Gautier, *L'Islamisation de l'Afrique du Nord*.

28   Ibid.

29   Articles on Libya, on Tunisia, on Algeria, and on Morocco, *The Catholic Encyclopedia*.

30   Henry Koehler, *L'Eglise chrétienne du Maroc et la mission franciscaine*, Paris, 1934.

31   *The Catholic Encyclopedia*.

32   St Louis died from pestilence having failed to convert the Sultan of Tunisia to christianity.

33   Bernard Lewis, *Jews in Islam*.

34   Koehler, *L'Eglise chrétienne du Maroc*

35   Ibn Khaldun, *Histoire des Berbères*.

36   *The Catholic Encyclopedia*.

37   André Raymond, *Grandes Villes arabes à l'époque otomane*, Paris, 1985.

38   Koehler, *L'Eglise chrétienne du Maroc*

39   *The Catholic Encyclopedia*.

40   Koehler, *L'Eglise chrétienne du Maroc*

41   Ibn Khaldun, *Histoire des Berbères*.

42   'Morocco', *Encyclopedia Judaica*, Jerusalem, 1971.

43   Directorate of Statistics, *Recensement de la population de 1960*, Rabat, 1965 – the only census to link religion and mother tongue.

Chapter 3

1   Claude Cahen, *Orient et Occident au temps des Croisades*, Paris, 1983.

2   Speech of Pope Urban II, reproduced by Foucher of Chartres, in Régine Pernoud, *Les Hommes de la Croisade*, Paris, 1982.

3   See Chapter 1.

4   Cahen, *Orient et Occident*.

5   Ibid.

6   Claude Cahen, 'Les Croisades', *Encyclopédie de l'Islam*, Paris, new ed., 1960; Joshua Prawer, *Histoire du royaume latin de Jérusalem*, Paris, 1969.

7   'It is impossible to believe in the existence of significant direct relations between the Muslim East and Europe before the end of the tenth century', Claude Cahen, *Orient et Occident*.

8   It is the practice today to describe as Arab everyone whose language is Arabic, whatever their religion. A detailed argument is provided by Maxime Rodinson in *The Arabs*.

9   'The Eastern churches, dogmatically separated and protected from outside interference by Muslim domination, seem never to have tried to resume contact with Rome.' Cahen, *Orient et Occident*.

10   According to Guillaume of Tyre. See Joshua Prawer, 'Minorities in the Crusader States', in Kenneth Setton, *History of the Crusades*, London, 1985.

11   The doctrine that Christ has two natures but a single divine will. It was declared heretical by the Council of Constantinople in 680.

12 Joshua Prawer, *Histoire du royaume latin de Jérusalem*, Paris, CNRS, 1969.

13 Ibid.

14 Gérard de Montréal, quoted in Pernoud, *Les Hommes de la Croisade.*

15 Claude Cahen, *La Syrie du Nord à l'époque des Croisades*, 1940.

16 Foucher of Chartres, quoted in Pernoud, *Les Hommes de la Croisade.* See also André Miquel, *Ousama – Un prince syrien face aux croisades*, Paris, 1988.

17 Pernoud, *Les Hommes de la Croisade.* From the same text, Amin Maalouf gives a more subdued translation: 'Now doubt invests the heart of a great number of these men when they compare their lot to that of their brothers living in Muslim territory. Indeed, the latter suffer from the injustice of their coreligionists, whereas the Franj act with equity.' *The Crusades Through Arab Eyes*, London, 1984.

18 Cahen, *Orient et Occident.*

19 Régine Pernoud believed that the Pope would only have promised eternal riches. Ibid. However, his view is contested by many historians.

20 Marcel Reinhard, André Armengaud and Jacques Dupâquier, *Histoire générale de la population mondiale*, Paris, 1966.

21 Josiah Cox Russell, 'The Population of the Crusader States' in Setton, *History of the Crusades*, Breast-feeding is an intermediary factor which affects fertility.

22 Joshua Prawer, 'Social Classes in the Latin Kingdom of Jerusalem: The Franks', in Setton, *History of the Crusades.*

23 Prawer, *Histoire du royaume latin*; Cahen, *Orient et Occident.*

24 Cox Russell, 'The Population of the Crusader States'. The levels are clearly too high, but the difference is certainly plausible.

25 Ibid.

26 Cahen, *La Syrie du Nord.*

27 Prawer, 'Social Classes'.

28 Prawer, *Histoire du royaume latin.*

29 Ibid.

30 Letter from a crusader, Cahen, *La Syrie du Nord.*

31 Prawer, *Histoire du royaume latin.*

32 See Chapter 1.

33 Some men born to mixed marriages were also included.

34 Ibid. The rural population was estimated at 250,000 inhabitants, by counting the villages currently existing (900) and during the Crusades (1200), distinguishing small villages (10 to 15 families) and large (20 to 40 families) between Beirut and Daron, Aqaba and Amman, on the basis of five members to a family. 30,000 non-Franks lived in the towns.

35 22,000 men in arms, being one-fifth of the total population, represented the whole of the male population of military age. Prawer, *Histoire du royaume latin.*

36 'The Maronites', *New Catholic Encyclopedia.*

37 Cahen, 'Croisades', *Encyclopédie de l'Islam.*

38 Setton, *History of the Crusades.*

39 Prawer, *Histoire du royaume latin.*

40 'There were perhaps [some attempts at rapprochement] in Syria and the neighbouring countries at the time of the arrival of Latin missionaries, but these

efforts were in vain precisely because of the impossibility for the Christians to avoid becoming politically suspect if they came close to them.' Claude Cahen, 'Dhimma', *Encyclopédie de l'Islam*.

41 The fact that the Eastern Christians were not members of the Latin Church made them distrustful toward the Crusaders. This is why they declined to collaborate. See Cahen, 'Dhimma'.

42 Ibid.

43 Guillaume de Rubrouck, *Voyage dans l'Empire mongol (1253–1255)*, Paris, 1985.

44 In fact the Mongols combined all the religions of Central Asia, including Nestorian Christianity. However Doqouz Khatoun, the wife of Hulagu, who held a strong influence in a civilization where women participated in public life, was Christian and anti-Muslim. Bertold Spuler, *Les Mongols dans l'histoire*, Paris, Payot, 1961.

45 Malouf, *The Crusades Through Arab Eyes*.

46 See Chapter 1.

47 Mohamed Ben Cheneb, 'Ibn Taïmiyya', *Encyclopédie de l'Islam*, 1st ed., 1913.

48 Gilles Kepel, 'L'Egypte aujourd'hui: mouvement islamiste et tradition savante', *Annales, économie, sociétés, civilisations*, Paris, July–August 1984.

49 R. Paret, 'Sirat Baïbars', *Encyclopédie de l'Islam*, 2nd ed.

50 Roman de Baïbars, *Fleurs de truands*, Paris, Sindbad, 1986.

51 R. Hartmann, 'Damas', *Encyclopédie de l'Islam*, 1st ed., 1923.

52 Gaston Wiet, 'Kibt', *Encyclopédie de l'Islam*, 1st ed.

53 A. A. Dui, 'Baghdad', *Encyclopédie de l'Islam* and Spuler, *Les Mongols dans l'histoire*.

Chapter 4

1 Ömer Lütfi Barkan, 'Research on Ottoman Fiscal Surveys' in M. A. Cook (ed.), *Studies in the Economic History of the Middle East from the Rise of Islam to the Present Day*, Oxford, 1978, gives the gross statistics of the census: the number of households. We have calculated from this the size of the total population, assuming five persons in the average household. Gilles Veinstein, 'Les Registres de recensement ottomans. Une source pour la démographie historique à l'époque moderne', *Annales de démographie historique*, Paris, 1990.

2 Muhammad Adnan Bakhit, 'The Christian Population of the Province of Damascus in the Sixteenth Century', in Braude and Lewis (eds), *Christians and Jews in the Ottoman Empire*, vol. 2.

3 André Raymond, 'Les provinces arabes (XVIe–XVIIIe siècle), in Robert Mantran (ed.), *Histoire de l'Empire ottoman*.

4 Subsequent censuses in 1897, 1906 and 1914 covered only a part of the Ottoman provinces.

5 Karpat, *Ottoman Population, 1830–1914*.

6 In fact the census covered males of all ages better than females. The census figures of 1881/82–1893 which are given in Table 5.5 have been obtained according to the following rule: we accept the gross figures of the Ottoman census when the female totals are higher than or equal to the male, otherwise we

NOTES 217

double the male total.

7 The administrative division at the time distinguished in descending order between the *vilaya* (province), the *sanjak* (department) and the *caza* (canton). Two provinces had special status of autonomy, the *mutasarrifiyya* of Mount Lebanon and Jerusalem.

8 André Raymond, 'Les Provinces arabes'.

9 Bakhit, 'The Christian Population' has examined some of them in depth.

10 Dominique Chevallier, *La Société du Mont-Liban à l'époque de la révolution industrielle en Europe*, Paris, 1971.

11 In the tables at the end of this chapter, we have used the most detailed figures, provided by Vital Cuinet, *Syrie, Liban et Palestine. Géographie administrative, statistique et raisonnée*, Paris, 1896.

12 At the time the vilayet extended from the mouth of the Orontes to Palestine.

13 Figures from 1914 census.

14 Bakhit, in 'The Christian Population', provides a rough guide to the registers. We have limited ourselves to the villages (and not the towns, to which there was considerable migration at this time) which were counted five times during the century. The following is our summary:

	1523	1543	1548	1569	1596
Muslims	7,546	9,718	10,467	15,885	9,261
Christians	6,914	9,428	15,885	11,816	10,556

It can be seen that this is an irregular series from which it is difficult to extract more than an average rate from all the data.

15 The net balance is the rate of natural growth minus the rate of emigration.

16 Elie Safa, *L'Emigration libanaise*, Beirut, 1960.

17 See Chapter 7.

18 Doris Behrens-Abouseif, 'The Political Situation of the Copts, 1578–1923' in Braude and Lewis (eds), *Christians and Jews*.

19 Jomard underestimated the Egyptian population by almost 2 million: the first demographic census of Egypt in 1846 gave a figure of 4.476 million. However, he does not appear to have been very wrong on the proportional shares of the religious communities.

20 Edme François Jomard, *Coup d'oeil impartial sur l'état de l'Egypte comparé à sa situation antérieure*, Paris, 1836.

21 Elsewhere, Jomard appears to have obtained – by mathemetical means rather than by counting on the ground – an estimate that is appreciably higher: 215–220,000 non-Muslims. M. A. El-Badry, 'Jomard et la démographie d'Egypte', *Population*, 6, Paris, 1991.

22 Letter from Pierre Plane, 13 July 1787, quoted by Daniel Panzac, *Quarantaines et lazarets. L'Europe et la peste d'Orient*, Aix-en-Provence, 1986.

23 Quoted by Chevallier, *La Société du Mont-Liban*.

24 Leila Tarazi Fawaz, *Merchants and Migrants in Nineteenth-Century Beirut*,

Cambridge Mass., 1983.

25 Chevallier, *La Société du Mont-Liban*.

26 LaVerne Kuhnke, *Lives at Risk. Public Health in Nineteenth-Century Egypt*, Berkeley, 1990.

27 Raymond, *Grandes Villes arabes à l'époque ottomane*.

28 Haroutune Armenian, 'Health Information System: Diversity of Data and Need for Integration', communication to the seminar of the International Union for the Scientific Study of Population, *Measurement of Maternal and Child Mortality*, Cairo, 1991.

29 The original figures from this census carried out by two French informers are provided by Chevallier, *La Société du Mont-Liban*.

30 See Chapter 1.

31 Philippe Fargues, 'La démographie du mariage arabo–musulman: tradition et changement', *Maghreb–Machrek*, 116, 1987.

32 The relations between repudiation and fertility are complex and do not always work in the same way. Ibid.

33 Kamal Salibi, *The Modern History of Lebanon,* London, 1965.

34 Ibid.

35 With two short exceptions: the ephemeral 'Umar Pasha (1842) and the *musarrif* Ismail Haqqi Bey (1917).

36 The ruling dynasty in Riyadh today. This is a remarkably persistent project which, at the end of the twentieth century, is still working from Najd to raise up Islam from its apathy.

37 Salibi, *Modern History of Lebanon*.

38 Ibid.

39 The name given to it during the civil war of 1975–90.

40 Salibi, *Modern History of Lebanon*.

41 In an area twice as small as Lebanon today, it comprised the mountain and its seafront, with the notable exception of Beirut and the main coastal towns.

42 Atiya, *A History of Eastern Christianity*.

43 See Chapter 8.

44 This is suggested by Aziz S. Atiya, ibid.

45 This was noted by the British diplomat Mark Sykes, *The Caliph's Last Heritage*, London, 1915.

46 R. Janin, *Eglises orientales*, Paris, 1926 – but 200,000 according to an Orthodox source: A. Diomedes Kyriakos, *Geschichte der Orientalischen Kirchen von 1453–1898*, Leipzig, 1902.

47 See Pierre Rondot, *Les Chrétiens d'Orient*, Paris, 1955 and Table 8.18.

48 Chevallier, *La Société du Mont-Liban*.

49 H. A. R. Gibb and H. Bowen, *Islamic Society and the West. A Study of the Impact of Western Civilization on Muslim Culture in the Near East*, vol. I, *Islamic Society in the XVIIIth Century*, London, 1950.

50 Atiya, *A History of Eastern Christianity*.

51 With the exception of Lebanon, with was divided between 1842 and 1860, into two *qaimaqamiyya*.

52 Emmanuel de las Cases, *Le Mémorial de Sainte-Hélène*, Paris, 1968.

53 Moshe Ma'oz, 'Communal Conflict in Ottoman Syria during the Reform Era: the Role of Political and Economic Factors' in Braude and Lewis (eds), *Christians and Jews.*

54 André Raymond, 'Les Provinces arabes'.

55 Daniel Panzac, 'Affréteurs ottomans et capitaines français à Alexandrie', *Revue de l'Orient et de la Méditerranée modernes*, Aix-en-Provence, 1982.

56 An allied theme is developed by Samir Amin, *The Arab Nation: Nationalism and Class Struggles*, London, 1978.

57 Raymond, 'Les Provinces arabes'.

58 Fernand Braudel, *Civilisation matérielle, économie et capitalisme, XVe–XVIIIe siècle*, vol. 3, *Le Temps du monde*, Armand Colin, Paris, 1967.

59 Ottoman registers in Muhammad Adnan Bakhit, 'The Christian Population of the Province of Damascus'.

60 This reconstruction was done by André Raymond, *Grandes villes arabes* who also provided a series of estimates for other towns: Aleppo, 120,000 inhabitants, 12,000 Christians, a few Jews; Mosul, 55,000 inhabitants, 6,000 Christians, 1,000 Jews; Baghdad, 90,000 inhabitants, 10,000 Jews; Cairo, 260,000 inhabitants, 10,000 Copts, 5,000 Syrians, 5,000 Greeks, 2,000 Armenians, 3,000 Jews.

61 Amnon Cohen, 'On the Realities of the Millet System: Jerusalem in the Sixteenth Century' in Braude and Lewis (eds), *Christians and Jews in the Ottoman Empire*, vol. 2.

62 Raymond, *Grandes villes arabes.*

63 According to the Ottoman register of 1523: 3,715 Muslims, 407 Christians and 72 Jews; Bakhit, 'The Christian Population of the Province of Damascus'.

64 Volney, *Travels through Egypt and Syria*, Dublin, 1793.

65 On the demography of Beirut, see Youssef Courbage and Philippe Fargues, *La Situation démographique au Liban*, vol. 2, Beirut, 1974.

66 Henri Guys, the French consul in Beirut, estimated in 1830 that the population of Beirut already comprised 50 per cent Christians and 50 per cent Muslims. *Beyrout et le Liban. Relation d'un séjour de plusieurs années dans ce pays*, Paris, 1850.

67 Fawaz, *Merchants and Migrants.*

68 May Davie, 'Ville, notables et pouvoir: les orthodoxes de Beyrouth au XIXe siècle', *Bourgeoisies et notables au Maghreb et au Machreq*, Grasse, 1991.

69 Dominique Chevallier, 'Lubnan', *Encyclopédie de l'Islam*, new ed., 1966.

70 Known as the 'barcelonnettes'.

71 Anouar Abdel-Malek, *L'Egypte moderne, idéologie et renaissance nationale*, Paris, Anthropos, 1970.

72 This is shown in the statistics of school attendance collected by Vital Cuinet, *Syrie, Liban et Palestine*. For an account on Lebanon see especially Boutros Labaki, *Education et mobilité sociale dans la société multicommunautaire du Liban. Approche socio-historique*, Frankfurt, 1988.

73 Quoted by Moshe Ma'oz in 'Communal Conflict'.

74 See Chapter 8.

Chapter 5

1 The borders of Anatolia change over time; here it it taken to comprise present-day Asian Turkey, including Armenia and Kurdistan.

2 Eight million according to Speros Vryonis, *The Decline of Medieval Hellenism in Asia Minor and the Process of Islamization from the 11th through the 15th Century*, Berkeley, 1971; 7 million according to Josiah Cox Russell. See also Speros Vryonis, 'Religious Change and Continuity in the Balkan and Anatolia from the 14th through the 15th Century,' in Vryonis (ed.), *Islam and Cultural Change in the Middle Ages*.

3 V. L. Ménage, 'The Islamization of Anatolia,' in Levtzion (ed.), *Conversion to Islam*.

4 Before Mantzikert, the Seljuks hesitated between two victims: the heretical Egypt of the Fatimids and the Byzantine Empire of the infidels. See Jean-Paul Roux, *Histoire des Turcs*, Paris, 1984.

5 Marco Polo, *Le Devisement du monde. Le livre des merveilles*, Paris, La Découverte, 1980.

6 Bernard Lewis, *Istanbul and the Civilization of the Ottoman Empire*, Norman Okl. 1963.

7 François Taeschner, 'Anadolus', *Encyclopédie de l'Islam*, 2nd ed.

8 Cox Russell, 'The Population of the Crusader States', in Setton, *History of the Crusades*, vol. 5, estimates that in the year 1200 the Christian population of Anatolia was 3 million and the Turkish population 4 million.

9 With the appearance of the first nationalist movements at the beginning of the twentieth century, some promoted a Turkish society including all the people of Turkish ethnic origin, while others claimed a Turanian society including all those whose language was Turkish.

10 Feroz Ahmad, 'Unionist Relation with the Greek, Armenian and Jewish Communities of the Ottoman Empire, 1908–1914' in Braude and Lewis (eds), *Christians and Jews in the Ottoman Empire*, 1982.

11 'The mixture of truths, half-truths and error [on the origin of the Turkish people] was proclaimed as the official doctrine and teams of researchers set to work to "prove" its various propositions', according to Bernard Lewis, 'History Writing and National Revival in Turkey', *Middle Eastern Affairs*, IV, 1953.

12 Ö. L. Barkan, 'Les Déportations comme méthode de peuplement et de colonisation dans l'Empire ottoman', *Revue de la faculté d'économie d'Istanbul*, XI, XIII, XV, Istanbul, 1953.

13 Ömer Lutfi Barkan, 'La "Méditerranée" de Fernand Braudel vue d'Istanbul', *Annales, Economies et Civilisation*, 2, Paris, 1954.

14 H. A. Gibbons, *The Foundation of the Ottoman Empire*, Oxford, 1916.

15 Claude Cahen, *Pre-Ottoman Turkey*, London, 1968.

16 See for example Marcel Reinhard, André Armengaud, Jacques Dupaquier, *Histoire générale de la population mondiale*, Paris, 1966.

17 William McNeil, *Population and Politics since 1750*, Charlottesville, 1990.

18 Osman Turan, 'L'Islamisation dans la Turquie du Moyen Age', *Studia Islamica*, 10, 1959.

19 Gibbons, *The Foundation of the Ottoman Empire*.

20 Claude Cahen, 'Le problème ethnique en Anatolie', *Cahiers d'histoire mondiale*, II, 2, 1954. See also his commentary on Speros Vryonis, 'The Decline of Medieval Hellenism', in *International Journal of Middle East Studies*, 34, 1973, where he charges him with under-estimating the weaknesses of Byzantium.

21 Paul Wittek, *La Formation de l'Empire ottoman*, London, Variorum Reprints, 1982.

22 Marco Polo, *Le Devisement du monde*.

23 Ibn Battuta, *The Travels of Ibn Battuta*, vol. 2, tr. H. A. R. Gibb, Cambridge 1962.

24 See Chapter 1.

25 Ibn Battuta, *The Travels of Ibn Battuta* and Ibn Khaldun, *The Muqaddimah*.

26 Cahen, *Pre-Ottoman Turkey*.

27 Vryonis, *The Decline of Medieval Hellenism*.

28 W. C. Brice, 'The Turkish Colonization of Anatolia', *Bulletin of the John Ryland Library*, 38, 1955–6.

29 These orders which originated in Khorasan became very popular in Anatolia from the thirteenth century.

30 Cahen, *Pre-Ottoman Turkey*.

31 R. M. Dawkins, 'The Crypto-Christians of Turkey', *Byzantion*, 8, 1933.

32 The Turkish Muslims who cohabited with the Christians enjoyed rights to a mosque and were subject to the jurisdiction of an Islamic judge; Robert Mantran, *La Vie quotidienne à Istanbul au temps de Soliman le Magnifique et de ses successeurs*, Paris, 1965.

33 Ibid and Lewis, *Istanbul*.

34 Except the 'empire' of Trebizond which survived until 1461.

35 Dimitri Kitsikis, *L'Empire ottoman*, Paris, 1985. According to Claude Cahen: 'To present the Ottoman Empire as a Greco–Turkish empire is slightly simplistic but not devoid of reality.' Claude Cahen, *Pre-Ottoman Turkey*.

36 See Chapter 5.

37 Kemal Karpat, 'Millets and Nationality: The Roots of the Incongruity of Nation and State in the post-Ottoman Era', in Braude and Lewis (eds), *Christians and Jews*.

38 Bernard Lewis, *The Emergence of Modern Turkey*, London, 1961. See also Bernard Lewis, 'Some Reflexions on the Decline of the Ottoman Empire', *Studia Islamica*, 1959, p. 23.

39 For the sixteenth century see, Ömer Lutfi Barkan, 'Contribution à l'étude de la conjoncture démographique des pays méditerranéens au XVIe siècle', *Actes de l'Union internationale pour l'étude scientifique de la population*, London, 1969. For the nineteenth century see, Kemal Karpat, *Ottoman Population, 1830–1914, Demographic and Social Characteristics*, Madison, 1985.

40 Robert Mantran, *Histoire de l'Empire ottoman*, Paris, 1990 and Karpat, 'Millets and Nationality'.

41 Benjamin Braude, 'Foundation Myths of the *Millet* System' in Braude and Lewis (eds) *Christians and Jews*.

42 Lewis, *The Emergence of Modern Turkey*.

43 There are several interpretations of the Qur'an, of which four are codified – the Hanbali, Maliki, Shafi'i and Hanafi.

44 Lewis, *The Emergence of Modern Turkey*.

45 Braudel, *Le Méiterranée*.

46 Reinhard, Armengaud and Dupaquier, *Histoire générale*.

47 Lewis, *Istanbul and Civilization*, pp. 112–13.

48 Barkan, 'Les déportations'.

49 V. L. Ménage, 'Devshirme', *Encyclopédie de l'Islam*, 2nd ed.

50 Barkan, 'Les déportations'.

51 Cem Behar, *The 1300 (1883) and 1332 (1905) Tahrirs as Sources for Ottoman Historical Demography*, Istanbul, n.d.

52 Suraiya Faroqhi, *Towns and Townsmen of Ottoman Anatolia*, Cambridge, 1984.

53 The treaty of Kutahya which was signed in 1833 a few kilometres from Istanbul, acknowledged Muhammad Ali as having sovereignty over Syria and Cilicia.

54 Robert Davidson, 'Turkish Attitudes Concerning Christian–Muslim Equality in the XIXth Century', *American Historical Review*, LIX, 1954.

55 Paul Dumont, 'La période des *Tanzimat* (1839–1878)' in Mantran, *Histoire de l'Empire ottoman*.

56 Details of the censuses and estimates are to be found in Karpat, *Ottoman Population 1830–1914*. Salaheddine Bey (1867), Ritter (1872–74), the census of 1881/1882–83, estimates for 1894, 1895, 1896, 1897, census of 1906–7, estimates for 1914.

57 Between 1906 and 1914, the population of the province of Edirne fell from 1,334 million to 631,000 as a result of territorial losses. Our reconstruction concerns the territory in 1914. For the province of Aleppo, additional estimates were taken from Vital Cuinet, *La Turquie d'Asie*, Paris 1896, in order to take into account the populations that were divided between Turkey and Syria after the war.

58 See Chapter 5.

59 Rate calculated with 1888 as the base year of the 1881/1882–93 census (recommended by Karpat, *Ottoman Population*).

60 Mantran, *Histoire de l'Empire ottoman*. This figure includes not only the Greek and Armenian emigration, but also that of the Arab Christians.

61 Excluding foreigners, who were largely Christians.

62 Mantran, *Histoire de l'Empire ottoman*. and Karpat, *Ottoman Population*. Of 2 million Muslim immigrants, three-quarters settled in the Turkish part, and one-quarter stayed in the Arab provinces: Syria, Lebanon, Jordan, Palestine, Iraq. Of the 300,000 Christian immigrants from the Empire, three-quarters came from Turkey and the remainder from the Arab provinces.

63 The net effect of migration compensated for the naturally weaker growth of the Muslims; for this reason the confessional distribution changed little.

64 More than 52,000 *piadeh* and *musellem*, 10,000 *timariots* in service and 10,000 footmen assigned to them, being a total of 72,000 in the military between 1520 and 1535; Barkan, 'Essai sur les données statistiques'.

65 See Chapter 5 and Karpat, *Ottoman Population*.

66 Karpat, 'Millets and Nationality'.

67 *The Treatment of Armenians in the Ottoman Empire*, London, 1916

68 On the capitulations, see Chapter 4.

69 Alan Duben and Cem Behar, *Istanbul Households – Marriage, Family and Fertility, 1880–1940*, Cambridge, 1991.

70 Nassau Senior, *A Journal Kept in Turkey and Greece*, London, 1856, quoted by Richard Clogg, 'The Greek Millet in the Ottoman Empire' in Braude and Lewis (eds), *Christians and Jews*. Furthermore, 'abortion and the shocking prevalence of unnatural crime among the Mussulmans' were suggested by the British consul as significant factors responsible for the weak population growth of the Turks. This passage in his report was later expurgated from the official published version.

71 By relating children of less than ten years to women of fertile age (20 to 50 years) we can obtain an indicator of fertility for the ten previous years. This has been calculated for each province of the empire in 1894 and correlated to the proportion of non-Muslims. The two indicators have a statistically significant positive correlation of +0.50.

72 In the 1950s the Greeks began to study Turkish, Alexis Alexandris, *The Greek Minority of Istanbul and Greek–Turkish Relations 1918–1974*, Athens, 1982.

73 Braude and Lewis (eds), *Christians and Jews*.

74 This was soon to be three and a half times, if we consider the demands put forward at the conference of Sèvres by the Kurds, who claimed the same land in Turkey as the Armenians.

75 Justin McCarthy, *Muslims and Minorities: The Population of Ottoman Anatolia at the end of the Empire*, New York, 1983.

76 Abdolonyme Ubicini and Pavet de Courteille, *Etat présent de l'Empire ottoman*, Paris, Dentu, 1876.

77 The withdrawal of the Russians, after the Brest–Litovsk Treaty in 1918, from Turkish Armenia which they had occupied since 1916; the rejection by the US Senate of the proposal by President Wilson in 1920 to create an independent Armenian state under an American mandate, incorporating the four Turkish *vilayet* with a large Armenian population (Erzurum, Trebizond, Van and Bitlis); the occupation of Cilicia which was put under a French mandate and followed by the withdrawal of the French troops in 1921.

78 Gérard Chaliand and Yves Ternon, *Le Génocide des Arméniens*, Brussels, 1980.

79 *The Treatment of Armenians in the Ottoman Empire*.

80 Kamuran Gürün, *The Armenian File – The Myth of Innocence Exposed*, New York, 1985. In the 1914 census, 1.204 million Armenians were counted; the figure of 1.3 million takes into account natural growth and the classification of 60,000 Armenian Protestants in the Protestant *millet*.

81 *The Treatment of Armenians in the Ottoman Empire*.

82 McCarthy, *Muslims and Minorities*, simply used the 'stable population' model to correct the age pyramid and the male–female ratios. The interest of his work lies in the calculations by *vilayet*.

83 Chaliand and Ternon, *Le Génocide des Arméniens*.

84 Obviously Toynbee and Lepsius were not able to estimate the number of converts; by converting they became Turks and were removed from the statistics of the minorities. Their crypto-Armenian descendants in the region of Antioch are still officially Muslims, using Arabic as their spoken language and, it is said,

practising Christianity in secret.

85 Chaliand and Ternon, *Le Génocide des Arméniens*, estimate the number of victims at between 1.2 and 1.5 million

86 Report of the Ottoman Minister of the Interior to the Grand Vizir dated 7 December, 1916; quoted in Gürün, *The Armenian File*.

87 This percentage takes into account the only people who risked deportation, that is the mass of the Armenians apart from the residents of Istanbul and Smyrna, and some 200,000 people who were already refugees in the Russian Caucasus.

88 Kamuran Gürün estimates the Armenian refugees in the Caucasus and Russia at 420,000, which is double the figure of Toynbee (183,000) or Lepsius (244,000). He estimates the number of those who stayed in Turkey at 124,000, which is higher than the figure given in the tables of the Turkish census of 1927 according to the criteria of religion (77,000) or language (65,000).

89 McCarthy, *Muslims and Minorities*.

90 Ibid.

91 The massacres have been estimated using the following equation: (Armenians of Anatolia in 1914) + (Armenians of Istanbul and European Turkey in 1914) − (Armenian migrants) − (Armenians of Anatolia in 1927) − (Armenians of Istanbul and European Turkey in 1927). No doubt inadvertently, McCarthy has forgotten the term (Armenians of Istanbul and European Turkey in 1914).

92 Richard Clogg, 'The Greek Millet' in Braude and Lewis, *Christians and Jews*.

93 Before he was known as 'Ataturk', the preferred epithet for Mustafa Kemal was 'Ghazi' (the victor of the holy war), in homage to his victory against the Greeks. Furthermore, 'Even today ... after thirty-five years of the secular Republic, a non-Muslim in Turkey may be called a Turkish citizen, but never a Turk'; in Lewis, *The Emergence of Modern Turkey*.

94 *Annuaire statistique de Turquie*, Ankara, 1930.

95 Bernard Lewis, *Le Retour de l'Islam*, Paris, Gallimard, 1985, p. 384.

96 In 1923 they were 250,000 (crude estimates of the Greek Orthodox Patriarchate of Constantinople); the increase probably arises from the placing of 38,000 Greeks in the city under allied occupation. They were drawn by the mirage of 'Greater Greece'.

97 The Muslim population of Greece declined less because of its greater fertility. Of the 141,000 Muslims counted in 1940, 125,000 remained in about 1980 (68 per cent Turks, 22 per cent Pomaks and 18 per cent Tziganes). On the Muslims of Greece, see Panayote Elias Dimitras, 'Minorités, un plus ou un moin pour la Grèce?', *L'Evènement européen*, Paris, October 1991.

98 The Hellenic Greeks were in no way different from the Turkish Greeks, except by their ancestors who came from the provinces of the empire incorporated into Greece after 1830.

99 The Arab Christian community was a victim both of religious and linguistic homogenization and of the political situation; the transfer to Turkey in 1938 of the *sanjak* of Alexandretta, which was part of Syria under the French mandate, pushed it to an exodus.

100 Alexandris, *The Greek Minority*.

101 The spoils extended even to the countryside; see Daniel Panzac, 'L'enjeu du nombre. La population de la Turquie de 1914 à 1927', *Revue des études méditerranéennes et sur le monde musulman*, 50, Aix-en-Provence, 1988.

102 Lewis, *The Emergence of Modern Turkey*. For further information on the *dönme* see Edgard Morin, *Vidal et les siens*, Paris, 1988.

103 Non-Muslim men of between 18 and 45 years who were enrolled in the army were confined in special camps during the Second World War.

104 Lepsius would have maintained that Enver Pasha, Tala'at Pasha and Jamal Pasha, the members of the triumvirate responsible for the Armenian massacres of 1915, were in fact atheists and that the fight was between Armenians and Turks and not Muslims and Christians.

105 The expression 'peuple-classe' comes from Abraham Léon, *La conception matérialiste de la question juive*, Etudes et documentations internationales, Paris, 1968.

106 Assuming a natural growth rate similar to that of the Christians in Lebanon.

Chapter 6

1 The thread which links the Crusades, the European expansion in the nineteenth century and the birth of the Israeli state is recognized by the Israeli historian Joshua Prawer: 'The country [Palestine] had itself been sunk in a long oblivion until the sound of the cannon in the nineteenth century reminded Europe of the grand epoch of the Crusades, and the ploughing of the Jewish peasant led the way to a new settlement', *Histoire du royaume latin de Jérusalem*.

2 For example, André Chouraqui, *Les Juifs d'Afrique du Nord entre l'Orient et l'Occident*, Paris, 1965.

3 Out of 800,000 people of French nationality. Pierre Nora, *Les Français d'Algérie*, Paris, 1961.

4 G. Acher, 'Le Peuplement espagnol dans l'Algérie occidentale', *Bulletin de Géographie d'Aix–Marseille*, 1, 1955.

5 Marc Baroli, *Les Français en Algérie*, Paris, 1967.

6 Laraoui, *History of the Maghreb*.

7 The Archbishop of Algiers, Charles Allemand Lavigerie, the founder of the order of the Pères Blancs and the Soeurs Missionnaires d'Afrique, authorized the conversion of Muslims. 'Lavigerie', *New Catholic Encyclopedia*, New York, 1968.

8 Jacques Berque, *Le Maghreb entre deux guerres*, Paris, 1962. However, they may have been more numerous; Berque uses as his source the paper *L'Humanité*, which was inclined to deride the church in the 1930s.

9 Canon P. Repeticci, *L'Algérie chrétienne – Esquisse historique*, Algiers, 1930. Canon Jules Tournier expressed a similar idea in *La Conquête religieuse de l'Algérie*, Paris, 1930.

10 Victor Demontès, *L'Algérie économique. Un siècle de colonisation: Evolution historique de la colonisation de l'Algérie*, Algiers, 1930.

11 Charles-André Julien observed without complacency: 'The greater part of the colonials believe that colonization would no longer be possible if they did not show the indigenous people that they were superior to them. In addition

they do not mix with them or learn their language.'
Charles–André Julien, Introduction to Nora, *Les Français d'Algérie.*

12 Ministère de l'Agriculture et du Commerce, *Annuaire statistique de la France*, Paris, 1878.

13 North Algeria only: this is the official figure, but is an under–estimate.

14 Berque, *Le Maghreb entre deux guerres.*

15 Gouvernement générale civil de l'Algérie, *Etat de l'Algérie*, Algiers, 1881.

16 G. Yver, 'Algérie', *Encyclopédie de l'Islam*, 1st ed. 1913; Nora, *Les Français d'Algérie.*

17 Quoted by Jacques Taïeb, 'Les Juifs du Maghreb au XIXe siècle. Aperçus de démographie historique et répartition géographique', *Population*, 2, 1992. This statement concerning Tunisia would no doubt be true of all the Jews of the Maghreb before the Crémieux Decree.

18 The quantification of Algerian Judaism is made difficult because of this. The censuses no longer distinguished between naturalized Jews and those of French origin. Until 1936, however, the census forms retained the following question: 'Are you an Israelite naturalized by the decree of 1870 or the descendant of Israelites naturalized by this decree?' Ibid.

19 Yvonne Queney, 'Les Etrangers non musulmans en Algérie au recensement de 1954 – Comparaison avec le recensement de 1911', *Bulletin de la section de géographie*, Paris, 1965; G. Acher, 'Le peuplement espagnol'.

20 The Kabyles among others rebelled against the Crémieux Decree and the demise of Napoleon III.

21 René Ricoux, *La Population européenne en Algérie pendant l'année 1884*, Philippeville, 1885; Victor Demontès, *L'Algérie économique*, vol. 2: *Les populations algériennes*, Algiers, 1923.

22 Acher, 'Le Peuplement espagnol'.

23 Ricoux, *La Population européenne en Algérie.*

24 Acher, 'Le Peuplement espagnol'.

25 Berque, *Le Maghreb entre deux guerres.*

26 Ibid. The same view is put forward by Laraoui, *History of the Maghreb* and Baroli, *Les Français en Algérie.*

27 Demontès, *L'Algérie économique.*

28 At their high point, the kibbutz contained only 5 per cent of the Israeli population.

29 The crude birth rate increased from 26 per thousand in 1830–34 to 41.4 per thousand in 1856–62, then declined to 29.1 per thousand in 1897–1904. As for the crude death rate it stayed close to 50–51 per thousand until 1855 and then remained around 33 per thousand in the second half of the century; Demontès, *L'Algérie économique*, vol. II, *Les populations algériennes.*

30 Nora, *Les Français d'Algérie.*

31 Philippe Marçais, 'Algérie', *Encyclopédie de l'Islam*, 2nd ed.

32 Ibid.

33 P. Berthaut, *Rapport presenté au congrès des ingénieurs agricoles à l'Exposition coloniale de 1931*, quoted in Berque in *Le Maghreb entre deux guerres.*

34 Julien, *Histoire de l'Afrique du Nord.*

35 René Hoffherr and Lucien Paye, 'Evolution du peuplement en Afrique du

Nord', *Congrès international de la population*, Paris, 1937.

36 Quoted by Berque, *Le Maghreb entre deux guerres.*

37 René Ricoux, 'Recherches sur la mortalité de la première enfance en Algérie', *Annales de démographie internationale*, 1882.

38 Raymond Pearl, *The Biology of Population Growth*, New York, 1925.

39 Quoted by Berque, *Le Maghreb entre deux guerres*. He points out 'to what extent literary aestheticism, however benevolent, can fail to recognize the movement of history.'

40 For a critical approach to the birth rate, see Jacques Breil, 'Essai de détermination du niveau et des tendances de la fécondité des musulmans d'Algérie', *Congrès mondial de la population – Rome 1954*, New York, 1955 and Jean–Noël Biraben, 'Essai d'estimation des naissances de la population algérienne depuis 1891', *Population*, 4, 1969.

41 In fact the French statistics had under-estimated the population growth of the Muslims.

42 Berque, *Le Maghreb entre deux guerres*. Elsewhere, Berque has stated: 'In the inter–war period, the indigenous person became more and more a specialist concern. His true nature was of interest only to the revolutionary, the researcher or rare hang-overs from the past. Who, or rather what is he to the European? A threat, an opportunity, a thing to use or, at best, to humour.'

43 The quotation is from René Hoffherr and Lucien Paye, *Evolution du peuplement*. G. Mesnard added: '*and I add, the political one*'.

44 William Vogt, *Road to Survival*, New York, 1948. This was the first and most famous attempt to relaunch Malthusianism.

45 G. Mesnard, 'La Régression relative des Européens en Algérie', *Congrès international de la population*, Paris, 1937.

46 Demontès, *L'Algérie économique.*

47 See the conclusion of this chapter.

48 Mesnard, 'La régression relative des Européens en Algérie'.

49 Colonial agriculture did not only favour the movement of settlers and civil servants, but also that of the Muslim wage–earning class. Thus, 200,000 Moroccans were settled permanently in Algeria. *Situation démographique régionale au Maroc*, Rabat, CERED, 1988. Conversely, a Frenchified Algerian elite participated in the administration of Morocco.

50 In Morocco the progress of foreign colonization would have pushed back the indigenous ownership from 9.2 million hectares in 1917 to 8.3 million in 1927 and 7.5 million in 1936. Berque, *Le Maghreb entre deux guerres.*

51 Laraoui, *History of the Maghreb.*

52 *Le Cri du Maroc*, March 1926, quoted in Berque, *Le Maghreb entre deux guerres.*

53 Haïm Zafrani, *Mille Ans de vie juive au Maroc, Histoire, culture, religion et magie*, Paris, 1983.

54 Several hundred Christians of European origin remained after independence and took Algerian nationality. Some descendants of Kabyles who had converted to Christianity did not rejoin the religion of their ancestors. There is no incompatibility between Algerian nationality and Christian religion.

55 After Algerian independence, less than 7 per cent of Algerian Jews

emigrated to Israel compared to 93 per cent to France.

56 Berque, *Le Maghreb entre deux guerres*.

57 Expressed, for example, by Francine van de Walle, 'Qu'est-ce qu'un francophone?' *Colloque de démographie et destin des sous-populations*, Liège, 1981.

58 Data from the 1987 Algerian census.

59 The components of the increase in the French–speaking population in Algeria are as follows: 69 per cent comes from the growing rate of bilingual French–Arabic education; 31 per cent from population growth.

60 Reconstruction from the censuses close to independence and more recently – for Algeria 1954, 1966 and 1987; for Tunisia 1956 and 1984; and for Morocco 1951, 1960 and 1982. These censuses classify the literate population according to the language or languages read and written: French, Arabic, French and Arabic and so forth. The statistics have been interpolated to estimate the French-speakers at independence and extrapolated to supply the current numbers. Children of less than ten years (or less than six years) are assumed to reach the same rate of French speaking as their immediate elders, whence there is a slight under-estimate because of the increase in the French-speaking population over the generations. These data, which refer to the reading and writing of the language, are more restrictive than those which would have been obtained if spoken language (one–third or above in Algeria) or comprehension had been the criteria used.

61 Jean Bourgeois-Pichat, 'La France dans le monde', *Population*, 4–5, 1990.

Chapter 7

1 Sabri Geries, *Les Arabes en Israël*, Paris, 1969.

2 Ibid.

3 The Mutasarrifiya of Mount Lebanon, see Chapter 4.

4 Bernard Lewis, 'La Carte du Proche-Orient', *Le Débat*, 58, Paris, 1990.

5 These and the following figures for the Ottoman period are taken from Justin McCarthy, *The Population of Palestine. Population Statistics of the Late Ottoman Period and the Mandate*, New York, 1990 and from Roberto Bachi, *The Population of Israel*, Paris, 1974.

6 The figures are challenged by different sources:

Source	Muslims	Christians	Jews	of which Ottoman Jews
Ottoman census	515,481	69,456	?	31,671
McCarthy (corrected census)	602,377	81,012	60,000	38,754
Bachi (various sources)	525,000	70,000	94,000	?

7 Nathan Weinstock, *Le Sionisme contre Israël*, Paris, 1969.

8 These rates can be found, for example, in McCarthy, *The Population of Palestine*.

9 Perhaps even more if we take into account the under-registration of the birth of girls: 91.4 girls were registered in 1926 for 100 boys, rather than the

normal 95.3. Thus the rate of birth was probably 63.5 per thousand.

10 See Chapters 5 and 8.

11 Israeli statistics add the inhabitants of East Jerusalem and the Golan Heights to the Arab Israelis. In this chapter they are added to the populations of the other occupied territories since the annexation has not been recognized by the international community. The figure of 2.2 million Palestinians living in Gaza, the West Bank and East Jerusalem is contested; a census held in May 1994 shows a population size close to 3 million.

12 The 1950 law which offered all Jews the right to emigrate to Israel was completed in 1952 by the law of citizenship, which allowed all Jewish immigrants to become Israeli citizens from the time of their arrival.

13 George Dussault, 'Israël: l'enjeu démographique', *L'Afrique et l'Asie modernes*, 143, 1984–5.

14 M. J. Weitz, member of the governing party MAPAM–MAPAI in 1967, in a statement made to *Davar* (the official daily paper of the trade union federation, the Histadrut) 29 September, 1967. Quoted by Eli Lobel, 'Les Juifs et la Palestine'.

15 840,000 according to Elias Sambar, *Palestine 1948. L'expulsion*, Les livres de la revue d'études palestiniennes, Washington, 1984; 750,000 according to George Kossaïfi, 'L'enjeu démographique en Palestine' in Camille Mansour (ed.), *Les Palestiniens de l'intérieur*, Les livres de la revue des études palestiniennes, Washington, 1989. Roberto Bachi puts the figure lower, at between 614,000 and 626,000 (*La Population d'Israël*).

16 Weinstock, *Le Sionisme*. On the same subject see in particular Geries, *Les Arabes*, Camille Mansour (ed.), *Les Palestiniennes de l'intérieur* and Charles Kamen, 'After the Catastrophe II: The Arabs in Israel', *Middle Eastern Studies*, January 1988.

17 Geries, *Les Arabes*.

18 Except, recently, to perform the pilgrimage to Mecca.

19 Total number of Palestinians resident outside the borders of the mandate (Israel, Gaza, West Bank).

20 The Arab Israelis have a low infant mortality rate, but not one equal to that of the Jews:

Infant Mortality Rate Per Thousand	Jews	Arabs	Excess of Arab Mortality Rate
1975–9	15.0	31.1	107
1980–84	11.8	22.5	91
1985–89	9.0	17.1	90
1988–92	7.7	14.5	88

Source: *Statistical Abstract of Israel*, 45, Jerusalem, 1994.

21 See Chapter 8.

22 In Chapter 8 we explain why these factors have not been significant in the occupied territories.

23 M. Al-Haj, *Social Change and Family Processes. Arab Communities in Shefarim*,

Boulder and London, 1987.

24 Doris Bensimon and Eglal Errera, *Israéliens, des Juifs et des Arabes*, Brussels, 1986.

25 Sergio Della Pergola and U. O. Schmelz, 'Residential Distribution Aspects of Immigration Absorption in Israel', *Séminaire sur les phénomènes migratoires, l'urbanisation et la contre-urbanisation*, Amalfi, 1991.

26 A district in the north, excluding the Golan Heights. In the north in the broadest sense (Galilee, Haifa, Sharon), that is to say in the body of the districts where the Arabs are strongly represented, the Jews are 65%.

27 In the localities of less than 20,000 inhabitants, at the end of 1990 there were 437,000 Arabs against 326,000 Jews.

28 Excluding East Jerusalem and the Golan Heights.

29 Bensimon and Errera, *Israéliens*.

30 Benjamin Gil, *Projections of the Population of Israel (1955–1970)*, Jerusalem, 1958. This assumed that in 1993 the non-Jews would have fallen to 9.2% – compare this to the 17.3 % that Bachi found for the same year.

31 Bachi, *The Population of Israel*. Bachi overestimated the relative growth of the Arabs: by mid-1993 they were 15.3% of the population of Israel, East Jerusalem and the Golan Heights.

32 Nine per cent is an extrapolation in 1993 of the 1958 projection; 17.3% is the number projected by Bachi in 1993, excluding East Jerusalem and the Golan Heights.

33 Dov Friedlander and Calvin Goldsheider, *The Population of Israel*, New York, 1979.

34 Nick Eberstadt and Eric Breindel, *Realities behind Camp David: Demographic Aspects of Politics of Peace in the Middle East*, Center for Population Studies, Harvard University, 1978.

35 *Projection of Population in Israel up to 2010 – Based on the Population in 1985*, Central Bureau of Statistics, Jerusalem, 1988.

36 Over a longer period, 1978–89, Israel recorded 217,000 immigrants giving a balance of migration of 85,000, that is 39%; Central Bureau of Statistics, *Monthly Bulletin of Statistics*.

37 Ibid., December 1991.

38 Ibid., October 1991.

39 The one-million threshhold may be reached earlier since these projections underestimate Arab fertility which is continually recovering; the Israeli demographers took this phenomenon into account for the Christians but not for the Muslims. In addition, since Jewish immigration was far lower than forecast, the proportion of Arabs in the total population will grow at a higher rate.

40 In the area formed by Israel and the occupied territories, 500,000 additional immigrants from the ex-Soviet Union would only delay by five years the date when the Palestinians become the larger group.

Chapter 8

1 Quoted in Anouar Abdel-Malek, *Anthologie de la littérature arabe contemporaine*, vol. II, Paris, 1965.

2 Kemal Karpat, *Ottoman Population, 1830–1914*.

3 For Mount Lebanon we have used figures from Vital Cuinet, *Syrie, Liban et Palestine. Géographie administrative, statistique et raisonnée*, Paris 1896.

4 The *nahda* or Arab renaissance included many Christian writers.

5 Feroz Ahmad, 'Unionist Relation with the Greek, Armenian, and Jewish Commmunities of the Ottoman Empire, 1908–14' in Braude and Lewis, *Christians and Jews in the Ottoman Empire*.

6 Georges Corm, *L'Europe et l'Orient*, Paris, 1989; Edgard Morin, *Vidal et les siens*, Paris, 1988.

7 The statistical annuals are a legacy of Muhammad Ali and have been published annually since 1907. Until 1952, including the years of the British mandate, they were drawn up in French and reflect the impact of the scientific missions sent to France in the nineteenth century. Death certificates contained a wealth of details concerning the district and the cause, but only from 1944 was religion included, and then irregularly.

8 See Chapter 5.

9 The crude death rates given in Table 8.4 are taken from the Registrar General without adjustment. During the Nasser period Christian mortality seemed to be abnormally low, probably because of non-declarations.

10 The statistics provide only one rate in the last 15 years, that of 1980.

11 But not necessarily more reliable information: in Palestine under the British mandate deaths were under-registered. Life expectancy at birth was over-estimated but religious differences remained apparent.

12 Georges Kossaïfi, *Contribution à l'étude démographique de la population palestinienne*, Paris, 1976, vol. 1.

13 Department of Statistics, *A Survey of Palestine*, Anglo–American Committee of Enquiry, Jerusalem, 1946, vol. 1.

14 Georges Kossaïfi, *Contribution à l'étude démographique*.

15 The Israeli Arabs certainly enjoy the lowest infant mortality of all Arab populations. However they exceed, sometimes considerably, that of the Israeli Jews. See Chapter 7.

16 The name adopted by the Shi'i movement lead Imam Musa Sadr in the 1970s.

17 Hoda Zureik, Haroutune Armenian et al., *Beirut 1984: A Population and Health Profile*, Beirut, 1985.

18 Philippe Fargues and Myriam Khlat, 'Child Mortality in Beirut: Six Indirect Estimates Based on Data Collected at the Time of a Birth', *Population Studies*, 43/3, 1989.

19 See Chapters 4 and 5.

20 Philippe Fargues, 'Un siècle de transition démographique en Afrique méditerranéenne, 1885–1985', *Population*, 2, 1986.

21 Births are slighty under-registered in the Egyptian registry and adjustments are proposed in *The Estimations of Recent Trends in Fertility and Mortality in Egypt*, Committee on Population and Demography, Washington, 1982.

22 Pierre Rondot, 'L'évolution historique des coptes d'Egypte', *Cahiers de l'Orient contemporain*, 2, 1950.

23 Laurent et Annie Chabry, *Politique et minorités au Proche-Orient*, Paris, 1984.

24 Otto F. A. Meinardus, *Christian Egypt. Faith and Life*, Cairo, 1970.

25 Volney, *Voyage en Egypte et en Syrie*.

26 Laurent and Annie Chabry, *Politique et minorités*.

27 The real figure in the census of 1986 is 2,829,349 Christians of all rites, Copt and non-Copt.

28 Christian Cannuyer, *Les Coptes*, Brussels,1990.

29 Rondot, *Les Chrétiens d'Orient*.

30 Fifty years ago, some conversions to Islam still occurred but they were too rare to explain the falling proportion. '[The Copts] see no more reason to continue to belong to a sect which differentiates them from their neighbours without giving them anything in return', noted Charles Issawi. Quoted by Pierre Rondot, who observed that 'each year several hundred Copts pass over to Islam', *Les Chrétiens d'Orient*.

31 The series which enable us to calculate the composite index of fertility, births by religion and age of the mother in the Israeli Arab population are only available from 1955.

32 No other national group appears to have had such a fertility rate. Kenya was said to have a record level in 1980, when it had a total fertility rate of 8.5.

33 Palestinians are, with the Lebanese, the most educated among the Arabs – in particular the women.

34 See Chapter 7.

35 Quoted by Jean-François Legrain, 'Mobilisation islamiste et soulèvement palestinien, 1987–1988', in Gilles Kepel and Yann Richard (eds), *Intellectuels et militants de l'Islam contemporain*, Paris, 1990.

36 Until the Taif agreement it was as follows: 54 Christian deputies (30 Maronite, 11 Greek Orthodox, 6 Greek Catholic, 4 Armenian Orthodox, 1 Armenian Catholic, 1 Protestant, 1 representative of the other minorities) and 45 Muslim deputies (20 Sunni, 19 Shi'i, 6 Druzes).

37 The distribution by religion in the two censuses is very different. The figures for the various Christian communities in 1922 and 1932 were as follows: Maronites, 32.7 and 28.8%; Greek Orthodox 13.4 and 9.8%, Greek Catholics 7.0 and 5.9% Others 2.1 and 6.8%. For Muslims the were: Sunnis, 20.5 and 22.4 %; Shi'a, 17.2 and 19.6% , Druzes 7.2 and 6.8%. See Said Himadeh, *Economic Organization of Lebanon and Syria*, Beirut, 1936.

38 The Taif accords increased the number of Muslim deputies to 54.

39 The Christians also held the majority position in the administration with 53% of posts in the public services.See Boutros Labaki, *Education et mobilité sociale dans la société multicommunautaire du Liban. Approche socio-historique*, Frankfurt, Deutsches Institut für Internationale Pädagogische Forschung, 1988.

40 An inquiry conducted in 1987 by Robert Kasparian shows both a low birth rate (8% aged 5 and under in the total population, that is a crude birth rate of about 16 per thousand) and moderate marital fertility (on average 3.3 children on the 15th anniversary of marriage in the 1970–74 cohorts). The age at marriage for women has increased and is now on average 26.5 years for the first marriage. Comparative statistics are not available for Muslims. Robert Kasparian, *Enquête sur la famille chrétienne au Liban*, Beirut, 1990.

41 Kasparian (ibid.) does not provide information on births by period or by

women's age. However, the age structure enables us to estimate the fertility rate by multiplying by seven the ratio of children under 5 years to women of 15–49 years.

42 Estimate for 1975 by Salma Husseïni Moussawi, *Redistribution de la population du Liban pendant la guerre civile (1975–1990)*, Ecole des hautes études en sciences sociale, Doctoral thesis, Paris, 1992.

43 Quoted by Jean-Pierre Péroncel-Hugoz, *Une croix sur le Liban*, Paris, 1984. Was Bashir Gemayel unaware that the Turkish period had been favourable to Christian demography?

44 If Christians could prove that one of their ancestors had lived on the territory that later became Lebanon, they could win the right to Lebanese nationality.

45 This is also true of the Christians in Jordan and Syria. The only index that we possess of their fertility (ratio of children to women, see Table 8. 16) reveals a great difference among denominations in the former country, where they are largely Orthodox, but less in Syria which has a greater diversity and large rural Catholic communities.

46 May Davie, 'Ville, notables et pouvoir: les orthodoxes de Beyrouth au XIXe siècle', paper presented to the conference on *Bourgeoisies et notables au Maghreb et au Machrek*, Grasse, 1991.

47 See Chapter 5.

48 Particularly in the town of Zahleh.

49 The Lebanese survey in 1971 gave the Druze a very moderate fertility, lower than that of the Maronites. *Al-Usra fi Lubnan (La Famille au Liban)* 2 vols., Beirut, 1974. Perhaps the Druze, who had been closed to conversions since Caliph Muqtana Baha al-Din had so decreed in 1043, had a weak population growth as a result of being an isolated group?

50 With the exception of Sunnis in Denniya and the Jabal Qammoua.

51 Alan Duben and Cem Behar, *Istanbul Households.*

52 With the exception of the Bosnians and the Bulgarians, Youssef Courbage, 'Les transitions démographiques des musulmans en Europe orientale,' *Population*, 3, 1991.

53 The Christian religious schools – Protestant College, Notre-Dame de Jamhour, Soeurs de Nazareth and so on – and the Lycée franco-libanais de Beyrouth have always been patronized by the Sunni upper and middle class.

54 Volney, *Voyage en Egypte et en Syrie.*

55 This is the fertility figure for 1984; *Family Planning in Rural Lebanon; 1983– 1984*, Beirut, Lebanon Family Planning Association, 1985. This survey did not provide statistics that would allow a comparison of fertility in the two regions studied – the South and West Beqa'a which have a large Shi'i majority – with that of Christian families. See Kasparian, *Enquête sur la famille chrétienne.*

56 Fawaz, *Merchants and Migrants* 1983.

57 Etienne de Vaumas, 'La répartition confessionelle au Liban et l'équilibre de l'Etat libanais', *Revue de géographie alpine*, XLIII/III, Grenoble, 1955.

58 Husseini Moussawi, *Redistribution de la population du Liban.* See also the work of Abdo Kahi in Nabil Beyhum, *Reconstruire Beyrouth. Les paris sur le possible*, Lyon, 1991.

59   The rhythm method among the Lebanese Christians, coitus interruptus among the French.

60   Boutros Labaki recently published an inventory of the role of the religious institutions, Christian and Muslim, in the promotion of education in Lebanon, *Education et mobilité.*

61   'Alexandria, so peaceful in appearance, was not a secure place for Christians', Lawrence Durrell wrote, however, in the first book of his quartet. *Justine.*

62   In the census of 1937, Alexandria had 596,385 nationals and 88,351 foreigners, of which 36,822 were Greek, 22,881 were British and 14,030 were Italian.

63   10,834 foreigners in the 1986 census, out of 2,896,459 inhabitants.

64   These towns were established in 1860 and 1863 by the Suez Canal Company.

65   There were 2 million members in 1948, of which 1 million were in Egypt. *Atlas mondial de l'Islam activiste*, Paris, 1991.

66   The whole of Middle and Upper Egypt which begins at Giza and ends at Aswan.

67   Jacques Berque, referring to the end of the nineteenth century , has observed that: 'The Copts, who are the oldest peasantry in Egypt, practise occasional occupations. For example, everything concerned with cadastral surveys and taxes; compromising occupations. He who remains closer than all others to the timeless land, sometimes allows himself to be tempted by the expatriation of language and behaviour ... While his community is dispersed but united, it nevertheless leaves its mark – a different shade, sometimes a contrast – in the Muslim city. A secondary axis which is seeking a direction.' *L'Egypte, impérialisme et révolution*, Paris, 1967.

68   Assassinated in 1981 by the Islamic fundamentalists, Anwar al-Sadat had in 1973 nominated a governor to Asyut, Muhammad Osman Isma'il, of whom Gilles Kepel recalls that until 1982 he applied himself to encouraging the Jama'at Islamiyya so that they would fight against the communists. He adds that the subsequent prodigious development of the university Islamist associations was due to the dynamics they were themselves able to set in motion. *The Prophet and the Pharaoh*, London, 1983.

69   The current proportion is not known.

70   Despite some mishaps quoted by Christian Lochon, 'Les Communautés chrétiennes en Syrie à la fin du XXe siècle,' communication to *Journées de l'association française pour l'étude du monde arabe et musulman*, Tours, 1991.

71   He belonged to the pro-Iraqi wing of the party.

72   Quoted by Olivier Carré, *L'Utopie islamique dans l'Orient arabe*, Paris, 1991.

73   The Alawis are a branch of the Shi'a. Founded by Muhammad Ibn Nusayr (884) who called himself the incarnation of the Holy Spirit, the community rejects various ritual obligations of Islam. It survives only in Syria, and in a very small number in Lebanon and Turkey. Louis Massignon, 'Nusaïriya', *Encyclopédie de l'Islam.*

74   Rondot, *Les Chrétiens d'Orient.*

75   Generalizing to the whole East from the Lebanese case, Etienne de

Vaumas noted: 'The Oriental is infinitely less attached to his land than the Western peasant, his community is infinitely more important to him than the land ... From this arises the tendancy to form extensive diasporas worldwide.' Etienne de Vaumas, 'La répartition confessionelle'.

76 Boutros Labaki has clearly shown the wide range of causes of this emigration, 'L'émigration libanaise en fin de période ottomane (1850–1914)', *Hannon, revue libanaise de géographie*, XIX, Beirut, 1987.

77 15,000 and 8,000 departures per annum respectively, Youssef Courbage and Philippe Fargues, *La Situation démographique au Liban*, vol. II, Beirut, 1974.

78 The Lebanese Maronites are proud of their emigrant communities across the Atlantic. As the memories have blurred over the century, they tend to overestimate the number of Lebanese, whether true or sympathizers, among the migrants. Other Lebanese migrants of more recent departure, the Shi'a in Africa, maintain an active community solidarity.

79 By definition the migrant cannot be recorded in the country of departure. Someone is needed to supply the information, usually a member of the family, but not everyone has such a person, particularly the old migrant. The census very probably under-estimated emigration (254,000 in 1932), which has been more reliably estimated by Elie Safa as 1,214,500 in 1959 (*L'Emigration libanaise*, Beirut, 1960).

80 We have seen in Chapter 5 that the opposite was true in the last century.

81 Today Christians represent 2.1% of the Arabs who live in Israel and the occupied territories and 4 per cent in Jordan.

82 UNRWA counted 130,500 Palestinians resident in the camps in Lebanon. However, the majority lived outside the camps and therefore escaped the statistics.

83 Courbage and Fargues, *La situation démographique au Liban*, vol. II.

84 Transferred to Tunis in 1982, the Palestinian Central Committee withdrew its assets from Lebanese banks; from 1984 the economic crisis in the Gulf limited the remittances of migrants' savings.

85 Kuwait and Bahrain are the exceptions. They both produce reliable statistics on their foreign residents. However, the details are too rudimentary to inform us on the confessional composition of the Lebanese diaspora. We know only that the proportion of Christians among the foreigners (all nationalities) was 23.5% in the last census of Bahrain (1981) and that it has evolved as follows in Kuwait: 1957, 10.5%; 1965, 10 per cent; 1970, 8.7%; 1975, 8.6%; 1980, 11%; 1985, no information on religion. The coincidence between the increasing proportion of Christians in Kuwait and the civil war in Lebanon is too tenuous to be an indicator.

86 The *caza* is the smallest administrative unit; Lebanon contains 24. Effectively they were all mixed before 1975, although this does not mean that all the villages were.

Index of Names and Terms